RAMMER JAMMER
YELLOW HAMMER

RAMMER JAMMER YELLOW HAMMER

A Road Trip into the Heart of Fan Mania

WARREN ST. JOHN

THREE RIVERS PRESS
NEW YORK

Copyright © 2004 by Warren St. John

All rights reserved.
Published in the United States by Three Rivers Press, an imprint of the Crown Publishing Group, a division of Random House, Inc., New York.
www.crownpublishing.com

Three Rivers Press and the Tugboat design are registered trademarks of Random House, Inc.

Originally published in hardcover in the United States by Crown Publishers, an imprint of the Crown Publishing Group, a division of Random House, Inc., New York, in 2004.

Library of Congress Cataloging-in-Publication Data
St. John, Warren
Rammer jammer yellow hammer: a journey into the heart of fan mania / Warren St. John.—
1. Football fans—Southern States—Social life and customs. 2. Recreation vehicles—Southern states. 3. Alabama Crimson Tide (football team). 4. University of Alabama—Football. I. Title.
GV959.S87 2004
796.332'63'0975—dc22

ISBN 0-609-80713-7

Printed in the United States of America

Design by Lenny Henderson

10 9 8 7 6 5 4 3 2 1

First Paperback Edition

For my parents

A singular example of mental perversion, an absurd and immoral custom tenaciously held fast in mob-mind, has its genesis in the partisan zeal of athletic spectator-crowds. I refer to the practice of organized cheering, known in college argot as "rooting."

—G. E. Howard, *Social Psychology of the Spectator*, 1912

You Will Suffer Humiliation When the Team from My Area Defeats the Team from Your Area

—Headline from the *Onion*, 2001

CONTENTS

RAMMER JAMMER YELLOW HAMMER

INTRODUCTION

AT SOME POINT IN THE LIFE OF EVERY SPORTS FAN THERE comes a moment of reckoning. It may happen when your team wins on a last-second field goal or three-point basket and you suddenly find yourself clenched in a loving embrace with a large hairy man you've never met and with whom you have nothing in common except allegiance to the same team. Or it may come in the long, hormonally depleted days after a loss, when you're felled by a sensation oddly similar to the one you felt when you first experienced the death of a pet. In such moments, even the fan who rigorously avoids anything approaching self-awareness is sometimes forced to confront a version of the question others—spouses, friends, children, and colleagues—have asked for years: "Why do I care?" In very general terms that's what this book is about—the human obsession with contests.

I grew up in Alabama—possibly the worst place on earth to acquire a healthy perspective on the importance of spectator sports. If you were a scientist hoping to isolate the fan gene, Alabama would make the perfect laboratory. People in Alabama have a general interest in almost all sports—the state is second only to Nevada in the amount of money that its citizens bet on sports, despite the fact that in Alabama, unlike Nevada, sports gambling is illegal. But the sport that inspires true fervor—the one that compels people there to name their children after a popular coach and to heave bricks through the windows of an unpopular one—is college football. A recent poll by the *Mobile Register* found that 90 percent of the state's citizens describe themselves as college football fans. Eighty-six percent of them pull for one of the two major football powers there, Alabama or Auburn, and 4 percent pull for other teams—Florida, Notre Dame, Georgia, Tennessee, and Michigan, or smaller schools like Alabama A&M or Alabama State. To understand what an absolute minority nonfans are in Alabama, consider this: they are outnumbered there by atheists.

My team is the Alabama Crimson Tide. Growing up a Tide fan in the 1970s gave me an unrealistic sense of what it means to be a fan, for the simple reason that in the 1970s Alabama won, and being a sports fan is largely about learning to cope with losing. In most sports there is just one champion per year—every four years if you're into a sport like World Cup soccer—so for the overwhelming majority of fans, losing at least once a season is a near certainty. In my childhood, this small kink in the works of the fan's life went more or less unexposed.

The primary agent of this obfuscation was a man named Paul "Bear" Bryant, the gravelly voiced football coach with an old-growth frame who coached Alabama to six national championships and who, when I was eleven, set the record for the most wins of any college football coach in history. Along the way, the Bear, as he was called for taking up a childhood dare to wrestle a bear at a local fair, became a populist hero who hovered over the consciousness not just of every little kid in the state but of nearly every adult as well; his photograph, usually in his houndstooth fedora, hung on the wall of every barbecue and burger joint from Mobile to Muscle Shoals. His exalted status was proclaimed on thousands of bumper stickers, T-shirts, and homemade shrines. Socially and historically, the Bear was a complicated figure; he waited until 1970 to integrate the Alabama football team, and on matters of race Bryant was more or less silent. Given his stature in Alabama at the time of the civil rights struggle, that silence could only be interpreted as a tacit, if not wholehearted, endorsement of the status quo. But to a kid who didn't yet understand the connection of sports to culture and politics, these were incomprehensible complexities at the time. To me back then, the Bear was just a football coach.

Early in the morning of October 17, 1982, a Sunday and my thirteenth birthday, my father woke me and told me to put on a sweater and some khakis, to tuck my shirt in, and to get a move on. He had a friend who owned a local lawnmower dealership that sponsored *The Bear Bryant Show*, the Sunday morning postgame recap that enthralled Tide fans the way televised papal sermons seize the attention of devout Catholics, and the friend had managed to get me invited on the set. I didn't know this at the time, but I had an inkling where we might be headed—besides church, little else of importance happened early on Sunday mornings in Birmingham, and I was fairly sure that my birthday present wasn't going to consist of a morning of hymn singing at Independent Presbyterian. But the other possibility—that I was going to stand face to face with the most revered man in the state of Alabama and the architect of more joyful Saturdays in my young life than I could count—was too terrifying to contemplate. I had an exaggerated view of the man; once in grade school I looked at a picture of Mt. Rushmore and noted what a poor job the sculptor had done of capturing the Bear's likeness, and that he'd forgotten the hat.

We rode in silence through the empty streets, past the Tudor and clapboard houses with lawns like swatches of green felt, past the red clay outcroppings near Birmingham's iron ore seam, and up the winding road to the television studios, where Bryant taped his show for broadcast that afternoon. The parking lot, which overlooked downtown Birmingham, was empty save a few cars and some smashed soda cans. As soon as I got out of the car, I spotted Bryant's bodyguard, a black university policeman named Billy Varner, who was sitting at the door in front of the studio, a wide-brimmed trooper's hat low over his eyes. I'd seen him standing on the sideline of every Alabama game I'd been to, and in almost every television shot or photograph I'd ever seen of Bryant. The Bear couldn't be more than a few feet away.

"How's the Coach?" my father asked as we walked by, using the man's proper title, as all Tide fans knew to do.

"Not too good," Varner replied.

The day before, Alabama had lost to Tennessee, something that hadn't happened since my first birthday, in 1970. Varner had the Sunday morning *Birmingham News* at his feet; the outcome of the game was front-page news. Bryant was sixty-nine, and even as a kid, I sensed something ominous about the loss. It broached the unspeakable possibility that perhaps the old coach was losing his stuff. I walked through two sets of large steel doors, and there he was: a glowering hulk of a man with a voice so deep it seemed to vibrate the floor. He was sitting behind a desk like a news anchor, on a sky blue soundstage hung with signs advertising Coca-Cola and Golden Flake potato chips. His gray hair was slicked back, his cheeks were still red from the game-day sun. But his face was fixed in a steely grimace, and his eyes were bloodshot and wet, as though he hadn't slept. The Bear looked like he was grieving. I felt a pang of resignation: my one chance to meet the Bear and his mood was positively black.

I sat on a stool behind the cameraman as Bryant mumbled gravely through the show and took the blame for each fumble, each missed tackle, and each dropped ball. This was the Bear's way, and it bothered me tremendously. I knew exactly who had fumbled, and it hadn't been Bear Bryant. The captain was trying to go down with the ship, but at least one passenger wouldn't let him.

After the taping, Bryant got up slowly from his chair and stood on the set looking dour and preoccupied. He turned around and noticed me, then approached and stuck out his hand in a distracted, obligatory way. We shook, and his pillowy palm seemed to engulf my arm.

"I wanna play football," was all I could think to say.

"I'm sure you'll do fine at it, son," he said, and that was all. This wasn't going to be the day to get motivational platitudes from the Bear. I wasn't even disappointed; at the age of thirteen I knew enough about football and human emotions to feel badly for the old man. Losing to Tennessee, I figured, was hell on all of us.

My father asked Bryant if he wouldn't mind posing with me for a picture. Without so much as a word, the Bear put his arm around my shoulder and forced an unconvincing smile. We stood there in front of the Coca-Cola sign in this uncomfortable pose as my father fiddled with his camera, stalling in the hope that Bryant might loosen up. After forty-five nerve-fraying seconds, the Bear leaned over to me and thundered, "Son, I don't think your father knows what the hell he's doing." We both laughed and in the photo that now hangs on my office wall we look like old cronies sharing an inside joke.

Two months later, Bryant retired, and fulfilling his prophecy that he'd die without football, he succumbed to a heart attack a month later. I skipped school the day of his funeral and made my mother drive me to Elmwood Cemetery for the burial. Thousands of Alabamians lined the forty-five-mile stretch of interstate between the university campus in Tuscaloosa and the cemetery in Birmingham. Bryant's hearse and the three-mile procession of cars and buses behind took farewell laps around Bryant-Denny Stadium on campus in Tuscaloosa and Legion Field in Birmingham before heading to the cemetery, where I stood with ten thousand other mourners. Each Alabama win had served as a kind of temporal hash mark on the green turf of my youth, and after Bryant died I felt that field had turned brown.

It took getting away from Alabama to develop a little perspective on being a fan, and perspective came quickly when I arrived at Columbia University in New York in 1987, coincidentally during what would become, by my sophomore year, the longest losing streak in the history of college football. The Lions lost an astonishing forty-four games in a row, beating Northwestern's previous record by ten games; an entire class of players graduated without achieving so much as a tie. It was quite an adjustment to go from counting up a record number of wins under the Bear to the inexorable accumulation of a record number of losses at Columbia. And just as disconcerting: no one at Columbia seemed to mind. Columbia was a kind of inverse Alabama; where 90 percent of Alabamians had a favorite team, a similar percentage at Columbia seemed not to know the rules. In Alabama, life more or less came to a halt on football Saturdays; in New York, almost no one went to Columbia games except for their comedic value, or else to witness some sort of losing milestone. Throngs of Columbia students crammed onto a New Jersey Transit local for the 1987 Princeton-Columbia game, just to see what they hoped would be the loss that propelled Columbia past Northwestern's miserable streak. The Columbia fans, if you can call them that, wore Princeton orange and black and cheered wildly when Princeton scored. Some students unfurled a huge banner that read GO COLUMBIA—BEAT NORTHWESTERN! When Princeton won—as we knew they would—the Columbia students toasted the loss with champagne, celebrating the fact that we were, indisputably, the worst team ever. I can trace my first feelings of self-consciousness about being a sports fan to that cool October Saturday in New Jersey, because here's the thing: I wanted Columbia to win. Try as I might, I couldn't hope to lose. I couldn't mock football. I was not a sports dadaist.

There were other revelations, and usually they came care of some form of public ridicule. I was ribbed for hanging the photograph of the Bear and me on my dorm-room wall. Actually, at first, I wasn't ribbed at all; no one knew who the old man was—they assumed he was my grandfather. When his identity was discovered, the ridicule began. I don't remember what was more unsettling, taking endless flak for having a picture of a football coach on my wall or the realization that there were people roaming the world who at close range could not recognize Bear Bryant.

Once I spent three hours listening to an Alabama-Auburn game on the telephone; there was no broadcast of the game in New York, so

I called my parents in Alabama and had them lay the receiver next to a radio. When my friends realized what I was doing with a telephone next to my ear for three hours—well, suffice it to say there was more ridicule. And when an undefeated Alabama team lost to Auburn my junior year, I anesthetized myself with a steady drip of keg Budweiser. The next morning I woke up on my dorm-room bed, fully clothed and in the fetal position. My roommates reported that I'd taken refuge there at some point in the fourth quarter and had wept myself to sleep. I wasn't in any shape to dispute this version of events, but again, was it so strange?

At some point, I began to get the clear impression that it was strange. The problem wasn't that others thought my behavior was pathological, it was that I myself began to think something was a little . . . off. I'd gone to Columbia to study humanism and the great books—to become a rational being. Crying one's self to sleep over the failure of a group of people you've never met to defeat another group of people against whom you have no legitimate quarrel—in a game you don't play, no less—is *not* rational. It didn't make me feel any better about myself that while I was obsessed over college football, others were obsessed with pro football, baseball, basketball, and soccer. At the time, I failed to grasp how much we had in common.

One of the most comforting experiences for anyone who considers himself weird in some way is to find other people in the world who are, in the same way, weirder. For me, this experience took place, plainly enough, care of the local TV news in Birmingham. Just about the time I was beginning to wonder if I should enroll in some sort of twelve-step sports fan recovery program, I went home from college to visit my family for Thanksgiving—no coincidence, the very week of that year's Alabama-Auburn game. A few days before kickoff, I was flipping through the channels when I landed on a live broadcast from the parking lot of Legion Field, where the big game was to be played. As part of the week-long coverage that typically precedes that game, a local station was doing a lifestyle piece on people who drive motor homes to Alabama football games. That's when I saw a scene that would define fan devotion for me for years to come.

A little background: In the early 70s, some mad football fan someplace—a lot of people contend that place was Birmingham—got it in his head to drive a motor home right up to the stadium on game day, probably for the simple reason that motor homes have bathrooms and therefore provided this fan and his beer-drinking buddies the luxury of a place to take a leak during their pregame tailgate party. Whatever the original motivation, the idea caught on; other people got it in their heads to drive their motorized bathrooms right up to the stadium on game day. The more people who did this, the harder it became to get a good parking place, so a few enterprising fans decided to show up not on game day, but a day or two before game day. After all, in addition to bathrooms, motor homes have beds, and kitchens and televisions—in fact, everything you need to squat someplace until the authorities run you off. More and more people came earlier and earlier, forming, over time, a large diesel-powered movable feast, the main course of which was a Saturday football game.

RVs completely changed the fan experience. Before, football games were circumscribed events. They took place inside a stadium on Saturdays and lasted about three hours, after which everyone went home. Logistical problems like traffic, the need for tickets, the need for those bathrooms—set games off from the rest of life. RVs blew open the experience. The event was no longer confined to three hours—it could last three days. In the South, the Midwest, and other pockets of fan mania throughout America, it's not unheard of these days for fans to arrive in their motor homes a full week before kickoff—to drive directly from one game to the next. Futhermore, games no longer took place simply in a stadium, but in the neighborhoods around the stadium and on the open highways that brought fans together. The people who sought out the scene were necessarily among the most devoted. While there are plenty of obsessive football fans out there who've never set foot in an RV, for those whose passion for football was unchecked, the RV offered the possibility of total immersion.

Of all these convoys, Alabama's is among the largest. This is so for a number of reasons: for starters, because so many Alabamians are football addicts, and because the state's geographical position—within a half day's drive of the campuses of most of Alabama's

Southeastern Conference foes—makes RV-ing practical. The weather is a factor too; in the South, it doesn't get particularly cold until December, so fans cans tailgate comfortably for most of football season. At a typical Alabama game, between 250 and 800 motor homes show up, depending on the opponent and the venue. If you have never seen 800 motor homes in a single place, let me tell you, it is a strangely impressive sight. Consider that a motor home is exactly as big as its name suggests—it's as though someone put four wheels and a transmission on a standard American two-bedroom ranch dwelling and drove it off the lot. Eight hundred of these things amount to a modest-sized American neighborhood; and here's the thing—most of the time, these modest-sized neighborhoods are being driven into towns that *already have* neighborhoods, towns like Oxford, Mississippi; Gainesville, Florida; and Athens, Georgia. When hundreds of motor homes appear in one of these idyllic college towns, well, invasion is just too measured a word. The vehicles cram together in tight little perpendicular clusters, like bacilli in a petri dish, and fill every available empty space. It's not unheard of for a visiting team's motor home convoy to shut down an opposing team's town with a weekend-long traffic jam—totally overwhelming the place, confounding the local police, and causing university officials to abandon their well-conceived parking schemes. (To members of the convoy, this is considered the height of accomplishment.) At big games, motor homes are so tightly packed that a person could nearly circle the entire stadium by walking along their rooftops, although as I learned firsthand, you should never walk along the rooftop of a stranger's motor home because there's a decent chance he will shoot you.

At any rate, a local news crew is broadcasting from Legion Field. The camera pans across a parking lot and finally comes to rest on a massive contraption that has a name painted on its side like a ship: the *Crimson Express.* Motor homes come in three basic categories: the plastic ones that look like children's toys, the large boxy ones that look like a country-and-western star's tour bus, and the sleek aluminum ones that resemble a 737 with the wings lopped off. The *Crimson Express* is of the 737 variety. The reporter boards the craft and finds the owners, a middle-aged couple who seem entirely too subdued to own something as outrageous as the *Express.* The husband is thin and tan, with a perfectly maintained plank of hair on his head. He bears a striking resemblance to the country singer George Jones. His wife too is thin and tan, and oddly, she looks a bit like Tammy Wynette, who was once married to George Jones. The reporter probes the couple's devotion to Alabama football, and they say they haven't missed a game in about fifteen years. So the reporter idly asks what sort of things they've given up in pursuit of the Tide.

Let's see, the man says in a soft Southern drawl. *We missed our daughter's wedding.*

You what?

We told her, just don't get married on a game day and we'll be there, hundred percent, and she went off and picked the third Saturday in October which everybody knows is when Alabama plays Tennessee, so we told her, hey, we got a ball game to go to. We made the reception—went there soon as the game was over.

I'd wandered through the motor home encampment at Alabama football games since I was a kid, but until I saw the local news that night, I'd never thought much about what was really going on. People were taking their houses to football games—packing up their lives in big rectangular canisters, driving for hours or days at a time in order to live as close to games as possible. And not just that, but if the owners of the *Crimson Express* were to be believed, they were also taking their homes to football games, in the sense that that word suggests the locus of one's emotional comfort and well-being. I couldn't help comparing my own devotion to Alabama to that of the owners of the *Crimson Express;* I felt suddenly inadequate. I didn't remotely measure up. But it was clear that the same mysterious fascination that compelled me to listen to football games on the telephone moved others to totally rearrange their lives, to uproot themselves, and to shelve their familial obligations. But where did that fascination come from?

It would be easy, perhaps, to dismiss such hardcore fans as freaks, except for the fact that the world is practically brimming over with them. Open your daily paper's sports pages to the box scores. You might want to pause and ask yourself why your hometown paper devotes an entire section to sports. The implication is that the readers' need to know the outcome of sporting contests ranks up there in importance with their need to know about global politics, business and the arts. Compare that with the amount of column inches per week on religion; it's not even close.

For each box score, consider how many moods hung in the balance over the game's outcome. Maybe tens of thousands attended in person. They may have "gone wild," or "gone crazy," in the telling clichés we use to describe the behavior of fans. Thousands more—millions more if we're talking about a big play-off game in some sports—watched at home or listened on their car radios. If it was a close game, it's possible that some of these people had the most intense emotional experiences of their lives, more acute than anything they'd felt at home with their spouses or kids. If this sounds like hyperbole, think of the most emotionally intense moments in your own life—when you realized you were in love, when your child was born, or when someone you cared for accomplished something important, like graduating from college. You were profoundly happy, but you probably didn't hug the stranger sitting next to you. Most likely, you didn't "go wild." You probably didn't tear down a goalpost.

Now look at all the other box scores in sports pages and consider how many hundreds of thousands of Americans were on similar trips last night. Think about all the newspapers published in the world today, all their sports pages and box scores. Now think, if you can grasp it, of all the people in the world last night who watched sports. America has football, baseball, and men's and women's basketball. Europe, South America, Africa, and parts of the Middle East have soccer. Canada and Russia have hockey. The Japanese like baseball too, and also Sumo wrestling; Pakastanis, squash and cricket. Car racing is popular the world over. In Afghanistan there is a traditional game that involves two teams fighting on horseback for control of a ram's carcass. There's probably some kind of box score for that. (Cowboys 10,

Rams nothing?) It's dizzying, especially when you realize that what you just got your head around was one day's worth of sports in the world, and that the cycle will repeat itself this evening. Millions more moods will hang in the balance, and the papers tomorrow will be full of another round of box scores. And so on, like the tides.

Given the torrential emotional outlay contests inspire on a daily basis, it's amazing that human beings find time even to govern themselves. And yet—what is at the heart of every democracy but yet another contest—elections. We've even adopted the lingo of sports to describe our politics—the campaign is a "race"; and debates are scored like boxing matches. Constant polls amount to a sort of real-time scoreboard; election day is the buzzer. Perhaps this is the secret enduring quality of democracy: whichever way the ideological winds may be blowing, the public is always hungry for a good race. Even our judicial system is powered by contests—what is a trial but an intellectual sporting match? Everywhere you look, it seems, humans are compulsively gathering around to watch two sides battle it out. In this context, it was hard to see the couple aboard the *Crimson Express* as doing anything but steadfastly pursuing a universal human urge, third perhaps only to hunger and sex in its power over humankind.

For over a decade, whenever the subject of fans came up, I deployed the story of the wedding skippers as a kind of archetypal example of how far people would go. There was something interesting about the way people reacted. Most seemed to think the couple aboard the *Crimson Express* were nut jobs, or worse. Some used terms like "child abuse," or compared the couple's passion for football to alcoholism. Skipping a child's wedding for a football game for these people was simply *beyond.* To people in this camp the most disturbing detail of the story was that the couple had made the reception. They weren't not talking to their daughter; the family hadn't experienced some irreparable rift. They just weren't missing football games for her.

A not insignificant few, however—an unscientific estimate would be 25 percent or so—had a different view: they blamed the daughter. These people wanted to know what kind of person would force someone they loved to make such a choice. Those who blamed the daughter usually shared something in common: they were fans too. If they knew anything about Alabama football, they were likely to condemn the daughter even more harshly for the simple reason that she had scheduled her wedding for the day of the Tennessee game. Tennessee is a huge Alabama rival. You don't devote your life to Alabama football and miss the Tennessee game. Interesting too was that while those who thought the parents were bonkers usually reacted with a chuckle and a shrug, those who blamed the daughter were more likely to get *angry* over the story. When I told the tale to one hardcore fan I met in Florida, he shook his head woefully and said simply: "Bitch."

Whatever someone's reaction to the tale of the wedding skippers, other questions always seemed to follow: What exactly were the mechanics of devoting your life to college football? What did these people do for a living? You don't have endless amounts of free time and $300,000 to spend on a motor home by doing just anything; and yet, people who have come into such bountiful trappings of leisure aren't necessarily the kind of people you picture in motor homes at football games. And what about all those people in those other motor homes—what did they do? What familial sacrifices were they making? Was it possible to find someone out there whose attachment to a football team was more intense than his attachment to life itself? And the overwhelming question was, Why?

In the late spring of 1999, another team I'd foolishly adopted, the New York Knicks, lost in the play-offs. I should've been prepared—the Knicks always lost in the play-offs—but there I was again at the threshold of despair. I had a familiar internal dialogue: I blamed the players, then the coach, then the management, and of course the referees, and then I scolded myself for even bothering to care. Why was I letting something as far removed and trivial as a basketball game plunge me into a funk? It was a familiar, nagging question that still seemed to me as mysterious as it did years before when I'd first become aware of my susceptibility to sports.

A month or so later, I was visiting my family in Alabama when the wedding skippers came up with friends in conversation. More than a decade had passed since I had seen them on local television proclaiming their devotion to the Tide, and in the intervening years, I'd begun to doubt that they actually existed. Perhaps I'd imagined them as a kind of defensive hallucination to justify my own obsession. At any rate, I had some time to kill, and I wondered if I might actually be able to track them down.

One of the wonderful things about life in a moderately populated state like Alabama is that if you spend years driving around in a wingless 737 with *Crimson Express* painted on the side, people more or less know where to find you. I made a few calls to some Alabama fans I knew, and in no time at all, I had a name and phone number for the owners of the *Crimson Express*—or at least, *a Crimson Express*. The couple's name was Freeman and Betty Reese, and they lived in a suburb of Birmingham called Trussville, barely half an hour from where I grew up. I picked up the phone, dialed their number, and after a single ring, a gentleman answered in a familiarly soft voice and with an air of puzzlement, as if he were surprised anyone had called at all. I introduced myself as a reporter working on a piece about motor homes and football, and asked if I had the owners of the *Crimson Express*. Indeed I had, Mr. Reese said. A few minutes later, I was in a car on my way to meet them.

The Reeses live in a new subdivision next to a golf course, and their house is easily located, thanks to the big 737 without wings parked in the driveway, facing out and ever ready, like a fire truck. When I pulled in, the Reeses emerged from behind a glass storm door at the front of their house and introduced themselves. They were both older than I'd imagined, white haired with thin, tan legs emerging from matching red shorts. Mr. Reese wore a golf shirt and Mrs. Reese wore an Alabama football T-shirt. Mrs. Reese apologized for the state of the yard; the house was new, she said, and they were just now settling in, having recently moved here from a larger house a few miles away. The move had gone smoothly, she said, but for one hitch: there wasn't space enough in their new home for all their Alabama memorabilia; they'd had to put their entire " 'Bear' Bryant room" into storage.

"Sometimes you just have to move on," Mr. Reese said.

Mr. Reese gave me a tour of the interior of the *Express*—through the kitchen (larger than the kitchen in my New York apartment), the bathroom, and to the master bedroom in the rear with a queen-sized bed, all of it decorated in a faded red and cream color scheme, like that of a 70s disco. The driver's seat of the *Express* sat in a kind of well, with a steering wheel the size of a hula hoop and nearly as many switches, levers, and gauges as an airplane cockpit. Mr. Reese pointed to a button and raised his eyebrows with an impish look.

"Push it," he said.

I did: the Alabama fight song blared from the roof-mounted air horns at roughly the decibel level of a civil defense siren. As the tune played—and played—Mr. Reese gazed dreamily through the windshield, as though he'd been transported to . . . well, who knew? I had the distinct feeling it was a stadium someplace.

I sat on one of the banquettes facing Reese. We talked for a moment about the Crimson Tide's chances next season. "I'm optimistic, Lord knows," he said. It occurred to me that spending $300,000 on a motor home to follow your team in was nothing if not an act of optimism. Eventually, I got around to what I thought might be a sensitive question: Are you the couple, I asked Mr. Reese, who skipped their daughter's wedding to go to the Tennessee game?

"Oh *that*," Reese said, nodding, a little guiltily, it seemed. " 'Fraid so, yes sir. That'd be us. You know we made the reception—drove to it straight from the ball game." He paused for a moment. "I'm still paying for it."

"So why'd you do it?" I asked.

Reese collapsed his brow, pursed his lips, and nodded pensively, a look that suggested I'd asked a very good question, but not one he had ever pondered before in his life. We sat silently, except for the roar of the air conditioner, and after a long minute Mr. Reese shrugged and shook his head.

"I just love Alabama football, is all I can think of," he said.

* * *

My meeting with the Reeses inspired me to look further into the mysteries of being a fan. I wanted to understand how and why something so removed from our lives—something that doesn't affect our jobs, our relationships, or our health (hangovers notwithstanding)—affects us so much emotionally. It seemed to me at the time that whatever the answers, they would be writ large in a subculture that was built around fandom—the Alabama RV scene. My interest was not in the RV scene as an example of some eccentric, marginal freak show but as a tinctured version of whatever it was that motivated me to listen to football games on a telephone, and whatever it is that drives interest in all the box scores in today's newspapers—the almost universal fascination with sports. I went back to New York, took a leave from my magazine job, and soon after set out to attempt to join the RV-ers, to see what came of it. This book is the result.

Finally, a disclaimer. More than once in the course of my research, I looked up from my notebook into the face of a fan who was curious—sometimes, malevolently so—about what I was writing. This exercise produced a number of friendships, several threats of violence, and on my very first weekend out—in Nashville at the Alabama-Vanderbilt game—an exchange that occurred in various forms perhaps a dozen times during the fall.

A fan in cut-off blue-jean shorts, an Alabama T-shirt, a mustache, and a cheek full of tobacco asked, "Whachu writin'?"

I'm researching a book about fans, I said.

So you just picked Alabama out of a hat, the man asked declaratively. *You're not like an actual Bama fan, right?*

I've liked Alabama since I was a kid, I said.

A knowing smile crept across my interrogator's face.

Ho. Ly. Shit, he said. *You get paid to go to Bama games . . .*

Not exactly, I said. I go to games as research and—

Don't bullshit the bullshitter, good buddy. He was now vigorously patting me on the back. *You get PAID to go to Bama games! Sunuvabitch. Hey boys! Y'all get over here. This fella gets paid to follow the Tide!*

I then found myself surrounded by a group of people who treated me as though I had just unlocked the riddle of the meaning of life, and who wanted to know every last detail of the publishing business—that beneficent industry that funds people to follow the team of their choice so long as they agree to carry a notebook and pencil with them for the journey. At any rate, the disclaimer is this: I have every reason to believe the world will soon be flooded with works of a genre that might be called the Alabama fan travel memoir.

I accept blame only for this one.

Chapter One

Hallways on Wheels

> *Does anyone know where I might be able to locate a pic of the New Bama Logo? I want a pic large enough to print and use for a tattoo that would be about 6 to 7 inches tall.*
>
> —BULLETIN BOARD POST FROM ED HAMES, AKA "BAMAFANFORLIFE"

SO I HAVE A MISSION, BUT THERE ARE CERTAIN LOGISTICal issues I have to work out. How exactly does one join an RV caravan? I could always simply show up at the parking lot of the first game of the season, against Vanderbilt in Nashville, and impose myself. I have a trump card in the form of that photograph of Bear Bryant and me, which I figure for Alabama fans might act as a kind of press pass to the soul. There is another strategy more enticing than simply crashing the party: trying to get invited to it, on someone else's RV. But resolving to get invited aboard a stranger's motor home and actually getting invited, I learn in short order, are two very different things. Absent an attempt to track down a specific RV like the Reeses', I find that in the summer months it's oddly difficult to locate any RV-ers at all. The RVs that fill the highways and stadium lots in the fall seem to disappear without a trace in the warmer months, perhaps parked by their owners in backyards in a kind of inverse hibernation, or perhaps driven out west to tour the national parks. There are no Alabama fan motor home associations to contact; there is no Bama RV Club. Perhaps the whole point of RV-ing is to disconnect from the grid to chase after one's passions; to such people, the inability to be organized—or even found—could be a kind of virtue. So I go to the one place where even the least organized and most elusive people are sure to have a presence: the Internet.

There are literally hundreds of Alabama fan sites—TiderInsider.com, BamaMag.com, BamaOnline.com are the biggest, along with countless personal pages, the cyberspace equivalent of bumper stickers, where fans declare their love of the team for anyone who happens to click by. None, though, are devoted to RV-ers. I sign up for an e-mail listserv called Bamafan, a kind of live wire into the collective unconsciousness of Alabama fans, and within minutes of my signing up, e-mails begin to appear in my mailbox at a machine-gun rate from people with names like Bamadog, Krymsonman, Crimson Jim, and the Alabama Slamma. I've tuned in to to a kind of philosophical debate: Are there any circumstances under which it is permissible for an Alabama fan to pull for Tennessee? A fan named Tommy e-mails the group that when a Tennessee win would benefit Alabama, he actually finds himself humming "Rocky Top," the Tennessee fight song.

"You certainly don't know what it's like to really hate Tennessee if you pull for them AT ALL," a poster named Tiderollin' responds. "I'd cheer for Florida, Auburn, Notre Dame, Russia, and the University of Hell before the words 'rocky top' would ever come out of my mouth."

I send the group an e-mail of my own explaining my mission and asking, with the sort of straight-forwardness I expect someone like Tiderollin' might appreciate, if anyone would be willing to offer me berth aboard a motor home. Within a few hours, responses begin to trickle in. A woman replies offering to tell me the story of how she came to have the word *Bama* tattooed on her leg. Another offers the use of some photographs he thinks might go well in a book about Alabama fans:

> *My family are all BAMA grads . . . and we all made a trip in '95 to China. I have a shot of all of us holding a large BAMA flag on the Great Wall of China*

just outside of Beijing. If you are interested in using this photo in your book we could probably work something out.

I get a number of other encouraging e-mails, wishing me luck, but no invites on RVs. Eventually, Bamadog writes to suggest I contact Tide Pride, the booster office of the University of Alabama. "They may or may not have information on the people you're looking for," he writes helpfully, before signing off, "Dawg."

It turns out even University of Alabama officials are at a loss to name the people who crowd their campus on game weekends. A man named Wayne at the school's booster office laughs when I explain my mission, then quickly tries to dissuade me. RV-ers, he says, can be disagreeable people. "They show up on Monday and park where students are supposed to park," he says. "We tell 'em, 'You gotta wait till Friday afternoon to park there,' and they just get upset with you. Some of these people feel like they deserve everything. It gets too much sometimes. They's people who go too far." It seems significant that a university official charged with inciting fan zeal believes the RV-ers are too zealous. I sense that Wayne is reluctant to help me; something like 95 percent of the RV-ers, he says, never attended the university—they simply like the football team. The implication is that while the university had no role in shaping these disagreeable people, it has to answer for them. I press for names.

"You could try a fellow in Clanton," Wayne grumbles before hanging up. "Name is Skeeter Stokes."

Skeeter Stokes answers when I call and is happy to talk. He's the semiretired owner and manager of the Clanton Chevrolet dealership and has been going to Alabama games for thirty years. He still attends most home games, he says, in an Allegro motor home, typically with a Chevy Blazer in tow—a kind of escape pod once the mother ship is fully set up in the lot. Stokes is eighty-five years old and, at least on the phone, sounds every bit his age. The image of an eighty-five-year-old man on the highway in a vehicle the size of a Greyhound—with an SUV in tow—is sobering. Perhaps this is what Wayne means about going too far.

The rest of our conversation yields two bits of valuable information. The first is that there is no way in hell—his words—that I'll be invited to spend a weekend with Skeeter Stokes aboard his RV. Second: Over the years Stokes has compiled a list of names and phone numbers of RV-ers he's met at Alabama games.

"It's out in the motor home," he tells me. "You welcome to it."

So I spend the next few days working my way down Stokes's list. My first call is to a man named Wayne Snead of Snead, Alabama, the owner of a $400,000 Bluebird motor home. Mr. Snead of Snead isn't into the hard-drinking life around the stadium; he and his wife prefer to be near the team, so they stay in the parking lot of the team's hotel. I speak to a man named Rudy Valley, whose job—leasing beach furniture to a significant portion of the Florida panhandle—neatly conforms to the seasonal rhythms of football; he closes shop just before the first kickoff each year. Valley puts me in touch with a moderately coherent man known to me only as "The Night Mayor," because of his insomniac tendency to wander the lot into the morning hours. When pronounced with an Alabama drawl, the name is a pun on "nightmare," a fair description, I'm told, of this man after a few drinks. The Night Mayor gives me the number of a friend, a motor-homing Bama fan who, by coincidence, happens to own a bar. And so on.

Whatever alarm these people feel at having a stranger ask details of their personal lives is offset by the flattery of encountering a stranger who is interested. Each has a story about going too far, a story or bit of personal data they report with an ambivalent mixture of shame and pride. Wayne Snead tells me about the time he drove to an uncle's wake in his fully provisioned RV, ready to hit the road as soon as he'd paid his respects. Rudy Valley boasts that he has $200,000 worth of Alabama football memorabilia in his home and that his motor home cost him more than his actual house. A man in Delaware named Jeremy tells me of his hard-fought but ultimately successful effort to convince his wife to name their daughter Crimson. And these aren't social misfits, at least not exactly. Wayne runs a successful farm supply business in Snead. Rudy Valley's beach furniture leasing business is among the most successful in Florida. Jeremy has a Ph.D. in molecular biology.

Besides being zealots for the Crimson Tide, most everyone I speak with shares something else in common: a belief that the world does not understand them. Each has a story of mockery at the hands of spouses, coworkers, or friends. Each has in his life the equivalent of the Reeses' daughter—someone who has tested, provoked, and frustrated them, someone who didn't just not understand but who actively agitated against their obsession, who made the frustrating (although perfectly rational) argument that a lifetime's outlay of energy and emotion for a sports team was not recoupable, no matter how many victories or championships.

I figure this feeling of being unappreciated may be my in. What we fans need, I argue, is for a reporter to tag along in one of their RVs for a season and to translate the experience for everybody else, to make them understand. With this, everyone heartily agrees. There is certainly no more deserving subject matter for a book, the fans say, than fans themselves. And when I suggest that I should be that reporter and my interview subject should be that Alabama fan, and that we should spend a few months together on an RV, the reply is always the same: Not on your life.

I'm near the end of Skeeter Stokes's list when I place a call to a man named Corky Williford from Dothan, Alabama, who as quickly as anyone lets me know that I will not be riding with him and his wife at any point during the football season. Williford nevertheless seems friendly enough—he tells me I'm welcome anytime to visit his RV at the stadium, to eat barbecue and "drink good booze," as he puts it. So I ask, based on his knowledge of the convoy, what the chances are of my getting a single invitation.

"Not good, son," Williford says, not unsympathetically. "There's a saying: no matter how big a motor home is, it's only built for two. Once you get in one, no matter how big it is, it's just a hallway on wheels." My best bet, Williford says, is to get a motel room near Vanderbilt Stadium on the first weekend of the season, and then to glom on the RV scene there. I thank him for the insight and resolve to begin my reporting on foot.

Two days later, I receive the following e-mail:

> *Saw your post on Bamafan . . . we live in South Carolina, but you're welcome to join us from here.*
>
> *ROLL TIDE!!!*
> *Chris & Paula Bice*

Chris and Paula Bice, I learn in subsequent e-mails, live in Simpsonville, South Carolina, outside Greenville, and travel to games in something called a Winnebago Warrior. Chris Bice e-mails a photograph; if the typical motor home is a hallway on wheels, as Williford said, this is a linen closet. It's short and boxy and looks more or less like the *Crimson Express* cut in half. I'm in no position to get uppity about the make and model of motor home I'll stoop to travel in, so I find myself in an interesting position: doing everything I possibly can to join two perfect strangers for a weekend in what amounts to a modestly large car. Bice tells me to call him at work, so on a weekday in early August I oblige. He answers in a deep, edgy baritone, and seems excited to hear from me.

"Hey, Roll Tide," he says when I introduce myself.

"Roll Tide" is Alabama's battle cry, but among fans, it's the ultimate all-purpose phrase, like *prego* in Italian or *namaste* in Nepali, an acceptable substitute for hello, goodbye, nice to meet you, and Amen.

"Roll Tide," I say.

We chat for a few minutes about the team—Bice has high hopes, mainly because of Shaun Alexander, the Tide's star running back. I ask how many games Bice expects to attend.

"We're going to all of them this year except the away game at Florida," he says. "Florida is where I might end up killing somebody."

Bice leaves me to mull this comment as he tends to a squawking radio in the background. I hear him blurt a string of unintelligible numbers and commands—he's obviously a dispatcher of some kind. He picks up the phone again, and I get a few biographical details: he and his wife Paula are in their midthirties and are both originally from Birmingham. They've been Alabama fans since childhood; their first date was to the 1983 Alabama–Ole Miss game, which Alabama won 40-0. The Bices started RV-ing to games in Paula's parents' Winnebago Brave, and later in their thirty-three-foot Itasca Windcruiser, a "lap-of-luxury type thing," Chris says. Paula's father died in a car fire in 1991, and they got rid of the Itasca. A few years later Chris and Paula began to peruse the classifieds in the *Greenville News* for their own motor home. They bought the Warrior, used, for twenty-five grand.

About my invitation, Chris says, there's just one thing. He's hasn't exactly cleared it with Paula. "I'm fine with it," he says. "But she said, you know, 'What if he's a weirdo or something?' I said, 'Hey Paula, that's the whole point: *we're* the weirdos.' " Apparently Paula was unmoved by this line of thinking. So Chris and I agree to a tentative plan: I'll drive from New York to South Carolina on the Thursday before the game, go out with the Bices to a local farm league baseball game, and if I don't register code red on Paula's internal serial killer detector, we'll leave for Nashville on Friday morning. The radio squawks and Bice asks me to hold. I hear him chattering into a microphone, then distinctly, the words *"Clear to land."*

"What do you do for a living?" I ask when Bice picks up the phone.

"Air traffic control."

"Do you need to go?"

"No, it's pretty slow right now."

Later I ask Bice if he'll be taking his Winnebago to all the games or if he'll fly.

"Oh I don't fly," he says.

"Why not?"

"It's not safe," he says, and hangs up laughing.

* * *

I've got over a month to kill in New York before heading south to meet the Bices, and I spend the time reading up on the team, memorizing the roster, correlating names and numbers. The weeks before a season starts are the most sublime in a fan's life. Each day the anticipation builds, and unlike during the season, no loss can mar the glee or the sense of infinite hope. We have Alexander, a running back who in his freshman year ran for an incredible 291 yards against LSU—281 of them in the second half alone. He's now a senior. We have Chris Samuels, a bulldozer of an offensive lineman who clears the way for Alexander. There's a streaking receiver named Freddie Milons, a sophomore whose performance in practice is already inspiring the sorts of fan paeans on the Internet that usually follow only a big, game-winning run. And we have two excellent quarterbacks, Andrew Zow, the starter, who is black, a drop-back passer with a howitzer of an arm; and Tyler Watts, a white freshman with Hollywood looks and a thick battering-ram frame for running.

The question mark, though, is the coach, Mike DuBose. DuBose is a native of Opp, Alabama—short for "opportunity"—a name that neatly foretold his career in football and his improbable rise to the near-holy post of Alabama head coach. DuBose was a stump-necked linebacker under Bear Bryant in the 1970s—he made a famous fumble-causing tackle in the 1972 Tennessee game that allowed Alabama to come back and win, forever solidifying his position in Bama lore—and went on to coach defense as an assistant under the revered Alabama coach Gene Stallings. When Stallings left unexpectedly, fans nominated DuBose to replace him on the strength of his defense and his ties to Bear Bryant. The school administrators heeded their wishes, but with reservations. DuBose is not the sort of polished presence university presidents typically like to have representing their schools. His Opp upbringing has left him with a phonetics-wrecking south Alabama accent, which sometimes makes him sound as though his mouth is full of Gobstoppers. He talks almost exclusively in memorized sound bites—his favorite, "a tremendous challenge and a tremendous opportunity," applies to almost every situation. He regularly invokes his devout Christianity in awkward, heavy-handed ways, crediting God with victories that might better have been put on his players. On the sideline DuBose wears a polyester-blend white golf shirt with white polyester slacks—kind of a high school football coach's get-up—in a place where people expect their coach to dress for football games the way he would for church.

In two years as head coach, DuBose hasn't fared well, just 11-12.

He's had a legitimate excuse though; he took over in the aftermath of a recruiting scandal for which Alabama was ultimately forced to cut its annual offering of football scholarships, hopelessly thinning the ranks. Alabama fans—not usually the forgiving type—seem to have understood, so far at least, because of DuBose's lineage to Bryant and his local roots. He's family.

This year, however, DuBose's excuses have run out. The impact of the recruiting sanctions is passing. We have talent, and expectations have grown. A big loss or two, and the fans could begin to turn on DuBose; his speech tics and sartorial quirks could, like bad habits in a failing marriage, begin to grate. To keep the fans on his side, DuBose simply has to win. It won't be easy—Alabama plays Arkansas, who embarrassed us last year 42-6; then Florida in Gainesville, where the Gators haven't lost in five years. We play Tennessee, the defending national champions; then Mississippi State, with their ferocious defense, and, at season's end, hated Auburn, away.

In addition to those formidable foes on the Alabama schedule, Mike DuBose faces a fearsome off-the-field opponent as well: a man named Paul Finebaum. Finebaum—ubiquitous as a newspaper columnist, talk radio host, and evening sportscaster—is as obsessed with Alabama football as the most die-hard fan, but from the opposite perspective. He's an antifan, a tireless shit stirrer and controversy monger whose specialty is not X's and O's—you'll never hear him debating the finer points of a blocking scheme or talking about the pros and cons of man-to-man coverage over zone—but instead: firings, scandals, NCAA investigations, the impact of a bad season on the job security of university officials, the personality flaws of various coaches. The intro to his daily call-in radio show offers an only slightly hyperbolic boast of Finebaum's strange but ineluctable power over Alabama fans: against a background of raucous heavy-metal power chords, an announcer cheerily declares: "It's the *Paul Finebaum Show:* where legends are made, and most coaches *are fired*!"

Finebaum has made a career, quite simply, of offending Alabama fans. He stumbled into this role in the early 1980s when, in his first story as a sports reporter at the *Birmingham Post-Herald*, he exposed the illegal recruiting of a star Alabama athlete. He was sued (unsuccessfully) and denounced statewide for his scoop—his bosses quickly made him an opinion columnist "for liability reasons," he says—and from his editorial post he continued to offend the locals: "Welcome to the State of Alabama—Loserville, USA," began a typical early piece. He mocked Bear Bryant and Pat Dye, the Auburn coach, with abandon. He insulted players. He taunted fans. But a funny thing happened. The more egregiously Finebaum offended Alabamians, the more eager they were to buy the *Post-Herald* to read him. Finebaum got his own local television show, and the radio show—it started at two hours and now spans four—is by far the highest-rated talk show in Alabama. These new venues gave Finebaum more opportunities to offend, which he seized enthusiastically. He published a joke book called *I Hate Alabama*, which was a hit among Auburn fans, and, ever the entrepreneur, repackaged the very same jokes under the title *I Hate Auburn*, which sold well among the Alabama crowd. (Not one to let an opportunity slip away, Finebaum published the same joke book under fifty different titles, exploiting nearly every major rivalry in the country.)

When he wasn't offending in print, he was offending on air. After Alabama head coach Ray Perkins's losing season in 1984, Finebaum broadcast a parody tune on his radio show called "Dig 'Im Up," in which he suggested that Alabama would be better off with the corpse of Bear Bryant on the sideline than with a living Ray Perkins.

Finebaum is perhaps not the most likely Alabama sports shock jock. For one thing, his air is more that of a professor than a jarhead. He never yells on the air, and his delivery is low-key and caustically dry. In person, he's physically slight and distinctively bald. Finebaum is also Jewish, which in a Bible Belt football state might provoke more commentary were it not for another detail in Finebaum's background that went much further in defining him as an outsider than his ethnicity or religion: Finebaum is a graduate of the University of Tennessee, one of Alabama's most hated rivals. Even circumspect Tide fans harbor a suspicion that he has been sent here as part of a plot to undo us. Consequently, Finebaum, for all his commercial success, doesn't have an easy life in Birmingham. Fans carry anti-Finebaum banners to games—GO TO HELL FINEBAUM is a typical message. He's been heckled on the putting greens at charity golf tournaments and, once, chased through a parking lot by an enraged fan. When Finebaum spoke to a local high school assembly, a student released a live possum into the audience, causing panic. (It's a measure of Finebaum's unpopularity that instead of disciplining the student, the high school's administrators banned any future appearances by Paul Finebaum.) He is sued with regularity, most recently by a rival Birmingham sportscaster whose softball interview techniques Finebaum compared on the air to fellatio. (Finebaum's professional peers resent him not because of his stance on football matters but because of his Arbitron ratings.)

Finebaum also gets death threats. He says he doesn't take them seriously, but he lives in a gated community with a full-time security guard, just in case. In the introduction to a collection of his columns, a friend wrote, "If Finebaum were found dead facedown in a Birmingham drainage ditch, the list of prime suspects would immediately be reduced to 200,000."

For the last two years, Finebaum has been a relentless badgerer of Mike DuBose, a man he has adjudged an incompetent of the highest order. (Finebaum calls him the "Flop from Opp.") DuBose's woeful record has provided plenty of material, but last spring Finebaum thought he had something really juicy to dig into—a rumor, started on Internet bulletin boards, that DuBose was having an affair with a secretary in the athletic department. DuBose denied the rumor—at a charity golf tournament in the south Alabama town of Dothan he told the media, "There is absolutely no truth or basis to any of these rumors you may have heard involving me or other university employees"—but that didn't stop Finebaum from knocking on his door unannounced in Tuscaloosa and having a sit-down with DuBose's wife, Polly, who had been DuBose's high school sweetheart, while the coach was out. Under the headline "Polly DuBose Stands by Her Man," Finebaum wrote what to the naive eye—and surely to the DuBoses—seemed like an almost maudlinly sympathetic portrait of a deeply religious woman who'd been injured by some terribly vicious rumors. Between the lines, though, it was clear Finebaum thought—or at least hoped—those rumors were true.

" 'When I first heard it, I couldn't believe they were talking about my husband,' " Finebaum quoted Polly DuBose as saying. " 'He's always been an honest man.' "

"Despite the pain this week, I was struck by Polly DuBose's remarkable outlook on this unfortunate situation," Finebaum added. "It had been difficult for Polly DuBose to talk about this subject. However at every fork in the conversation, she seemed to find a light . . . 'When you have faith in the Lord,' Polly DuBose said, 'He meets your every need.' "

So on Saturdays, DuBose will battle for his job against the Southeastern Conference's best football teams, and Monday through Friday, he'll face Finebaum in a lopsided matchup on a more ethereal playing field. DuBose is hamstrung by his earnestness, his linguistic difficulties; Finebaum has wit, and irony, and something else—a 5000-watt transmitter that broadcasts through three 300-foot towers northwest of downtown Birmingham. The towers stick impressively into the evening sky, like large electrified needles jabbed deep into the collective psyche of the Bama Nation. At the top, red lights slowly pulse, burning against the gloam like tiny droplets of fresh blood.

Chapter Two

Untold Sacrifices

IN EARLY AUGUST, THE FIRST ROBIN OF FOOTBALL SEASON arrives: *Sports Illustrated*'s annual College Football Preview issue. I open it with the anxious anticipation of a high school student ripping into a long-awaited letter from a college admissions office, eager to learn if we've been accepted or rejected. My yearly ritual, though, demands self-restraint: I begin at the beginning and, page by page, tick methodically through the rankings until I find my team. Too high a ranking and other teams will be gunning for us; too low, and it's a blow to the ego. Anything between 5 and 10 will satisfy. *Sports Illustrated* has picked Penn State to finish number 1; this I already know from the cover, which pictures a glowering LaVar Arrington, the Nittany Lions' star linebacker. I flip the page; Florida State, number 2. Flip again: Arizona, number 3. (*Arizona?*) And so it goes, past 5 and 10 and 15 (15!) before I turn the page and encounter the Tide and a photo of a hard-charging Shaun Alexander, *SI*'s number 16. It's the equivalent of being wait-listed; they haven't counted us out, but they haven't pegged us as contenders either. I quickly rationalize the disappointment away. The less *they* expect—"they" being the collective consciousness of all football fans out there, as represented by the editors of *Sports Illustrated*—the better. We'll sneak up on them, and make them pay.

I have access to a steady flow of more optimistic predictions on our season care of the Bamafan e-mail list, which brims over with good news. Each day, I receive a fusillade of glowing reports on our players—their progress in the weight room, their grades, their family lives—and on our position coaches, our band, and even the condition of the turf in our stadium. The optimism is so plentiful I find that I have to ration it by leaving some of those e-mails unopened. And anyway, all the positive football talk has an unbearable Pavlovian effect on me, causing me to salivate psychologically for actual football. I have an urge to lean on the days and speed up time for that first kickoff, which though a little over a month away, seems as far in the future as those childhood memories of Bear Bryant are in the past.

I get an odd e-mail from Chris Bice, asking me what I think about "Bama's bad boy." I don't get the reference, so I call Bice for an explanation. He's incredulous that I haven't heard. A secretary in the University of Alabama athletic department has threatened to sue the school for sexual harassment, claiming she has been having an affair with Mike DuBose. The school is in settlement talks, Bice reports, and we'll know more in the next couple of days. Couldn't they fire DuBose? I ask. Bice says it's a possibility but that he doubts it; he thinks the whole thing will blow over in a day or two. Besides, who knows if it's true?—DuBose had denied it in the spring, he reminds me.

Between phone calls to friends at home and a lot of time spent surfing Tide fan sites online, I have the strange, out-of-body experience of following the biggest news story in Alabama from New York City, where the story barely registers a blip. All sports, like politics, I suppose, are local. News trucks have set up a vigil in front of the football building at the university; callers bombard Finebaum's show; newspapers that wouldn't touch the rumor in the spring before DuBose's denial are now churning out several stories a day on the scandal. I devour as much of this information as possible, sealed off in an emotional cocoon from those around me who are oblivious to the faraway catastrophe. I'm torn too. I was no big fan of DuBose's to begin with, but if he has lied to the public and his bosses, he should almost certainly be fired. Firing him might also preserve some of the school's dignity and perhaps offset some of the humiliation the team will have to endure. On the other hand, firing a head coach less than a month before the first game will almost guarantee a miserable season—a petty concern in the big picture to be sure, but in the self-interested calculus by which we tend to judge these things, not an insignificant one: I've already taken a leave from my magazine job and would rather not get stuck chronicling an excessively dismal year. And another petty but not insignificant concern: this is my team—I don't *want* them to have a miserable year.

Apparently, and not necessarily reassuringly, administrators at the University of Alabama—specifically the president and the athletic director—come down on the side of self-interest themselves. A woeful season will do nothing for their job security, and so they opt to settle the woman's claim and keep DuBose as coach. The university agrees to pay the woman $350,000—money the school will get by docking DuBose's salary. DuBose is also put on probation for lying about the affair to his boss, athletic director Bob Bockrath, and a clause is added to DuBose's contract saying that he will be fired if he brings any more "disrepute, contempt, scandal or ridicule" on the university. Finally, Bockrath compels DuBose to make a public confession and apology. The university calls a press conference, and all those television trucks crank their generators and raise their satellite dishes to the sky to broadcast the sort of speech more typically given on a bar-room pay phone with a borrowed quarter. "This past May I addressed a matter related to my personal life," a bleary-eyed Mike DuBose says to the cameras. "My statement at that time misled all of you and I'm truly sorry. I made a mistake and made the situation worse with my response. To say I'm sorry is not enough."

A month before the season, and already I feel as though we've suffered our first loss—a blowout on both pragmatic and moral grounds. In his private purgatory, DuBose has had his authority undermined, which will surely impact the players and probably our performance on the field. And I can't help but feel that the school has copped out too and, by keeping DuBose, tacitly sanctioned his behavior. As with an actual loss, my despair is compounded by the thought of how delighted our rivals must be at our misfortune.

I'm not alone in my ambivalence toward DuBose. On the day freshman players report to campus for practice—traditionally, the beginning of daily news coverage of the new season and a time of unbridled hope—a *Mobile Register* poll reveals that roughly half of the state thinks Mike DuBose should quit. I turn reflexively to the Bamafan e-mail list, to sample the opinion of the hardcores. For them, the episode is all the more deflating because it feels so familiar. The DuBose scandal eerily tracks the script of the Monica Lewinsky–Bill Clinton affair: a media storm, an emphatic public denial, a bigger media storm, lawsuits, and finally, a humiliating public confession. Only to the hardcores, there is one important difference between the sex scandals: the DuBose scandal actually matters. Games could be lost, the team thrown into chaos weeks before the opener. By comparison, a constitutional crisis seems tame. What bothers them most is DuBose's incompetence in handling the matter. It's one thing to give in to temptation, the posts suggest, and another to do it so inartfully. If DuBose can't pull off a fake in his personal life, they wonder, how can he be expected to pull one off on game day?

* * *

Over the next week, Chris Bice sends a steady flow of upbeat e-mails—"I'm getting pumped!" one reads. "Come South Young Man!" another exhorts. Still another includes an invitation to a barbecue the Bices are throwing to celebrate the new football season. "Tailgate Party of the Century," the invitation promises. "Bring your own lawn chairs." Where once I was lobbying to get on board the Bices' RV, I'm now being lobbied. Worried fans want friends, and the more worried they are, the more they need each other's company. Chris's need to commiserate bodes well for my chances of securing an invitation on board his RV for the weekend. Paula still hasn't given her blessing, and when she hears my voice at the other end of the telephone, she still reacts like a woman who's received a collect call from a strange prison inmate. But following Chris' lead, I decide to be optimistic and to press on. In late August I receive an envelope in the mail from Chris that includes a detailed map to the Bices' house from New York City. My instructions are to call when I'm close; Paula will meet me at an exit ramp on her way home from work, and I can follow her to the house. I ask Chris what kind of car to look for.

"You'll know her when you see her," he says.

* * *

Before driving from New York to South Carolina, I decide to seek out the counsel of the man who knows more about RV-ing to football games than perhaps anyone: Tony Brandino. In the forty-three years between 1954 and 1997, Brandino attended 500 consecutive Alabama games. In a state where pretty much everyone knows somebody working on an improbably long attendance streak, 500 games in a row is considered a significant tally. Brandino had no intention of stopping at such a perfectly round number. A few days after number 500—a dismal 38-21 loss at Tennessee in 1997—he caught a flu that prevented him from attending number 501, against Ole Miss in Oxford. "I felt like death warmed over," Brandino wrote in *FANtastic*, his memoir. "My head was throbbing. My stomach felt like a canoe in the Gulf of Mexico. If I had made it to the stadium, I would've puked on everybody in sight."

No one seems to know precisely who drove the first RV to an Alabama football game, but Brandino was certainly one of the pioneers. According to Brandino—who's eighty-three years old and describes himself as "a semiretired residential hardware consultant"—RVs started showing up at Legion Field in the early 1970s, when he was well into his run. He immediately seized on the potential benefits of owning one. He could go to the stadium in the morning when there was no traffic, and spend the hours before the game in comfort. He could have a bathroom. After the games, he could make dinner and relax until the traffic cleared up, then leave when it suited him. He started out with a camper and soon upgraded to a proper motor home.

Brandino is the rare fan who can remember precisely where he was when he formed his bond with his team. It was in 1926, when an underdog Alabama played the University of Washington in the Rose Bowl, a game many southern historians consider the Big Bang of the South's obsession with football. Before the '26 Rose Bowl, teams from the two coasts dominated the sport, and no southern team had ever even been invited to play in the Rose Bowl. Alabama was undefeated that year and had allowed just seven points all season, so the Rose Bowl committee took a chance and invited them to play what most East Coast sportswriters would've called a "real team." The game came at a time when southerners were doing a better job than usual of embarrassing themselves—the Klan was in full force and the Scopes "Monkey Trial" had just been concluded, events, as the historian Wayne Flynt has pointed out, that prompted H. L. Mencken to suggest in one of his columns that southerners must have smaller brain cavities than other Americans. The southern media, with the help of the Alabama head coach, Wallace Wade, spun the game as a test of southern character. The fact that no such thing as Washington state existed during the Civil War was a minor glitch in the scheme, which the press was happy to overlook; they referred to the Huskies as the "Yankees from Washington," and Wade fanned the flames. Before Alabama set out on the three-thousand-mile train ride to Pasadena, he stocked the train with fifty-five-gallon barrels of local water, telling the press he didn't want his players to get sick from the "foreign" stuff. When Alabama fell behind 12-0 at the half, Wade grumbled to his team, "And they told me southern boys could fight."

Alabama came out inspired, scored twenty points in the third quarter, and won the game 20-19. At stops on the way home, the team's train was greeted by crowds and brass bands—a throng of a thousand people showed up to see them in New Orleans. Brandino was ten years old. There was only one house with a radio in his section of Woodlawn, Alabama, and when his older brother and some of the other kids went there to listen to the game, Brandino followed along. "Everybody started screaming and hollering," he says. "That's when the Bama bug bit me."

Brandino calls himself a "pure fan," by which he means one who didn't actually attend the University of Alabama. This is an interesting twist, since fans who are alumni often take a condescending view of fans who are not—the idea being that the latter are glomming on to the reputation of the school. In Brandino's view, alumni are just college types who are glomming on to the glory of his football team. An alumnus is compelled to pull for the school's team, this way of thinking goes; others make a meaningful choice.

His streak began in 1954, heading in to the lowest ebb of the school's program, under the hapless coach J. B. "Ears" Whitworth. Brandino and his brother went to fully nineteen games before seeing a victory. Brandino's relationship with Alabama progressed like a lot of successful marriages; it began out of infatuation and survived out of duty. Brandino stuck by the team during that terrible 0-17-2 streak under Whitworth, and the team was there for Brandino on Saturdays when he suffered a big loss as well, his brother's death of a heart attack in 1965. "I was down and out, as sad as a person can be," Brandino writes in *FANtastic*. "The Alabama football program came to my emotional rescue."

Brandino continued the streak without his brother—he kept a running tally of consecutive games on a small chalkboard that he displayed in the front window of his RV—and every few years Alabama made it worthwhile by winning a national championship—seven in all during his forty-three years. When the national media called on the university to supply the name of a devoted fan, the sports information office offered up Brandino. He was featured in *Time*, *Newsweek*, *Sports Illustrated*, and, over time, in pretty much every newspaper and on every local newscast in Alabama. When the *Wall Street Journal* did a story on the fans' reaction to the integration of the Alabama football team, a drawing of Brandino was on the front page. The coverage benefited Brandino and Alabama mutually; Brandino received the acclaim of being informally designated the school's biggest fan, and the university got out the message that its football team inspired loyalty of a staggering degree.

By the 1980s Brandino's streak was such an integral part of his life that even his long-suffering family wouldn't let him give it up.

When Brandino learned that Alabama had been invited to play in the Sun Bowl in El Paso, Texas, on Christmas Day, 1986, he announced to his family that the streak was over. "Having a damn bowl game on Christmas Day—that really goofed me off," Brandino says. "So I told them, 'That's it, I'm done. I'm not gonna go.' " But concerned that breaking the streak might send Brandino into a depression, his family—wife Marie, son Buster, and daughter Candy—moved into action. They planned a late Christmas dinner and arranged for Brandino to hitch a ride on the Alabama team plane, which left El Paso immediately after the game to get the players back to Alabama for Christmas with their families. Brandino made the Sun Bowl and Christmas dinner, and the streak survived. There's a touching section of *FANtastic* called "My Own Hall of Fame," in which Brandino pays tribute to those who helped him maintain the streak over the years. Under his friend George Shaw, for example, he writes, "On October 17, 1992, we were in Knoxville to play Tennessee. I had serious knee problems. Our seats were in the upper deck, which was too much for me. George Shaw and my son-in-law, Les Tucker, carried me up the stands."

He wrote this under the heading "Candy and Buster": "Thank you, dear children, for forgiving your father for being away so much chasing a dream. Also, thank you for going to so many games with me and on occasion, insisting I go to games without you."

"They knew it was my thing," Brandino tells me on the phone. "If your family is not willing to make untold sacrifices, it just won't work."

The week of game 500 the *Birmingham Post-Herald* put Brandino on the front page. During the game, cameras from ESPN and CNN trained on Brandino, and the Alabama cheerleaders and university president sought him out in the stands and presented him with a game ball signed by Mike DuBose. When the team lost the game, DuBose apologized to Brandino on live television. Not long after that five hundredth game, the Bear Bryant Museum in Tuscaloosa called Brandino to request the jacket and slacks he'd worn that day. The outfit and the chalkboard from Brandino's RV now reside behind glass at the museum, securing his reputation as the team's most devoted fan.

Brandino now goes to as many home games as possible, but he

rarely travels. He sold his RV, a move he regrets, he says, because after forty-three years of seeing games in person, watching them on television makes him uneasy.

"When I watch a game on TV," he says, "I feel like my body is here but my spirit is there."

Asking a fan why he or she likes a team is a lot like asking someone why they're in love with their spouse; all the rational reasons a person can muster don't explain the bond. But I figure that over the years perhaps hundreds of people have put the question to Brandino and that he might have something interesting to say on the subject.

"I just like the sport of football," he says, seeming annoyed, though it is unclear if this is because of the question or his inability to come up with an answer that satisfies him. "Like I told you," he says after a moment. "The bug bit me."

Like a lot of fans, Brandino's attraction to his team is so mysterious that he can describe it only as the act of some outside agent, like Cupid's arrow, or a terrible virus.

Chapter Three

Van Tiffins and Bama Bombs

SO ON A SCALDING LATE AUGUST AFTERNOON, I LEAVE New York City for South Carolina to meet the Bices. I'm making the trip in my beater—a ten-year-old Acura Integra that has been abused by the New York streets and has received only the most basic maintenance, which does not include fixing the long-broken air conditioner. In the heat I power along with the windows down and the sunroof open, which is comfortable enough so long as I keep moving. The first day, I make it as far south as Virginia before stopping for the night, and in the morning I'm off again. With each mile south I travel, the thermometer seems to tick up incrementally, so that by the time I reach South Carolina, with the hot wind rushing through the windows and sunroof, it begins to feel as though I'm driving headlong into a very large hair dryer. This is significant because I want to make a good impression on Paula Bice and to look, if not presentable, then at least not like a mountain man just returned to civilization. Outside of Greenville, South Carolina, however, the sight of myself in the rearview mirror is cause for alarm. Unshaven and with sweat-stiffened, windblown hair, I bear a striking resemblance to Ted Kaczynski, the Unabomber, on that fateful day when he was snatched from his mountain redoubt.

I call Chris from my cell phone, and he directs me to an interstate exit near downtown Greenville, where Paula will meet me on her way home. Pebbles plink against the undercarriage as I ease the Acura onto the shoulder and roll to a stop next to a patch of dry grass where crickets clatter noisily in the heat. With a few minutes to kill, I try to tidy up—I fish a clean golf shirt from my duffel and use a T-shirt to towel my forehead dry—but with no breeze, I begin to sweat steadily. Soon a black Volkswagen Jetta with tinted windows pulls up behind me, then eases by, like a squad car on patrol. The car has Alabama football logos plastered on the windows and doors. The license plate reads: CRMSNTD. A hand emerges from the driver's-side window and waves me to follow.

I trail the Jetta past shopping malls, a Wal-Mart, and then into the country, by pastures and long split-rail fences, before turning into a freshly built Colonial-style subdivision in the Greenville suburb of Simpsonville. Some kids are throwing a football in the streets, and in every third yard, sprinklers shoot little crystalline arcs of water into the air. I turn into a cul-de-sac, and the Bices' home immediately announces itself: A red and white Alabama Crimson Tide flag hangs limp above the front door, giving the house the appearance of a kind of embassy, and there's a land yacht in the driveway. But I'm confused; it's not the ratty-looking Winnebago Warrior but a massive, gleaming white thing with a green and blue abstract swoosh on its side, like a sneaker. I pull in the driveway behind it; the license plate reads: T1DE.

Just as I've parked, a man with a boxy build, short blond hair, and clean Teutonic features—think of a heavyset Billy Idol with a crew cut—emerges from behind the house, heaving a lawnmower that stirs a cloud of dust and dry grass clippings. He hits the kill switch, and the engine coughs to a stop.

"Chris Bice," he says between huffs. "Roll Tide."

"Roll Tide," I say.

"I'm Paula," says a voice behind me. Paula Bice is standing in the driveway with an armful of mail. She has a bob of brown wavy hair, rosy cheeks, and soft round features, like a peach. Chris is even sweatier than I am, and Paula looks at both of us with a twinge of disgust. It's a kind of bonding moment for Chris and me—we're comrades in filth.

"Roll Tide," Paula says finally. The three of us stand in the driveway on the verge of an awkward silence. I come up with: "Nice neighborhood."

"Hey, we like it," Chris says. "Guy across the street is a Michigan fan, guy over there is a Miami fan, guy over there played for Clemson, and the girl in the cul-de-sac went to Georgia."

I was referring to the houses, but never mind. Most Americans probably identify their neighbors by profession—the plumber next door, the school teacher across the street. The hardcore fan has a different classification system.

"What do you think?" Chris says, gesturing grandly toward the RV. "A new Hurricane—delivered yesterday. Wanted to surprise you."

"Wow," I say, with genuine awe. "It's huge."

And it is. The Hurricane is thirty-one feet long, six feet longer than the Warrior, and is decked out with amenities, which Chris enthusiastically catalogs: a built-in TV, a queen-sized bed where the Warrior had twins, a retractable awning, separate refrigerator and freezer, and a ten-cylinder Ford engine. Chris says he and Paula stopped by a local RV show a week ago just to look around when they came across it. At $57,000, it was out of their range, but the salesman offered them $19,000 for the Warrior on trade-in, and with no money down and a fifteen-year loan, their monthly payments would come to $495, just a few dollars more than they were paying each month for the Warrior.

"Two days later," Chris says, "we got a new RV."

Chris offers me a tour, so we take off our shoes and climb aboard sock-footed. My first thought upon climbing aboard the Hurricane is, where did it all go? A vehicle that from the outside looks as big as a house from the inside feels indeed like a corridor—a very crowded corridor. Behind the driver's seat, there's a banquette like you'd find at a diner, except that it converts into a bed. Behind that, there's a kitchen much like you'd find in a regular house—with a sink, microwave, and that two-door refrigerator-freezer. Aft of the kitchen is a bathroom, with a normal-sized shower stall, a vanity, and a toilet. All the way in back is the master suite, with a queen-sized bed that presents a kind of spatial riddle, like a ship in a bottle. It must've been installed before the roof was welded on. While on board, I meet the Bices' dog, a white Scottie-poodle mix named Larry; he'll be coming too. I'm beginning to appreciate Paula Bice's anxiety at having me along for the weekend. After cramming an entire suburban home's worth of appliances and furniture into a thirty-one-foot RV, there is precious little room for three people and a dog to live for a long weekend. We aren't going to be living with each other for the weekend so much as living upon each other.

And yet, the RV seems designed more for living than driving. Even in park, the Hurricane feels tender, like an overloaded dinghy. I ask the Bices if they've ever wrecked. Just once, Chris says; Paula's parents flipped their RV at an interstate rest stop when the cruise control wouldn't disengage.

"Mamma landed on Daddy, Tommy Dean broke his hip and wouldn't go to the hospital, Melanie was hit in the head with a can of beans and got a concussion. Daddy's arm scraped the pavement when the thing flipped on its side, and he had asphalt in his shoulder till the day he died," Paula says.

Chris catches a concerned look on my face as I ponder life with a shoulder full of road.

"Relax," he says. "This thing's got plenty of safety features. Watch this." He flips on the television, climbs in the driver's seat, and turns the key. The television goes blank.

"TV automatically shuts off when the engine's on," he says.

The Hurricane might not have air bags or antilock brakes, but at least we won't wreck because the driver is distracted by the late edition of *SportsCenter*. Perhaps the Hurricane was designed with football fans in mind after all.

Chris and I both clean ourselves up, and I'm even taken aback by the unfamiliar face that emerges when I've shaved and showered. Soon, we're off to the ballpark to see the local farm league team, the Greenville Braves. The game is a dud—a blowout by the visitors—but the Bices don't seem to mind. They didn't come to watch the game anyway, so much as to watch me. I'm on a tryout of sorts, to test my worthiness as both a fan and a traveling companion. We drink beer and gorge ourselves on stadium food—hot dogs, boiled peanuts, and for dessert, a curious form of ice cream that has been frozen in tiny balls, like BBs—and we compare our favorite Alabama games. I offer the 1985 Auburn game, won on the final play by Van Tiffin's fifty-two-yard field goal. Right answer; it's one of Chris's favorites as well. We compare superstitions: I never wear red on game day, and I never take a shaker into a stadium, acts that jinxed Alabama in our 1980 home loss to Notre Dame. Chris and Paula say they can't imagine not wearing red to an Alabama game, and as for shakers, Paula has been taking the same withered frond of a shaker to every Alabama game for the last twenty years. But they seem to appreciate my asceticism; resisting the urge to wear red takes willpower. Perhaps I'm a real fan after all. And yet, whenever I feel like I'm gaining ground with Paula, she asks a pointed question about life in New York—the crime rate, diseases, random acts of violence—and the mood turns cool. That a New Yorker might pull for Alabama seems unfathomable to her, and I get the feeling that the issue of my home address is the single biggest snag to my credibility.

After the game, we head back to the Bices', where, in the driveway, Chris and Paula engage in a heated conversation that apparently has to do with where I will sleep. I've offered to stay at a local motel, but perhaps fearing the karmic cost of being inhospitable to a fellow Bama fan, Chris is trying to broker a deal with Paula so that I can at least stay on the premises, if not in the house. Chris's gaze travels back and forth between the home parked temporarily in the driveway and the one parked permanently in the yard.

"Maybe you could stay in the mowder home," he says, as much to himself as to me. " I'll talk to Paula about it."

Inside, Paula offers me something to drink and opens the refrigerator to show me my choices. On the top shelf, there's a large jar full of a bright red liquid.

"What's that?" I ask.

"Bama Bombs," Chris says. "Maraschino cherries soaked in PGA."

I rifle through my database of college memories in a vain effort to recall what PGA stands for—

"Pure grain alcohol," Chris says helpfully.

"How long have they been soaking in there?" I ask.

Paula and Chris look at each other and shrug, a gesture I interpret as meaning: months. My curiosity has gotten me into trouble. Paula unscrews the jar and fishes out a Bama Bomb, which she holds delicately between her thumb and forefinger, as if it were the leg of an icky bug. I take a bite; a blob of napalm detonates on my palette. A Bama Bomb before kickoff is good luck, Chris explains, and when the cherries are gone, he uses the leftover liquid to make a cocktail; one part cherry-flavored PGA, one part Sprite.

"I call it a 'Crimson Tide,' " he says.

"Why don't you call it a 'Van Tiffin?' " I manage as the burning sensation subsides. Chris and Paula look at me quizzically.

"A 'Van Tiffin'?" she says.

"Yeah—cherry juice and Sprite with a kicker."

For a moment, the Bices are silent. Then slowly, reluctantly, it seems, a smile breaks over Paula's face. Without realizing it, I've engaged in one of the Bices' favorite exercises—taking some mundane accoutrement of life and appropriating to it a connection to Alabama football. The Bices use Tide brand detergent. The refrigerator magnets in the kitchen are little ceramic elephants, after the Alabama mascot. Their toothbrushes, garbage can, and bath mat are red, by design. Chris keeps only Kentucky bourbon in the house—none from Tennessee; if there were an Alabama-made brand, he'd drink that, but as it is, his brand reflects his hatred of the Tennessee Vols, the negative expression of his love for Alabama. As a house cocktail, the Van Tiffin fits right in.

"I think we got a new drink," Chris says, with a confirming pat on my back. "The Van Tiffin: cherry, Sprite, and a kicker."

The cocktail naming eases the mood, enough so that Paula and I can relax in the study, flipping through scrapbooks of newspaper clippings, photographs, and autographs from seasons past, while Chris sits at his computer beneath a ceramic bust of Bear Bryant, checking the day's e-mail output from the Bamafan list and updating a catalog he's compiling of vanity license plates that reference the Crimson Tide—Bamafan, Bamafvr, Bamacar, and so on; so far he's come up with 114 from fifteen different states. For the next three hours, we talk football—from the DuBose debacle with the secretary, to our beloved running back Shaun Alexander to the competition, which we have cased thanks to several scouting reports Chris has found online. For fans, this is bonding time; whatever differences we have melt away in the face of our shared restless anticipation of this weekend's game and the promise of a new season. Paula slips off to bed sometime just before two in the morning, as I'm flipping through a laminated collection of ticket stubs, and not long after, Chris sees I'm nodding off too.

"Lemme show you your room," he says. Chris points me toward a room across the hallway, and heads downstairs to walk Larry the dog. My eyes adjust to the darkness. The covers have been turned down.

* * *

"Wake up man, it's football season."

I open my eyes to see Chris Bice flitting past my bedroom door with an armful of tailgating gear. I look at my watch—it's 6:45 A.M.—and the Bices are in full swing. The window panes rattle as they bound up and down the stairs, and I can hear the constant jingle of Larry's collar as he trots behind them. I stumble downstairs to the kitchen, where I find Chris going over a packing list.

"Food: Check. Ice: Check. Clothes: Check. Drinks: Oh yeah. Radar detector: Hmm Mmm. Other:—" Chris looks me up and down. "Check."

The stereotype of hardcore sports fans holds that they are watchers, not doers. A glimpse of the Bices' preparations for the weekend shatters that myth. A dizzying amount of gear has to be packed on board: a half-dozen chairs, a folding picnic table, two coolers, a grill, two bicycles, a satellite dish, and a tangle of cables and wires. Then there are provisions for the dog and three people—Pop-Tarts, pretzels, milk, eggs, beer, Bama Bombs. The RV itself is connected with a tangle of hoses and cords, like a space shuttle; it will have to be undocked before it can be launched. Once at the stadium, most of this gear will be unpacked to make an outdoor living room, and then at the end of the weekend, we'll repack the RV and unpack it again when we're back home. The Bices will expend as much energy packing and unpacking their RV as many of the Alabama players will expend during Saturday's game.

It's time to do my share, so I grab a box of food and head outside into a scalding South Carolina morning. The Hurricane's air conditioner can't match the baking power of the sun, and with all systems running, the vehicle is only slightly cooler than my Acura with the windows down at highway speed. In the hour and a half it takes to pack the RV we become drenched in sweat. We take showers—Chris takes his with Larry (he tells me he prefers to RV with a clean dog)—and afterward Chris walks a final slow lap around the vehicle, his brow furrowed in concentration as he tests the compartment doors, the valve on the propane tank, and the fittings on the two bumper-mounted anti-deer whistles, which produce a high-frequency noise that supposedly sends deer scattering. You didn't want to be late to the game because you'd spent an hour scraping an unwitting mammal off your grill. There's one more chore before leaving: the Bices have three cats who stay behind and need food and water for the weekend. Paula tells me that one of the cats typically shits and vomits throughout the house as payback for being left behind, so a mess will await us when we return. She relates this information cheerily: another small price of devotion to team.

Chris tosses a small walkie-talkie to Paula, and she heads out into the cul-de-sac to guide us out of the driveway, barking commands like a veteran ground controller—"Turn right. Slow. Now left. Whoa—." The four back wheels of the Hurricane slide over the lip of the driveway, and the rear end of the vehicle lets out an awful scrape. The

Hurricane is clear. Paula climbs in. One last stop for gas, which I foolishly offer to pick up; the total comes to $107. Soon we're winding our way through the Blue Ridge Mountains on the long, swooping curves of I-40 toward Tennessee. At speed on the open road, the contents of the Hurricane rattle like beans in a mariachi gourd, so we have to shout to communicate. Despite the poor acoustics, Chris pops in a CD he'd bought from television; it's called *Jock Rock*, and soon we're tapping our toes to "Sweet Home Alabama." The Hurricane seems to handle well enough on empty roads, but tractor trailers pose a problem. When big rigs pull alongside, air rushes through the thin space between the vehicles, creating lift and literally sucking the vehicles together. When a truck clears, the vacuum is released, and the RV feels as though it's been pushed the other way by a strong crosswind. Each RV has its own feel on the road, and eventually Chris gets the hang of his new ride, so the push and pull of the wind becomes predictable, something he can steer for, like waves beneath a boat.

Chris passes the time with RV-lot war stories, which actually serve to put me on notice. Once a drunk guest in the Bices' RV woke up in the night and mistook a duffel bag full of clothes for the toilet, wetting a weekend's worth of clothes. Another time, Chris and Paula had helped haul an RV-ful of friends to safety after they'd become disoriented from carbon monoxide, a perpetual and deadly hazard of RV generators. I find the stories quite reassuring; if I don't poison the Bices with toxic fumes or piss in their luggage, I'll seem a model guest.

* * *

In the 1970s, a psychologist named Robert Cialdini found that fans were much more likely to wear their team's colors after a win than after a loss. Cialdini theorized that by wearing the colors of a winning team, fans were claiming a little of that superiority themselves, a phenomenon he called "basking in reflected glory." After two hours of surfing through the Blue Ridge Mountains, we're deposited into the piedmont of eastern Tennessee, near Knoxville, home of the University of Tennessee Volunteers, and evidence of Cialdini's theory abounds. Tennessee won last year's National Championship, and with the new season approaching, the state is awash in orange: on bumper stickers, flags, billboards, T-shirts, and baseball caps. At a gas station, we come across an offering of orange jerseys, T-shirts, hats, tennis shoes, mugs, and ponchos arranged like an altar beneath a large orange banner bearing a white "T." At the center of the altar: a television, constantly replaying a videotape of highlights from Tennessee's 1998 National Championship win over Florida State. A potbellied customer in an orange cap has been taken in by the sight. He stares at the television, slack jawed, in a trance.

"Disgusting," Chris says.

There's nothing intrinsically sickening about the color orange as far as I know, but I get a nauseous twinge myself. As Tide fans and therefore Tennessee rivals, we experience an equal and opposite reaction to all that orange; for us it's misery that's reflected.

A bit farther down the road, passing motorists begin to flip us off. In a sea of orange, our Alabama bumper stickers and that TIDE license plate are the equivalent of KICK ME signs taped to our backs. A truckful of Tennessee fans glares at us hatefully as they ghost by on the highway. A boy of perhaps twelve in the backseat of his parents' Lincoln gives us the finger. On my drive from New York to South Carolina, people on the highway had been my friends—strangers flashed their lights to warn of state troopers up ahead, and I got cheery waves when I changed lanes to let people pass. Now that football season has begun, the social landscape has changed. Factions have formed. We have friends *and* enemies—in our particular case, lots of enemies. When we see other Alabama fans, we wave enthusiastically; the more people flip us off, the more relieved we are to encounter the occasional friend. This is the difference between being a sports fan and the fan of a band or pop celebrity. When a carful of Eminem fans passes a car with a Kenny G bumper sticker on the highway, they don't roll down the windows in a rush to give the cool-jazz fans the finger. Being a music fan is its own end. Being a sports fan, though, is as much about opposing as advocating. To like one team is to dislike others—and there are lots of others. Past Knoxville we see RVs decked out in Georgia, Florida, and Auburn gear—half the American South it seems is barreling toward a football game in a land yacht. This means more honking, glaring, flipping each other off. The upside of all the negative attention is that the Bices and I bond more. We have common enemies, which means we are friends.

The reaction on the Vanderbilt campus is altogether different. We arrive in Nashville just after four o'clock. Paula unfolds a map and locates a small oval that represents Vanderbilt Stadium, and we're on our way through the city streets. With football our only concern, Nashville itself barely registers; it's just a two-dimensional backdrop of a skyline like the scrim behind the set of the local TV news. Soon we spot the rim of the stadium in the distance and pull in behind two other Alabama RVs to form a miniconvoy that trundles around the fringes of the Vanderbilt campus. Nearly everyone we pass stops what they're doing to gawk at us. But the locals aren't giving us the finger; they're pointing at us and laughing. Vanderbilt is a kind of Southern Ivy—a serious college, and hardly what you'd call a football school. The team usually finishes last in the conference, and the fans take an altogether measured approach in supporting them—visiting fans routinely outnumber Vanderbilt fans in Vandy's own stadium, for example, and you could drive around Nashville for months and not run into a single Vanderbilt fan in a motor home. We are an invading army in a place that doesn't mind being invaded. The hostile reaction around Knoxville had been validating; here, we are out of context. And as anyone who has ever seen a fan wearing face paint in any place other than a stadium surely knows, context is the hardcore fan's only cover.

"Motor home!" Chris is pointing off to starboard: a giant red superbus with an airbrushed mural of an elephant on its side, and it's just the beginning. Dozens of RVs stretch into the distance. The spread is set up along a busy campus thoroughfare, for maximum visibility. If we're out of context, the display says, we'll create one. Chris makes a quick move across traffic to slip past the confused-looking drivers of the two Alabama RVs we've been following; our friends are now competitors for a good parking space. We're greeted by a waving throng—another RV, more context. The lot is a crush not just of RVs but a crazy carnival of red and white golf carts, Jeeps, and crimson-colored Volkswagen Bugs and dune buggies. The difficulty of getting a parking place and the work that goes into setting up camp demands that anyone who wants to go anywhere after parking also bring another vehicle. Each RV has its own outdoor living room with a rug, folding chairs, coolers heaped with beer, and televisions in underneath compartments. Missing, though, is any sense of exuberance. The heat has induced languor, and it's all anyone can do simply to sit still in a folding chair, broiling even in the shade. There's a generator on each RV to power lights, water pumps, and the air conditioner, and besides creating a terrible racket—imagine a parking lot full of riding mowers at full throttle—they blanket the camp in a brown haze of exhaust. We pull in parallel to a long line of parked RVs and begin to unpack our own outdoor living room—a red Astroturf carpet, folding picnic table, a half-dozen folding chairs, two ice chests, the TV and satellite dish—but in the heat and befouled air, our living room is uninhabitable.

Our neighbors are a couple from Sylacauga, Alabama, named the Ogles. I introduce myself and am invited on board, out of the heat, and offered a sandwich. The Ogles are in their early sixties, and to them RV-ing to Alabama games is more than a simple recreational dalliance; it's the result of an attempt to reclaim their lives. Mr. Ogle worked on the floor of a printing plant for over twenty years; Mrs. Ogle was a dental assistant for nearly as long. They found their professional lives depressing, so they sold their house—it had a pool, a big yard, and bedrooms for their two children—bought a small cedar cabin with a twelve-foot by twelve-foot patch of grass for a yard and two rocking chairs on the porch, and put the rest of their money into a tractor trailer and RV. From Monday to Friday, the Ogles haul pipe across the South in the tractor trailer—Mr. Ogle does the driving and Mrs. Ogle rides shotgun and reads the Bible and the newspaper aloud. Then on Fridays, they return home, park the rig, get in their RV, and drive to Alabama games. Whenever the geography and the timing work out, they'll drive to a NASCAR race on Sunday. They get home on Sunday nights, get a little rest, and on Monday morning they pick up another load of pipe and hit the road again. The trucking gig grosses $100,000 a year, and being on the road, Mr. Ogle says, "is like being on vacation all the time."

The Ogles don't drink—their biggest thrill comes from helping stranded motorists and ministering to lonely truckers—and this fact alone says something about them: the Ogles are obviously very tolerant people. Being a teetotaler in an Alabama RV lot is like being a PETA member at a bow hunters' convention. But it also says something about the group: there's room for people who don't drink and who read the Bible aloud on the highway and minister to strangers. You don't have to be a loud, paint-your-face maniac who eats Bama Bombs for breakfast. The barrier for entry into the group is remarkably low: you just need to pull for the Crimson Tide.

The Ogles are so quiet and unassuming that I can't gauge their devotion. So I ask them to give an example of a sacrifice they've made to make a game. There's a long silence, which is taken over the whoosh of the air conditioner.

"Well my wife—" Mr. Ogle says eventually, pointing to Mrs. Ogle, "she had a gall bladder attack before the Alabama–Ohio State bowl game. The doctors thought they'd have to do surgery, but they got her eased up on Demerol, so the next morning I dragged her out of there and we made the kickoff."

Mrs. Ogle nods in assent. The whoosh of the air conditioner takes over again.

"I don't remember a whole lot about that game," she says.

I take leave of the Ogles and wander around the lot a bit to check the mood. For all the excitement and the jittery anticipation of tomorrow's matchup, the fans are in a rather surly state. A drunken RV-er named Randy explains the situation to me. The RV-ers are angry, he says, because they've been made to park farther from the stadium than in years past, and on asphalt instead of grass, which is contributing to the heat. Randy is wiry, sunburned, and has a little cap of blond hair that is short like moss.

"We used to could park over there," he says, pointing toward a patch of grass near the stadium. "Then they moved us to a field over there—" he points to his right. "Now we're just plain booted."

I ask who "they" is.

"How the hell am I supposed to know?" Randy says. "Some motherfucker at Vanderbilt University."

One of the core beliefs of the RV-ers seems to be that they are unwanted wherever they go, a not entirely imagined perception perhaps, given that even the University of Alabama doesn't know what to do with all of its motor-homing fans. But the feeling of being unwanted is even more acute on the road, where a host school's every act of planning is interpreted as an attempt to marginalize, inconvenience, and insult visiting RV-ers. We seem pretty close to the stadium to me—it's perhaps a third of a mile away—but we are not nearly close enough for Randy. I decide to forgo an argument, and instead accept Randy's offer of a cold beer. As we're sipping our brews in the heat, a carload of Vanderbilt students whizzes past shouting unintelligible insults.

"Fuckin' assholes," Randy says. "Tomorrow we're gonna kick some Commodore ass."

Back at the Hurricane I find Chris halfway inside one of the RV's rear exterior compartments.

"What's up?" I ask. Chris crawls out of the compartment. He's doused in sweat and there's a smudge of grease across his brow.

"Generator died," he says.

A dead generator is a bad thing; the generator runs the air conditioner; the air conditioner keeps us alive. Chris has a screwdriver in his hand, but he doesn't seem to have the slightest idea what to do with it. He sort of pokes the generator, as though he's trying to wake an old dog. Mr. Ogle steps out of his RV with a plate of pork chops he's planning to cook on an ankle-high minigrill. He sees us fumbling, puts down his barbecue fork, and comes over to help. After a composed minute inside the compartment, he emerges.

"I think it's your oil," he says. "A lot of these machines have an automatic shutoff if the oil gets low."

"Hey, if my oil was low, I'd quit too," Chris says. It's a quirk of his, I learn, to express empathy for animals and inanimate things, like engines. Later, we meet a couple with a dachshund they've trained to howl when it hears the Alabama fight song played on an RV air horn. Chris watches the show, then declares, "If somebody stuck my butt in front of a motor home and blew the horn, I'd howl too." In the case of the generator at least, his empathy is well placed. The oil trick works—the generator and air conditioner thrum to life. Chris, Paula, Larry, and I pile inside the Hurricane with a renewed appreciation of Freon and the mechanical gifts of our neighbors.

* * *

The last time Vanderbilt beat Alabama in Nashville was in 1969, the year I was born. Vanderbilt has lost twenty-five of their last twenty-six games to Southeastern Conference opponents. The school last won a conference championship in 1923. For a team like Alabama, with National Championship dreams, this was the kind of matchup that mattered only if you lost. Normally Alabama fans would approach the Vanderbilt game with insouciance bordering on arrogance (at least that was always my approach), but this is the first game of the season—always a crapshoot—and it's coming just three weeks after the DuBose meltdown, which only adds to the uncertainty. The game will show less about the team's raw talents than its ability to get over the damage caused by learning the coach has been doing a secretary in the football building. It's more about birds and bees than X's and O's.

I wake up on Saturday morning to a call-and-response rendition of "Yea Alabama!" the fight song, blaring from the air horns of an RV. It's seven-thirty. I have my first RV shower—picture bathing with a squirt gun—and head outside into a bolus of wet hot air. A night's worth of generator exhaust lies over the lot like morning mist on a river. The camp is coming chokingly to life. At ten minutes to nine, I spot my first beer drinker.

For the rest of the morning, enthusiasm builds. More Alabama fans show up in their cars and instinctively flock to the RV lot to tailgate with their own kind. There's a steady chorus of fans shouting "Roll Tide" across the lot, like birds chattering anonymously in a forest. Chris pours himself an Ancient Age and Mountain Dew in a Big Gulp–sized "go cup," as he calls it. We put out some water for Larry, and crank the air conditioner to high so that he isn't cooked medium-rare by the day's end. Paula packs a supply of washcloths and ice in Ziploc bags—emergency measures for when the heat stroke kicks in.

Just before leaving, Chris unscrews the lid on the jar of Bama Bombs and doles them out ceremoniously—Communion for fans. Paula digs out her lucky pom-pom, a stick with a few red scraps at the tip. Soon we're off.

Across the paved range around the stadium, people converge from every direction like water toward a drain. There is a confluence of dissonant sounds—wailing car stereos, the syncopated slamming of car doors signifying the arrival of more fans. Accents seemed to thicken, as if for emphasis. The sounds of marching bands—the low, muffled beat of bass drums; the rat-a-tat of the snares; and the fat, clean sound of brass—effervesce over the rim of the stadium. The day before the grounds were clean; now they are littered with garbage—plates, Solo cups, bags, strands of plastic from pom-poms, napkins, pieces of disposable tablecloths, beer can cartons—lots of beer can cartons. All of it sits festering in the stagnant air, which smells of charcoal and cooked meat, beer, cigarettes, whiskey, and exhaust.

As thanks for the ride, I picked up our tickets, three together in the Alabama section, facing the press box and unobscured from the searing sun, now directly overhead. It's possibly the hottest day of my life. Everyone—from fat guys to wispy little southern belles—is drenched with sweat. My shirt sticks heavily to my back. Paula, Chris, and I take turns putting the cold rags on our foreheads, but in no time they heat up and begin to feel like the steaming washcloths you get upon sitting down at a sushi restaurant. There are twice as many Alabama fans as Vanderbilt fans in the stadium—no surprise, really, because typically, Vandy students stay in their dorm rooms or frat houses for the first half, with the game playing low on the radio, and wander over to the stadium only if the score gets close. On a day like today, even a hardcore fan can see the virtue of this method of team support. Pretty soon, the players come barreling onto the field, and when they do, it's perfectly clear who will win. Vanderbilt, the home team, is wearing solid black jerseys, while Alabama is in white. We don't even have to try; we simply have to wait until sunstroke kicks in and fells their entire team.

It's a good thing, too. The Tide comes out playing sloppy football. The defense is confused and sluggish. The offensive line is out of sync, and players are jumping offside and holding. In the first half, the Tide gets eight penalties. We look preoccupied—exactly as you might expect from a team whose coach had been caught shagging his secretary. Vanderbilt scores first, early in the second quarter. We manage a drive at the end of the second quarter, and Alexander scores with less than a minute left in the half. When he breaks the goal line, Chris and Paula exchange a quick kiss, then turn and give dutiful high fives to me and all our neighbors. The game is tied at the half, and the three of us head for the shade beneath the bleachers. Amazingly, neither the Bices nor I feel the slightest bit of concern about the score. Playing Vanderbilt is like riding a roller-coaster—not in the sense of highs and lows, but in that we can experience the free falls and g-forces of a close game all with the knowledge that at the end, we'll pull safely into the station.

When the bands stop playing, we head out once again into the miserable heat and are greeted by a worrying sign: the Vanderbilt section is filling up. Their fans don't share our conviction that Alabama will win. No undergraduate at Vanderbilt University, it occurs to me, has even been alive for a home victory against Alabama, and they're putting a lifetime of frustration into every cheer. When Vandy kicks a field goal three minutes into the third quarter to go ahead, they jump through the air like spooked baitfish. The teams trade touchdowns, and at the end of the third quarter, the Commodores lead 17-14. Vanderbilt is not melting.

But there's only so long even a well-trained athlete can endure temperatures of ninety-something degrees and blistering midday sun in shoulder pads, a helmet, and a photon-slurping black jersey. Apparently the limit is about two hours and fifteen minutes, because that's how long it takes before Vandy begins their collapse. The first sign comes on a third down in their own territory early in the fourth quarter. The quarterback drops back, and Alabama defensive lineman Kindal Moorehead comes tearing through the line like a Sherman tank blasting through a hedgerow. The quarterback is quickly reduced to roadkill. He's helped off the field by teammates, and Vandy has to punt. Chris, Paula, and I exchange high fives.

In short order, Alabama pounds the ball down the field, and Alexander scores on a flitting three-yard run up the middle: more kisses and dutiful high fives. Vanderbilt's offense comes back on the field; the radiation sickness has fully set in. They give the ball right back to Alabama, and our quarterback, Andrew Zow, responds with a fifty-one-yard round fired over the heads of the defense to Alexander. Alabama has scored twice in three minutes; the Vanderbilt meltdown is complete. As their fans cascade down the stadium steps toward the exits, the Alabama band stands and shoulders its tubas, and we sing:

Hey 'Dores!
Hey 'Dores!
We just beat the hell out of you!
Rammer Jammer Yellow Hammer!
Give 'em hell Alabama!

The *Rammer Jammer* is a long-defunct campus magazine; the yellowhammer is the Alabama state bird, but these are meaningless allusions compared with the chant's real power, the dissonant clanging of all those vowels and that gloating line "We just beat the hell out of you." It's an awfully ungracious thing to say to your hosts after a great weekend, but perhaps part of the thrill of temporary superiority is being able to assert it, even ritually, and so the Bices and I sing as loudly as anyone. We stay in our seats as the stadium empties around us, all those fans and all that red rushing desperately into the shady portals. I feel strangely at ease with the Bices, and I sense they feel the same way, even Paula. What we have in common as Alabama fans, at this moment anyway, overrides whatever differences there may be between us. If Paula doubted that someone who lived in New York City could actually pull for Alabama, I imagine she was persuaded otherwise by the panic on my face and the desperation in my voice when Alabama fell behind.

The mood back in the RV lot is subdued. It wasn't an impressive win exactly, but the team hadn't come apart, which had been the big fear. We feel more relief than exuberance, and anyway, everyone is depleted and dehydrated from the afternoon-long sauna, which has managed to sober up even Randy, who's in the lot, bedraggled, sweating, and going over the details of the game with surprising coherence. With the game behind us, so is everyone's rationale for spending the night in a dismal parking lot off a major downtown thoroughfare. RVs are pulling out by the dozens, leaving black puffs of diesel soot in their wake. I begin to experience the anxiety of having stayed too long at a party.

The one creature who is not at all subdued or depleted is Larry, who greets us enthusiastically as we pile into the Hurricane. Something, though, is missing. Actually, two things are missing. The first is the monotonous drone of the generator in the rear compartment, and the second is cool air. The generator is dead, and it's only a miracle that Larry is not. Simultaneously, the three of us peek out the window in the direction of the Ogles, but their RV is gone. We'll have to fix the generator ourselves.

It's hopeless. The oil trick doesn't work this time, and Chris's aimless poking at the machine with a screwdriver doesn't inspire it back to life. An RV without air-conditioning in this heat is uninhabitable, but Chris has an idea: if we find an electrical outlet somewhere, we can hook up and run the air conditioner off shore power. He takes off to scout the nearby elementary school for an outlet from which we can "suck juice"—his term—and a few minutes later returns with some good news and some bad news; the good news is that he's found an outlet. The bad is that it is on an incline, beneath a streetlamp and next to an overfilled Dumpster. It's a sign of how desperate we are for cool air that these are perfectly acceptable trade-offs. We repark the RV, plug in, and the air conditioner comes to life.

Chris has to work the afternoon shift at the air traffic control tower on Sunday night, and he wants a little time to collect his thoughts before guiding aircraft safely to earth. So we wake up the next morning at 7:00 A.M. and get ready to go. Garbage festers in the lot, which looks like Max Yasgur's farm the afternoon after Woodstock. On Sunday morning, Nashville is as lifeless as a moonscape, and soon we're once again on the interstate, driving east toward Knoxville against a miles-long convoy of orange. There is one final task to accomplish while on the road: we have to empty the Hurricane's waste water tanks, a sixty-gallon tank that captures soapy "gray water" from the sink and shower, and a forty-gallon "black water" tank that holds sewage. You can't put this stuff just anywhere; Paula consults a telephone directory–sized volume that lists the amenities available at every interstate exit in America and finds a dumping station at a Flying J truck stop up ahead. She dons a pair of surgical gloves, connects an accordion-like blue hose to a fitting beneath the RV, deposits the other end into the top of a foul-smelling concrete cistern, and gives me a quick lesson on the finer points of conducting a procedure rather straightforwardly referred to as "a dump." The trick is to release the black water first, then to rinse the hose with the soapy gray water. Mission accomplished, Paula hoses herself down with the Hurricane's outdoor shower, HAZMAT-style, and we pull back on the highway.

We get back to the Bices' in the midafternoon. The house has been trashed by the cats—there are green, mucusy hairballs on the kitchen floor and on the living room carpet—but the Bices laugh it off. It seems unfair, after all, to get angry at the cats for doing to the Bices' home what we did, more or less, to the Vanderbilt campus. Lazily, we unpack.

So how did it go? Do the Bices like me enough to have me along again? I feel pretty good about the trip. Paula has warmed to me. I didn't confuse the duffel bag for a toilet. I helped out, by buying gas and tickets. I hung in there for the dump. But most important, Alabama won. Another result like that and my presence could become a talisman on par with Bama Bombs. I give Paula a farewell hug and follow Chris to work on my way out of town. He's agreed to show me the inside of an air traffic control tower, so I park out front of the Greenville Downtown Airport—a small airport for private planes known, if at all, as the departure point of Lynyrd Skynyrd's doomed 1977 flight, which killed six band members—and follow Chris up a series of stairs into the tower. Inside, Chris monitors traffic on a small green radarscope. It's overcast, and traffic is light, but every five or ten minutes a call comes in, and two little pinpricks of light emerge from the clouds on a steady slope to the runway. Any levity Chris showed at the wheel of the Hurricane on a weekend of tailgating has vanished. His delivery is robotic, almost grave. Pretty soon I get the feeling I'm in the way, so I say goodbye.

"So we'll see you in Birmingham?" he asks. Next Saturday's game is against the University of Houston at Legion Field in Birmingham. I say I'll be there.

"Well if you need a place to crash, man, there's a bed on the mowder home with your name on it."

There's only one thing to say in response: "Roll Tide."

"Hey man." Chris sticks out his hand. "Roll Tide."

Chapter Four

Coach Bryant's Gone

THE BICES WON'T GET TO BIRMINGHAM UNTIL FRIDAY night, so I make the five-hour trip in my car and keep an eye on the stadium to see when the Alabama RVs begin to show up. The first motor homes arrive at Legion Field on Wednesday afternoon, and by five o'clock, there are twenty in the lot, parked close together like a wagon train. The stadium is in a hard-luck neighborhood at the western edge of downtown Birmingham, where section houses once occupied by middle-class steelworkers have fallen hopelessly decrepit, with peeling paint, curling roof shingles, and, every fourth building or so, boards over the windows. In the public housing complex that abuts the stadium parking lot, sand separates the two-story red brick buildings where grass should grow. The stadium itself adds little cheer; it's a battleship gray structure atop a crosshatch of I-beams—in a steel town like Birmingham no one would've thought to slap a facade on something so beautiful as a girder—that hovers gloomily over the neighborhood like a summer thunderhead. In the middle of this dismal tableau there's a cluster of radiant white motor homes with brightly colored swooshes on their sides, flags overhead, and gleaming chrome wheels with lug nuts that shatter the sunlight like diamonds. A gaunt, leather-skinned parking attendant guards the lot. I give a quick wave as I roll by, and she responds with a jerk of her chin and a long tug on her cigarette.

I do a quick lap. There are lots of outdoor living rooms set up, but no one to be seen. It's too hot to be outside. A dry breeze curls around the East Stand and kicks up a cloud of brown dust. I see a man darting between RVs—checking out their undersides, then disappearing for a minute into a side compartment before reemerging. He looks curiously dutiful, like some sort of inspector, and has slicked-back black hair and a pencil mustache—a dead ringer for Schneider on *One Day at a Time.* I park the car alongside, get out, and introduce myself.

"Ed Cole," he says, sticking out his hand. "Mighty fine to meet you."

It turns out that Cole has been following Alabama football in an RV for nineteen years. Like one of those rocker kids from high school who ends up working at a guitar store, he has neatly merged his hobby with his profession: Ed Cole, football fan, sells RVs for a living. He works for a dealership with two big lots, one off I-20 on the way to Atlanta, the other in Panama City, Florida. His job is to ferry four motor homes to Legion Field on game weekends and to set up a temporary showroom, complete with all the amenities of a real tailgate party, to lure potential customers. Two coffin-sized coolers-full of Budweiser sit for the taking in front of Cole's RVs, as bait. Wednesday is setup day, Cole says. On Thursday, he "entertains full blast," which consists of "having drinks and lying to each other." Friday night is steak night. Just talking about it seems to get Cole excited. He rubs his hands together eagerly and shouts to no one in particular, "We gonna have us a TAIL . . . GATE . . . PARTY!"

Someone across the lot whoops in response.

Cole invites me aboard one of his rigs, a $289,000 model called a Dynasty. It has ceramic tile in the kitchen, double doors on the freezer/fridge, a washer/dryer, plenty of closets, a 350-horsepower Cummings diesel engine, and "automatic everything," Cole says. He's sold eighteen RVs in the last two weeks. Cole asks pointedly how much I make and how my credit rating is. I spare him the bad news, but the point is, Ed Cole wants to sell me a motor home. I tell him $300,000 is just slightly out of my range. The irony doesn't register; Cole wants to show me the $189,000 Diplomat next door.

Suddenly Cole furrows his brow and freezes in midstep, like a bird dog on a scent.

"Say," he says, "do you smell propane?"

I tell him I don't.

Just outside the Dynasty there is a smaller—much smaller—motor home with a FOR SALE sign on it. The RV is obviously used, and has an early seventies look to it, which I take to mean that it is a mid-eighties model, since motor home design seems to trail all other forms of design by a good fifteen years. The nose is pointy and triangular, kind of a beak, and the body looks just tall enough to stand in and just long enough to lie in; imagine a small garden shed strapped atop a Volkswagen.

"How much is that one?" I ask.

Cole, still frozen like a statue, snaps back to life.

"The LeSharo?" he says, peering out the window. "Cheap. Fourteen."

Fourteen thousand dollars for a glorified riding mower isn't cheap, but for $275,000 less than a Dynasty, it accomplishes the same basic tasks. The LeSharo has wheels, an engine, and a bed, and it's even customized for Alabama fans—it has faded Bama stickers baked onto its exterior and a spare tire cover with a big red "A" on it. Cole grabs a calculator and taps away while mumbling things like "one hundred and twenty months," "seven and a half percent interest," and "ten percent discount."

I'm still looking out the window at the LeSharo when my eyes are drawn to a peculiar site; across the lot a man is standing in the stairwell of his RV rotating his arms madly, like windmills.

"You could have it for $159 a month, nothing down," Cole says.

I have to remind myself that I don't want a motor home. At least I'm pretty certain I don't want a motor home. The idea was, I'd ride in *other people's* motor homes. In fact, I hadn't even considered it, but

Cole has got me thinking. For the price of a single night in a hotel, I can make a monthly payment on my own RV. There are any number of very solid arguments *against* buying an RV—they break down and leave you stranded on the side of the highway, for example, whereas hotels do not. Or: people flip them in interstate rest stops and end up with asphalt in their shoulders for the rest of their lives, as happened to Paula Bice's father. Motor homes get terrible gas mileage, or as one RV-er poetically put it, they "burn gas like you was flushin' the toilet." But I know better than to raise any of these points with Ed Cole. He's heard them all before, I imagine, and can flip them around on me and in no time have me mortgaged up to my ears. Still it's useful insight into how Cole had moved eighteen $300,000 RVs in two weeks. The average American considers a 300-horsepower motor home with double slide-outs and air bag suspension only slightly more attainable than a seaside mansion, so the first step for an RV salesman toward a sale is simply to make a potential buyer realize that owning an RV is possible. The notion has the inflating effect of telling someone that he's worthy of membership in a club he was sure would never have him. The one rub is that under Cole's financing scheme, I would be making monthly payments into middle age and certainly long after the used RV in front of me had been consigned to scrap. Well, one man's recreational vehicle is another man's loan vehicle.

I decide I should leave Ed Cole before inadvertently signing over my soul. I have an appointment, I tell him. I'll stop by later. Cole doesn't seem to believe me; but neither does he seem dejected. No sale goes down so easily. It's only Wednesday. There are two coffinfuls of Bud outside. There's steak night.

"Say," Cole says as I walk out. "You sure you don't smell propane?"

Actually, once outside, I do smell something unusual—a sulfurous vapor that has wafted over the camp, perhaps from one of the nearby steel mills. The man across the parking lot is still flapping his arms ridiculously in the stairwell of his RV. I walk over to see what's going on.

"Man!" he shouts when I get close. "Left on the propane stove. Liked to *knock me down*. I'm liable to blow up." The man stops flapping long enough to shake hands. He introduces himself as Donnie, then turns around and takes a deep sniff. The problem with propane is that it's heavier than air; instead of evaporating it puddles in boats and RVs like water, until someone with a match comes along. Donnie insists the RV has aired out plenty, and against my better judgment I follow him onboard for a tour. He rattles off the equipment list—mood lights, a 300-horsepower Caterpillar engine, two VCRs, a convection microwave, a 45-watt solar panel, and "plenty of Crown Royal and Kahlua."

"I got a motto," he says. "We can't be young, but we can be immature."

Donnie, it turns out, speaks almost exclusively in one-liners. When I ask him how long he's been an Alabama fan, he sticks out his lower lip, looks up at the ceiling as if he were doing complex math, and says, "Since I was a fetus." I ask what he does for a living and Donnie says he recently retired from Scott Paper for a new career as a kickboxer. He couldn't look less like an athlete—he appears to be in his fifties and has skinny legs and a protruding belly, and in silhouette could easily be confused with Kermit the Frog.

"A kickboxer?" I ask dimly.

"Yeah. I kick back on the sofa in my boxers."

There's a commotion outside, and Donnie and I rush out to see what's going on: a group of RV-ers on the trail of the propane leak have their noses in the air like a pack of hounds and they're coming our way. Donnie grabs the bottle of Crown Royal and heads out to greet them.

"I've hung out with y'all sober and I've hung out with y'all drunk," he says, raising his bottle into the air. "And let me tell you, *it's better drunk.*"

There's a circle of folding chairs outside Donnie's motor home, and once satisfied the threat of explosion has passed, everyone sits down, the faint scent of propane still in the air. I pop open a cheap folding chair of my own and join the group. Talk quickly turns to the DuBose situation.

"I wudn't gonna believe it at first," says Skipper, a burly, bugle-throated fan from Tuscaloosa. "And I believe in forgiveness. But a man with class should've resigned. That's what Coach Bryant would've done."

"Coach Bryant's gone, I heard the other day," Donnie says.

"Yeah I've been lookin' for him on the sideline," says Skipper. "Tell you sumpin'. When I found out it was true, I said we'll be a six and five team. And know what? That's what we looked like last week. A six and five team."

"You through?" Donnie says, perturbed. "They didn't show anything they didn't have to show."

"Aw, Donnie, that's silly. They still jumped offsides the whole game. Six and five. I'm entitled to my opinion."

Skipper's opinion can't be easily dismissed; he hasn't missed an Alabama game since he was ten years old. He's now fifty-six.

There's something about sitting in a folding chair that suddenly imbues the southern football fan with the storytelling powers of Homer. On Friday nights in the lot, you'll see dozens of clusters of folding chairs and, at the center of each one, someone telling a story. This is what Ed Cole meant when he said fans spent Friday nights "lying to each other"; being accurate in these sessions is never as important as being entertaining. For Donnie's crowd, the favorite topic seems to be Donnie himself. There's apparently a lot of material. There was the time in Raleigh a few years back, for example, when he and a carload of drunken Alabama fans got lost on the way to a local honky-tonk. A cop found them driving aimlessly around town, but instead of arresting them, he showed them the way to the bar. Raleigh isn't a half-bad town, everyone agrees, if a carload of drunks there can get a police escort to a pub.

In Omaha once, Donnie was having a hard time parking his RV and some of the locals started laughing at him. He took exception, got out of his RV, and exchanged insults with them. When the locals wouldn't back down, Donnie announced he was going to get his pistol. Violence was averted only because Skipper convinced the locals Donnie was "crazy from 'Nam," at which point they scattered as though they'd been teargassed.

That was the same trip, Skipper says, when Donnie met Ike

Richardson, the commanding officer of the USS *Nimitz.* Richardson was there to watch the game, and when Donnie found out who he was—namely, a man with personal control over a substantial atomic arsenal—he marched up to Richardson and asked how much it would cost to get him to "nuke Auburn."

Once, after Donnie asked a local country music singer for an autographed picture, his brother Robbie told the woman, "If you knew what he was going to do with that, you wouldn't sign it." When the woman asked what he meant, Donnie told her, "I'm gonna tape it to my blow-up doll."

The storytelling session—and the drinking—go on for an hour, at which point Skipper turns to me, points at my notebook, and asks accusatorily: "What the hell are you writing?"

I'd made clear to Donnie and his chums that I was a reporter, but apparently the information had been lost on Skipper, perhaps in the fog of cocktails. But his question suddenly seems to provoke the hostile interest of everyone in the circle. I explain myself: I'm researching a book about Alabama football fans and plan to go to every game this season with the RV crowd. Skipper rolls his eyes skeptically. Even Donnie, who an hour earlier was happy to give me a tour of his rig, now peers at me with a look of distrust. The bottle of Crown Royal beneath his chair is ominously close to empty. It turns out that there are two basic reactions in the RV lot to learning that I'm a reporter. A certain faction is curious, flattered perhaps by the idea that someone is interested in their stories. But the hardest of the hardcores have a more jaded attitude toward reporters. For one thing, it isn't news to them that they're news. They've been interviewed more times than a lot of minor Hollywood celebrities—by local newspapers and television crews and national magazine writers. A couple of times each year some graduate student in psychology or a sociology professor with a beard and Birkenstocks shows up at the lot with a clipboard and a number 2 pencil, to watch them and take notes, like biologists watching sea turtles on a beach. Last year, Skipper says, a professor from

Arizona shadowed him for months with a movie camera, filming him for the purposes of research.

"I believe he was getting stuff on us for the FBI," Skipper says. It's not at all clear that he's joking.

There's another strike against the press as far as Donnie's crowd is concerned, and that's that Paul Finebaum is a member of it. In Donnie's view, you can't say anything worse about a group of people than that. Once when Finebaum was doing a live feed from the parking lot of Legion Field on game day, Donnie tells me, he organized a group to sit in their RVs and blast their air horns whenever Finebaum went on the air. Eventually Finebaum got in his satellite truck and moved, to cheers. I sense an implicit threat in Donnie's retelling of this bold act: he's putting me on notice that he's capable of repulsing the enemy.

Donnie wants to know who I've interviewed so far, as a test of my methodology. I mention the Bices, the Ogles, Randy, the couple with a dachshund that howled when they played the Alabama fight song. Donnie shakes his head disapprovingly.

You haven't met the Show Chicken Man? he asks.

Not knowingly, I tell him.

You'd know if you had, Donnie says—*he drives a big RV with a bunch of champion show chickens in the hold.*

What about the Chicken Man? he asks.

I tell him I don't think so.

The Chicken Man—as distinct from the Show Chicken Man—Donnie says, *made a fortune building chicken houses across the South. He was diagnosed with cancer, sold his business, and put all of his money into a $1.2-million motor home and vowed to spend his last days following the Tide. Problem is, he got better. So now he's stuck with an RV that would've made Elvis proud.*

No, I say, I definitely haven't met the Chicken Man.

What about the Heart Guy? Skipper asks.

I don't bother to answer. The Heart Guy, he says, lives in Nashville and is awaiting a heart transplant there. If he travels farther than two hours from the hospital, he's automatically taken off the waiting list. But he refuses to miss Alabama games—only one of which this season takes place within two hours of Nashville. The Heart Guy, Skipper says, literally risks his life for Alabama football.

I'm beginning to think I'm getting my leg pulled. But the grave looks on the faces around me suggest otherwise. Well, if there are such people out there, I'm resolved to find them.

"You got a motor home?" Donnie asks sharply, to emphasize, it seems, my status as an outsider.

"Not yet," I say, words that startle me as soon as I speak them.

* * *

On Thursday afternoon the RVs arrive at Legion Field at a rate of about a half dozen every hour. The parking operation is under the command of a burly city employee named R. C. Hicks. He's suntanned the color of wet clay, wears a green Parks Department vest, and carries a clipboard and a walkie-talkie. Things aren't going well between Hicks and the new arrivals, for the simple reason that he has specific ideas about where and how they should park, and RV-ers hate being told where to park. RV-ers are like a more law-abiding faction of the Hells Angels; they have a special aversion to being told what they can and can't do, and one of the prime expressions of freedom to an RV-er is being able to set up one's rig without regard to city bureaucrats or the white lines on a blacktop. Further, friends who travel together in separate RVs sometimes like to park next to each other, alternating the direction of their rigs so they can square up their big retractable awnings, thereby doubling the space of their outdoor living rooms. Sometimes four RVs might park in a square with their awnings on the inside to form a huge covered living space. Such configurations are not an efficient use of space in a tight parking lot, but then people who drive vehicles that get eight miles per gallon aren't exactly efficiency-minded types.

Hicks, the lot attendant, wants all the RVs to park in the same direction and close together, so they can't unfurl their awnings at all. He uses his body, like that lone protester who stood in front of a tank in Tiananmen Square, to divert the big rigs into place. By the time an

RV-er has parked, gotten out, and realized that he is too close to his neighbor to deploy his awning, another RV has come alongside at Hicks's direction and hemmed him in. That's when the yelling begins. It's easy to imagine the situation getting out of control.

By Friday afternoon the lot is packed. A line of people are waiting to tour Ed Cole's RVs, or at least are feigning interest in his RVs as an excuse to drink his beer. No one is paying much attention to the LeSharo, but the door is open so I climb in. The accommodations aren't what you'd call comfortable—imagine a cot in a small U-Haul trailer—but it's functional, and there is a nifty feature that allows you to turn the living room into a shower, simply by lifting a floorboard to reveal a drain. I sit at the wheel and try to picture myself on the highway, lost in motor-homing reverie, but the image won't form. The imagination has its limits. Donnie walks by and sees me at the wheel.

"You ain't gonna buy that thing, are you?" he shouts at me through the windshield.

"I'm thinking about it," I yell enthusiastically.

"Have you driven it?"

"No. Why?"

"Everything on it makes noise but the horn."

* * *

The vibe in the lot is different from the week before. The University of Houston, Alabama's opponent this week, has only a few traveling fans, so there is no one to oppose us, and consequently, everyone seems exceedingly at ease. Late Friday afternoon, clusters of folding chairs shoot up like stands of mushrooms in a damp forest. A middle-aged man with white hair and a red face cruises the lot in a boatlike 1970s convertible, asking if anyone will give him five grand for it. So far, no takers. Red golf carts buzz around—it's hard to keep track of exactly how many there are because they constantly disappear and reappear from behind motor homes. A man wanders around the lot hawking framed prints depicting famous moments in Alabama football history.

A few white clouds are streaked across the sky like horse manes. Roof-mounted satellite dishes are silhouetted against the darkening sky and give the camp the look of a convention of lunar landers. After dinner, Donnie's friend Skipper sets up a karaoke machine between the RVs and the stadium. It's not some portable sing-along setup that you buy at Sears for a kid's birthday party, but rather a genuine nightclub-quality system with four wireless microphones, a monitor with computerized lyric scrolling, and big tripod-mounted speakers. The apparatus is powered by a gas generator and cranks out so much noise that, a year before, the Tuscaloosa Police Department sent a team in riot gear—"the SWAT team," according to Donnie—to shut it down. The police action prompted outraged RV-ers to take their case for karaoke to the University of Alabama administration, where they successfully obtained a guarantee that karaoke would be allowed in the RV lot without the threat of police raids.

I spend a good portion of karaoke night talking to a young man from Mississippi about the finer points of painting a ten-foot-tall portrait of Bear Bryant on the side of an RV—a task he is close to completing—while in the background various singers gleefully butcher "Let's Go to the Hop," "My Ding-a-Ling," a Ricky Skaggs version of "Little Maggie," and every half hour or so, the Alabama fight song, which brings everyone to their feet. During Hank Williams Jr.'s "Family Tradition," I find myself speaking to a spindly man with a mustache and a red baseball cap pulled low over his eyes. His name is Larry, but he prefers to be called the Hot Food Man, in recognition of his hobby: making the spiciest pickled foods in Alabama. (A community that comes together just eleven or twelve times a year apparently relies heavily on nicknames to keep its members straight.) Larry's specialties are hot pickled tomatoes, which he calls " 'maters," hot corn casserole, and hot "pencil cob corn," which in Larry's robust accent comes across as "pinthacaw corn"—leaving me for some time with the mistaken impression that it is a variety of corn grown by a little-known tribe of Native Americans from the Pinthacaw nation. As luck would have it, Larry has some hot food in his RV, and before I can tell him no thanks, I have a weak palate, he's off toward his RV and shouting, *"He gone try my 'maters!"*

"Thems 'maters so hot they'll make you wanna slap yo mamma," a friend of Larry's tells me. It takes me a moment to realize that the man means this as a good thing, wanting to slap one's mamma.

Larry returns a few minutes later with a plastic fork, and a paper plate with a blob of pickled cherry tomatoes in the middle. I take a tentative bite and instantly feel as though my head is dissolving. I bend over, gagging, which prompts Larry and his buddy to laugh hysterically and exchange repeated high fives.

"Hot ain't it?" Larry asks mockingly. He hands me a can of Bud, which I shotgun. But the beer only spreads the burning sensation around my mouth, like water on a grease fire. I'm sweating and sniffling wimpily, as Larry grabs a fingerful of tomatoes from the plate, leans his head back, and opens his mouth like a hungry baby bird. He carefully deposits the tomatoes deep in his craw, and chews them slowly and with relish, as if eating a wad of taffy. Finally he swallows.

"Shit's like ice cream to me," he says.

For the next half hour I sit with Larry, sweating profusely as he explains the intricacies of the pickling process. It's surprisingly interesting—not the details of pickling per se, but Larry's enthusiasm for it. There's something instructive in the obsessiveness of the Hot Food Man: football zealots are usually zealots about more than just football. Larry doesn't just make a few jars of somewhat spicy food every now and again; he's on a campaign to provide the state of Alabama with a steady supply of the hottest food imaginable, and is still perfecting his methods. When Skipper sets up karaoke, he doesn't buy a cheap karaoke machine, though that probably would do the job; he buys a professional sound system that scares the police into donning their riot gear. When fans decide to cook up a little barbecue for dinner, they don't throw a few meat patties on a portable George Foreman electric griddle; they roast up whole cows on grills that are portable only in the sense that they have trailer hitches and wheels. The RV-ers' ethic is everything to the max.

The Bices call me on my cell phone from the road; they're arriving late and offer a berth on board the Hurricane, which I gratefully accept. It's nice to see to them again when they arrive, and nicer still that the Bices seem happy to see me as well. We sit underneath the Hurricane's awning, going over a scouting report of Houston that Chris found online, and sometime after two I go to sleep, my nose still running from Larry's 'maters, the other Larry—the one covered in fur—curled up at my feet.

* * *

To accommodate TV coverage, the Alabama-Houston game kicks off at 11:30 A.M. Starting this early ensures that a decent portion of the fans in the stadium are hopelessly hung over, while another group is still drunk. Fans in the lot are groggy and quiet—there's a little less urgency to all those "Roll Tides" shouted skyward, a little less activity around the barbecue pits. The notable exception is Chris Bice, who seems to have an uncanny capacity to switch instantly from a deep sleep to a state of catlike alertness. He passes out a round of Bama Bombs, fills his "go-cup" with a bolt of Ancient Age and a dash of Mountain Dew, and leads us toward the stadium with the enthusiastic hip swivel of a racewalker.

It's a beautiful Saturday. The sky is clear, the sun shining brightly and dimmed only slightly by a fading haze on the horizon. In the brilliant morning light Legion Field looks noble and timeworn, as though chiseled from clean granite. The stadium is sold out, but not quite packed; some have stayed away because of the heat and the weak opponent. Our tickets are in the end zone, but we scan the upper rows between the forties and manage to find a trio of empty seats, as luck would have it, right next to a striking young southern belle. Pro football crowds consist mainly of well-fed, middle-aged males, but for the college game in the South there is an abundance of youth and women, many of them in sundresses that could easily be confused with lingerie. The young woman next to me is probably twenty or twenty-one, lithe and tall, with collarbones like wire hangers, perfectly pedicured toes the size of jelly beans, and a feathery bob of brown hair that rustles seductively against the back of her neck when she stands to cheer. A red silk sundress seems to have floated down over her frame the way a parachute might fall atop a small tree. She seems altogether too prim and refined to chat with a total stranger at a football game, but in the lull after an early Crimson Tide first down, I decide to give it a try.

"Great seats, don't you think?" I say.

"I don't give a damn about the seats," the young woman barks. "I just hope Alabama *kicks some ass*!"

A fan, I suppose, is a fan.

Actually, Alabama does kick some ass. On our first drive, Alexander bursts through the line and carves his way downfield for a twenty-five-yard touchdown. The belle shakes excitedly and screams, "*Yeah* Shaun! *Yeah* Shaun! *Yeah* Shaun!"

I hear the phrase perhaps two hundred times throughout the afternoon. It's Alexander's day. He runs for 167 yards and three touchdowns, and each time he scores, the belle shouts and shakes and the Bices kiss and then high-five everyone in our row. Alabama wins 37-10. It's cause for optimism. We can score points. The team played with confidence. Most importantly, the game demonstrates that the DuBose scandal hasn't completely occupied the team's headspace. There's hope.

After the game, we gather around the Bices' television and watch the Notre Dame–Purdue game. Perhaps the only thing as pleasurable to fans as watching their team win is watching a rival lose, and so when Purdue wins 28-23, we can hardly believe our good fortune. The Bices pull out Sunday morning. I make plans to meet them here next week for the Louisiana Tech game.

On my way out of the lot, I stop by Ed Cole's RV and make an appointment to test-drive the LeSharo on Monday morning.

Chapter Five

Worthless Shirts

LORE HOLDS THAT THE FIRST TAILGATE PARTY WAS HELD in 1869 at the first college football match, between Rutgers and Princeton, when fans cooked on the carriage they rode in to the game. In fact, tailgating, or at least a form of it, goes back much further—all the way at least to the eighth century B.C. It was then, the historian Allen Guttmann writes, that the first Olympic Games were held in Greece. There was no stadium in Olympia then—spectators, many of whom had traveled miles by sea and over mountains, watched the game from a mound of dirt—and since there were no hotels around, at the end of each day, Guttmann writes in his book *Sports Spectators*, "most of the spectators had to make do with tents or with nights under the stars." Ancient spectators had to deal with some of the same hassles as modern college football fans—the authorities who ran the Pythian games in Delphi, for example, tired of drunken fans and banned wine from the arena—but the fans then may have had a slightly tougher go of it: spectators at the Olympic Games spent their days under the careful watch of whip and truncheon bearers hired to keep them in line.

The Greek games were religious events, and it wasn't until Roman times, when chariot races and gladiatorial battles became popular, that spectator sports began to be staged simply for their entertainment value. Apparently little has changed in the last two thousand years. A historian who witnessed a chariot race in Alexandria in the first century A.D. wrote of the crowd, "When they enter the stadium, it is as though they had found a cache of drugs; they forget themselves completely, and shamelessly say and do the first thing that occurs to them." Even back then, fandom was viewed by some as unfathomably absurd. After attending a chariot race, the historian Pliny the Younger wrote this to a friend: "It surprises me all the more that so many thousands of adult men should have such a childish passion for watching galloping horses and drivers standing in chariots, over and over again. If they were attracted by the speed of the horses or the driver's skill, one could account for it, but in fact it is the racing colors they really support and care about, and if the colors were to be exchanged in mid-course during a race, they would transfer their favor and enthusiasm and rapidly desert the famous drivers and horses whose names they shout as they recognize them from afar. Such is the popularity and importance of a worthless shirt."

In the Middle Ages and Renaissance, Professor Guttmann writes, spectators were notified months in advance of pageants and tournaments, giving them plenty of time to make plans and to travel. Once there, the archery and jousting fields "were surrounded by gaily colored tents and stands were crowded with spectators," not unlike the modern RV lot. As at contemporary college football games, Guttmann points out, sometimes the behavior of spectators was of more interest than the contest itself: at the Strasbourg tournament of 1576, the big story wasn't the archery but a race by spectators to deliver a kettle of porridge from Zurich by water before the tournament started; the winner made it in nineteen hours, and the porridge was still warm. Anyone who has witnessed a barbecue cook-off in a modern stadium parking lot can appreciate the competitive intensity of that porridge race.

In the eighteenth and nineteenth centuries, fans in England

turned out by the thousands for horse races and rowing events—an estimated million people, for example, showed up on August 27, 1869, to watch Harvard and Oxford row against each other on the Thames—and, concession stands being what they were at the time, most of those in attendance were compelled to bring their own lunch. They no doubt called it picnicking, but the exercise bore a striking resemblance to what we now call tailgating. The automobile, and ultimately the motor home, opened the floodgates for fans who wanted to get to sporting events early, and football, which takes place on weekends, was timed perfectly to accommodate them. So the point is, from the earliest days of spectator sports, fans have never been particularly satisfied to show up just when the first discus is thrown, the first arrow launched, or the first ball kicked. They like to get there early and, if they win, to stay late. It's not just the contest, but the spectacle as well.

With this in mind, on Monday morning I show up at the lot of Colonial RV sales to test drive the LeSharo. Ed Cole, though, isn't there. He's off tending to more lucrative business. I'm referred instead to Bill Smith, his associate, who doesn't seem thrilled about getting saddled with the LeSharo sale himself. The lot is teeming with potential customers interested in six-figure models; I'm prepared to offer something in the mid-fours. I wait in front of Smith's desk as he talks languidly on the phone to a friend, waiting it seems, for me to get so bored I leave. There are a dozen "Salesman of the Month" plaques on the wall behind him, and on his desk, an overflowing ashtray and a bottle of Maalox. Smith is smoking desperately. He looks to be in his late fifties, is heavyset, and has jowls that jiggle when he speaks. When he sees that I'm not going anywhere, Smith hangs up the phone, annoyed. He roots through a pile of keys until he finds the ones he is looking for, and I follow him outside. The air smells of fiberglass, solvents, and new plastic.

With Smith sitting sullenly beside me, I ease the LeSharo out of the lot and into traffic. We are uncomfortable from the start. The vehicle is hot, its air conditioner ineffectual against the baking sun. We roll down the windows, but this seems only to annoy Smith further. The breeze tussles his hair unflatteringly and blows cigarette ashes into his face. I drive tentatively at first, but gradually I gain confidence and bring the vehicle up to speed. We're soon cruising in the midst of a fast-moving stream of traffic. A car cuts me off and I slam on the brakes.

"Goddamn!" Smith barks. "Stupid *sonuvabitch*!"

I'm relieved to see Smith pointing at the other driver. He lights another cigarette. I ask a lot of questions, as much to seem like a discerning buyer as out of genuine curiosity, but none of them elicit anything more than a one-word answer from Smith. When we get back to the lot, he makes no effort to sell, other than to tell me unenthusiastically that the LeSharo is a "great deal." The sale seems to hinge not on the LeSharo's merits, but rather on my ignorance. I tell Smith I want to think it over, and that I'll call him within a day. He shows no reaction, other than to release his tensed facial muscles from an expression of discomfort into one of utter blankness. We shake hands. I decide to get a little smarter.

If you call ten RV owners in Jefferson County, Alabama, and ask for the name of a good motor home repairman, seven of them will refer you to a man named D.A. Hare. Mr. Hare runs his own RV repair business out of a shop in Montevallo, and over the last three decades he's become intimately familiar with the design flaws of pretty much every model. I call and tell him that I want to know the ballpark value of a mid-eighties Winnebago LeSharo with mileage in the low fifties.

"How much does it weigh?" Mr. Hare asks. It is an odd question, but by a stroke of luck I had noticed a plaque on the interior of the LeSharo listing its gross weight at 6,700 pounds. I report the number to Mr. Hare.

"Well, scrap metal goes for a dollar every hundred pounds," he says. "You do the math."

I ask Mr. Hare if he might be a little more specific about the model's shortcomings. The request provokes a tirade, the finer points of which are lost on me, but the single feature that seems to consign the LeSharo to Mr. Hare's mental scrap heap is that it's powered by a Renault engine. Mr. Hare spits out the word *Renault* with disgust, as if it were the name of a venereal disease. I have no position on Renaults, but I'm pretty sure I don't want to find myself broken down in Opp, Alabama, trying to explain to a local mechanic that I need him to phone France for a spare part. I ask Mr. Hare to recommend a reliable model and a reputable dealer (the phrase causes him to cough laughter), and he suggests that I look for something called an Allegro. They're assembled in Alabama using good old American Ford or Dodge engines and chassis, he says. As for a dealer, he suggests Bill Burton at Burton Campers. "Ask for him personally and tell him Mr. Hare sent you," Mr. Hare says. "That way if you get screwed, you'll get screwed right."

On this puzzling note I hang up and strike out for Burton Campers, south of town. I tell a salesman there my price range, or lack of one, and he shows me the one thing on the lot I can afford: a conversion van with discolored mustard shag carpet on the walls and ceiling. A grease-covered mechanic sits at a pile of blackened metal parts on the garage floor next to the vehicle—the van's engine—and says he hopes to have the thing running "sometime this week."

The salesman looks at the mess and then at me, and I think I register a look of genuine sympathy.

" 'F'I'z you," he says, "I'd try lookin' in the paper."

On the Wednesday before the Louisiana Tech game I have neither a ride to the stadium nor an RV of my own. What's odd is that I find this to be a problem. I could drive a car or ride the bus to Legion Field the way I'd always done, but I'm beginning to feel that going any other way than in an RV would mean missing out. Now that I've experienced the torrent of stimuli that swirl out of three days at a stadium—the anxious buildup, the camaraderie, the flood of sound and colors, the game itself, the slow communal wind-down in the lot after dinner—all the other conventional ways of experiencing a game have begun to feel removed and incomplete. Perhaps once you've experienced a pursuit in its extreme, it's impossible to get the old rush from that same pursuit in a lesser form. A sailor who solos across the ocean will never get the same satisfying thrill from a day sail. Enthusiasts, like addicts, are forever upping the dose. Radio and television have always been last resorts for me—I can't remember watching or listening to a Birmingham game when I was actually in Birmingham. I imagine the difference between listening to a game and being there in person is like the difference between phone sex and the real thing. But strangely, I'm beginning to feel that getting to a game an hour or two before kickoff is to half-ass it. I'm beginning to understand what Tony Brandino meant when he said, *"My body is here but my spirit is there."*

The Bices have a full house for the Louisiana Tech game—relatives—but I have a lead on another candidate. On Donnie's advice, I put in a call to one Jerral Johnson, the Show Chicken Man. I'd been advised that the trick to catching Johnson is to call him at his barn between six and seven in the morning, when he feeds his chickens. So I call the barn at 6:30 A.M., and sure enough, Johnson answers the phone. I introduce myself and state my mission, and far from being alarmed, Johnson tells me I'm welcome to come up to Rainsville, Alabama, for a tour of his show chicken farm. After that, he says, I'm welcome to ride with him to Birmingham for the game, provided I find my own place to sleep. On Sunday after the game, I can ride with him back to Rainsville to pick up my car. We make a plan to meet in the parking lot of McDonald's in Rainsville at eight-thirty on Thursday morning. Johnson tells me to keep an eye out for a custom-painted red and white Saturn with Bama stickers on the windows and door handles and a large steel tow bracket on its nose.

"I'll see you in the morning then," Johnson says, as roosters crow in the background—lots and lots of roosters.

The McDonald's in Rainsville shares a busy central intersection with an Exxon station, a Taco Bell, a Chevron station, a Hardee's, and an auto parts store. Morning traffic consists mainly of big American pickups with rubber bed-liners, permanently mounted toolboxes, and mud on the side panels. It could be an intersection anywhere in rural America, except for one detail: every other pickup truck is fitted with a front license plate that in white letters on red background reads "BAMA." Rainsville is in the foothills of northeastern Alabama, a part of the state that heavily favors the Crimson Tide over Auburn, which is more popular in the southern flatlands, from Montgomery to the coast. Rainsville is just across the interstate from Fort Payne, the hometown of the country band Alabama. The word Alabama has such pleasing connotations in these parts that it's regularly applied to bands, businesses, boats, dogs—what have you. The terrain is hilly and marked by open green pastures interrupted by stands of red oaks and Bradford pear trees. Yesterday, the remnants of a Gulf Coast hurricane blew by, so the air is clean and the wind gusty.

At eight-thirty, a red and white Saturn with a BAMA plate on the front whips into the McDonald's parking lot. Jerral Johnson pulls up beside me and rolls down his window. He's wearing an Alabama baseball cap and has a coffee mug in the seat between his legs.

"Morning, buddy," Johnson says. The fact that we are both Alabama fans seems to preclude any more elaborate introductions; we're already buddies. He sips on his coffee. I offer my hand, and he reaches through the car window to shake.

"Let's go look at some chickens," he says.

I follow the Saturn out of town, turning onto a series of ever thinner and more decrepit roads, past fields polka-dotted with cattle and stubs of freshly harvested early corn. We come to a modern-looking log cabin home, and Johnson pulls off the road onto a black asphalt driveway that is distinct only in that it's in much better shape than the road. I tail Johnson toward a large beige corrugated-steel building the size of an airplane hangar, and as I approach, a massive RV emerges from the shadows. I can just make out the baroque airbrushed mural on its rear: a wild-eyed charging elephant.

We park our cars out front, and I follow Johnson inside the hangar and to a picnic table alongside the RV, where he offers me a cup of coffee. When I say I take milk, Johnson shovels four spoonfuls of nondairy creamer into my mug, gives a quick stir, and slides it across the table. Johnson is sixty-five years old but looks twenty years younger. He has muscular arms, wiry legs, a leathery farmer's complexion, and his jaw juts slightly to the side, so that he resembles the actor Jim Nabors. He speaks with the same powerful twang Nabors used as the character Gomer Pyle as well—he pronounces the word *hour* as "ire," and says "foller" instead of "follow." Based on the accent alone, it would be easy to stereotype Johnson as a man who'd never gotten off the farm, and yet all around there is material evidence to suggest otherwise: the new log cabin home across the road, the hangar, the RV, the Saturn, a pickup, and down in the hollow behind us, a show chicken operation with a few thousand birds. (I don't yet know much about the show chicken game, but I imagine it has the same catastrophic effects on one's personal finances as, say, owning a motor home.) Johnson clearly has disposable income, and he seems to be doing his level best to dispose of it. The RV, a massive contraption called an American Dream, cost him $195,000, he says, and that was before add-ons like the $1,200 custom awning or the $1,000 it had cost him to hire a Florida airbrush artist to copy the charging elephant from Johnson's favorite sweatshirt. Then there is the hangar we are sitting in, a custom-built two-RV garage that cost $35,000. There's fuel: his RV holds 150 gallons of diesel and manages around eight miles to the gallon. And add to that the Saturn, which Johnson had custom-striped to match the paint job on his RV. Probably three-quarters of the tow cars in the RV camp are Saturns, a fluke of consumer demographics, I had assumed, the way everyone drinks Budweiser and puts Kraft yellow mustard on their burgers. The fluke, though, is of mechanics: the odometers of certain Saturn models work only when the vehicles are in gear.

"When you pull 'em, they don't register the miles," Johnson says.

Those untallied miles might save a couple thousand dollars on the resale value of the car. If you're going to spend $195,000 on a motor home, you presumably have to make up the cost wherever you can.

Johnson grew up on this very farm—it was his "grandiddy's old homeplace," he says, which his parents inherited. They were sustenance farmers who ran a gristmill and a small grocery delivery business—a "rolling store," it was called—from a small concrete-block shack that stood where Johnson's RV hangar is now. Johnson spent his childhood working—he got up at dawn, fed the chickens, and "plowed that there field with a one-eyed mule," he says—and from an early age displayed a knack for business. By high school he'd saved enough money to buy a half share of his parents' grocery business from his father's partner. Through the grocery business he saved enough to buy a convenience store, and he ran that well enough to finance the purchase of another, and then another, until he owned fifteen. Along the way, Johnson had a revelation—in the summer, he found, southerners had an insatiable appetite for ice. He sold the stuff in boxes outside his stores, but he thought he'd make better money if he could produce ice himself. So he bought a half interest in a local ice company called City Ice. For his new business, Johnson came up with a slogan that captured his plainspokenness perfectly: "Ice Is Nice."

When Johnson bought into City Ice, the company was producing 60,000 bags of ice a year. In 1999, it produced 3 million—100 tons of ice every twenty-four hours in summer, when the machines "are running wide open," Johnson says. The company has eight trucks covering routes to 1,200 iceboxes across Alabama. Johnson sold half the business for $650,000 in 1992, and the cash gave him the chance to pursue what he calls "a lifelong dream for forty years": to see Alabama play in every stadium on its regular schedule.

"I wanted to be able to sit at home in my later years and visualize what it's like to be at each stadium in person," he says.

Johnson bought a used motor home in 1992 and in his first year went to four games. Alabama won the National Championship that year, and Johnson got hooked. He now has an "Alabama room" in his log cabin house; his king-sized bed is covered with a Bear Bryant quilt, and the coach's portrait is painted on the headboard. When football season is over, he follows the Alabama baseball and softball teams.

Johnson is keen to show off his chickens, so we make our way down a sloping dirt road toward a lightly forested hollow a couple hundred yards behind the hangar; as we approach the pens, the birds begin crowing frantically, like a kennel of eager hunting hounds.

"Let me hear y'all!" Johnson calls out.

Johnson walks into one of the cages and is promptly attacked by a small, khaki-colored chicken.

"Some of the males are so mean you can't hardly get in the cage with 'em," he says as the bird flogs away at his left leg. Johnson wrestles with it for a moment and manages to grab the chicken by its feet, then begins speaking to the bird in a droning mantra—"All right, let's hear you. Look at him. Look at him. Let's hear you. Look at him"—the poultry-world equivalent of horse whispering. The chicken calms down, then Johnson holds it high, like a falconer, and tickles its undersides. The chicken puffs up like a porcupine and crows raucously. That's how you show them, he says. When Johnson puts the bird down

I see that his hand is bleeding; the bird has punctured his skin with a single furious peck.

"What are these?" I ask, pointing toward a cage of Technicolor chickens.

"Don't know yet," Johnson says. "I'm experimentin'."

Johnson has had chickens since he was a kid, but it wasn't until a few years ago that he got into competitive breeding. He picked up a magazine on chicken shows and, figuring that he knew a few things about raising chickens, ordered a few starter birds. Chicken shows are like beauty pageants for birds, so Johnson had to learn the desired traits of each competitive breed, and had to master the finer points of dolling up the birds before contests—how to give chickens a pedicure and how to enhance the color of their feathers with old-fashioned human hair dye. Johnson hit the chicken show circuit, driving to shows in Virginia, Oklahoma, and Michigan with sometimes as many as 100 chickens in cages in the storage compartments of the American Dream. He started winning, which motivated Johnson toward two ambitious goals—to make a run for annual Point Champion and Exhibitor of the Year.

Johnson enters another cage and is again mauled.

"You don't get no money for it," he shouts over the squawking birds. "But the Old English Game Bantam Club of America prints a record book and if you win Exhibitor of the Year you get your name in it."

Johnson says he faces a tough choice. To make a run for Exhibitor of the Year, he'll have to miss some key Alabama games this year—Arkansas, Tennessee, and Auburn. On the other hand, he's got an excellent crop of birds, and figures this could be his best shot at a championship. It occurs to me that showing chickens and going to football games are simply different sides of the same coin. Both are contests, but each has its trade-offs. With football, Johnson is a spectator. He has no control over the outcome, but that shared helplessness is a source of bonding with all those other people out there who want the same outcome and are equally powerless to make it happen—people, in fact, like me. With chickens, Johnson is in control. Hard work and skill produce results, and individual effort is rewarded. The downside of breeding show chickens—like almost every kind of competitive or creative venture—is that it's largely solitary. Johnson might befriend breeders he respects, but they'll always be pulling for different chickens. He can be a watcher and have company, or a doer, and go it alone. Johnson says he's not sure which of his passions will win out.

"I'd split it fifty-fifty," he says.

We walk back up the dirt road to the RV shed, and on the way, Johnson says he's had a tough time going to games this year as it is. His best friend and traveling companion, an Alabama fan named Robert Robinson, died last year, he says. Johnson started going to games alone, but then he ran into Robinson, a childhood friend who lived nearby and had had to quit his job after suffering a heart attack. Robinson was going through a rough time financially—he managed a part-time job picking eggs in a local chicken house, but his bad health slowed him down—so Johnson came up with a proposal. He offered Robinson a job as his partner in the show chicken circuit and as driver of his RV. The arrangement was little more than a pretense to get around the fact Johnson was supporting Robinson, but it served them both. Robinson got financial help that allowed him to get out of the house and to go to football games, and Johnson got a buddy to travel with.

"I'd call him and say, 'Robert I got a job for you—get some worms and let's you and me go fishin,' " Johnson says.

For the next couple of years, Johnson says, he and Robert rarely missed a game. In the lot, they had come-one, come-all barbecues where Robinson sang gospel tunes, accompanying himself on guitar. They had success on the show chicken circuit as well, winning blue ribbons at some local contests. But then last year, Robinson experienced chest pains again and checked himself into the hospital. Soon afterward, he died of heart failure, Johnson at his side. Robert was buried with the Alabama fan equivalent of full military honors—his casket was crimson, with the University of Alabama seal on the outside of the lid and a crimson "A" sewn into the satin lining on the inside. Most of the flowers were Crimson Tide themed as well; there were red and white floral "A's" and a large floral rendering of Johnson's American Dream with a picture of Robinson in the driver's seat. Even the biblical reading, Ezekiel 20:29, invoked the Crimson Tide: "And I said unto them, 'What is the high place whereunto you go?' And the name whereof is called Bamah."

Johnson says he has some pictures of the funeral; I feel uncomfortable at the prospect of intruding on this private rite, but I get the feeling Johnson wants to show me. He roots around in the trunk of the Saturn and pulls out an envelope, from which he takes photographs one by one. He gives each a long, sad look before passing it to me. In the first, Robinson's casket is open, and his ashen face protrudes just above the rim. A floral RV is on the left and a large red and white letter "A" on the right. A portrait of Bear Bryant hangs on the wall above the casket, keeping watch over Robert's body. I hand the photograph back to Johnson, who is crying quietly.

"I didn't have no brothers or sisters," he says, "so he was my family. We didn't have no secrets."

I ask Johnson if the casket was custom made, and he says no, that the Wilson Funeral Home down the road keeps them in stock. Johnson says he wants to run into town to pick up some "baloney sticks" for the weekend; he has to pass Wilson's on the way, and so he offers to drop me off there if I want to see one. He says he'll pick me up on the way back.

The W. T. Wilson Funeral Chapel is in a kind of ranch house just off Alabama Highway 75, between Rainsville and Fyffe. Johnson pulls into the empty parking lot and lets me out. Inside, a large man with a loosened tie and dusty loafers jumps nervously from a chair. Wilson's Funeral Home is apparently not accustomed to drop-in customers, at least not live ones. I explain my mission and ask if I could have a look at an Alabama coffin.

"That all depends," the man says.

"On what?"

"On—you got any tickets to the Tennessee game?"

The man laughs heartily and sticks out his hand.

"Tom Wilson," he says. "I run the place." Wilson asks how I'd heard about him, and I tell him I've seen photographs of the Robert Robinson funeral.

"Robinson . . . ," he says, looking toward the ceiling and searching his memory. "Oh yeah—they wanted everything red, even the couches in the parlor."

Wilson leads me back to a somberly lit showroom full of caskets. The Alabama coffin fairly stands out: it's a big red box with the school logo on the top and a white velvet "A" sewn into the lid. Wilson says that the casket costs $1,999—$700 more than his most popular model, a standard coffin called the Going Home. Wilson says he sells a half dozen or so a year. That may not sound like a lot, but extrapolating from the mortality rates of Rainsville, a town of 4,400, I figure the annual figure statewide is probably in the hundreds. The oddest detail is that the coffin is affixed with a small round sticker that reads "Officially Licensed Collegiate Product," the same one you find affixed to sweatshirts and baseball caps.

"You gotta pay a royalty for using the emblem," Wilson explains.

The chief virtue of an Alabama casket—besides the color, of course—is that it's made of fiberglass, not wood or metal, which eventually decay. Wilson estimates a fiberglass Alabama coffin might last a thousand years.

Roll Tide indeed.

Before I can ask any more questions, a young man walks in and hands Wilson a piece of paper, prompting him to tighten the knot of his tie, and to pull a small brush from his coat pocket with which he whisks the dust from his loafers.

"Gotta run," Wilson says, giving the slip of paper a little shake. "Coroner call."

Johnson picks me up in the parking lot of Wilson's—he has three 4-pound logs of baloney in the backseat—and we head back to the farm. I carry the baloney sticks on board the American Dream; Johnson climbs in and tests his air horn by blaring the Alabama fight song inside the hangar. Soon we're trundling down the driveway and onto the distressed one-and-a-half-lane road that leads to town. Johnson slips a favorite tape into the tape deck—a friend of his playing the organ—and turns up the volume. The tune is "Off We Go into the Wild Blue Yonder."

Johnson's American Dream is an altogether different class of motor home than the Bices' Hurricane. It rides as smoothly as a Greyhound bus, has quick acceleration and brakes that "will damn stand you on your head," as Johnson puts it. He classifies his traveling experiences in it into two broad categories: times when he "got run off" and times when he "got good treatment." Good treatment is when "people stop by to offer you food or tickets or to get their picture taken with you or to tell stories." Getting run off is when "somebody stops by to tell you to move, to pay up, or that you're in violation of some reg-a-lation or other." The people who did such things, in Johnson's words, were "filling me full of shit." By coincidence, the times Johnson got filled full of shit often coincided with the occasions when Alabama lost. And in Johnson's parlance, Alabama was never simply beaten: the competition "beat the dawg shit out of us." Johnson had been at Tennessee when the Vols had beat the dawg shit out of Alabama, and at Auburn when they beat the dawg shit out of Alabama, and at both places he had likewise been filled full of shit. The worst had been the year before when he'd driven eight hours to Little Rock, where Arkansas beat the dawg shit out of Alabama; afterward, he'd been filled full of shit by, of all things, the highway. "That damn I-40 between Little Rock and Memphis," he says, "That sunuvabitch will damn beat you to *death*."

We pull up to Legion Field just before 2:00 P.M., our appointed rendezvous time with two other RVs owned by Johnson's friends, among them a couple named Bobbie and Bobby. Bobby is a retired freight train conductor, and he and Johnson park next to each other as often as they can. Johnson and the Bobbies want to leave enough room between their rigs to open their awnings, which means we'll have to get around R. C. Hicks, the parking lot czar. We lurk around the outside of the lot, and when Hicks heads off to the opposite side to harass some RV-ers over there, we blast in and lay claim to a large patch of gravel on the stadium's southern side. Johnson flips on the automatic levelers. They hiss and hum until the RV is brought flat.

There are over two hundred motor homes around us, but above all one stands out: our next-door neighbor's Champion, a dilapidated army-green job that looks as though it's rolled off the set of *The Grapes of Wrath*. The headlights and round, mouthlike grill make the thing look alive and piscine, like a bass. A man in his mid-thirties is sitting out front in a folding chair with a Solo cup in his hand.

"I call it the Toad," he says when he sees me checking out the thing. "All these others—the hundred, two hundred thousand dollars jobs—they all look alike. When people see this thing, they know I'm coming."

He introduces himself as Ron St. John. It's an interesting experience meeting someone with your same, not entirely common, last name who also drives around in a jalopy he calls the Toad. Ron proffers that perhaps we're cousins. I tell him I'm a reporter, and he seems to recoil at the possibility of having a distant relative who works in the media at least as much as I recoil at the thought of having a distant relative who drives a Toad. We agree that we are probably not related after all. Ron is from Panama City Beach, Florida—a five-hour drive by car—and yet here he is midday on Friday, enjoying a cocktail in the lot. I ask if it's difficult to get Fridays off to get to the stadiums early.

"Nope," Ron says with a smile. "I just call in sick every Thursday."

Our chat is interrupted by a commotion down the row: two women have attacked R. C. Hicks. One has him by the hair, the other has snatched his walkie-talkie and is shouting obscenities through it at his supervisors. Hicks has apparently imposed his heavy-handed parking rules on the wrong people; as the women engage him, one of their husbands comes barreling through the lot to claim his space. The women scatter, and for a moment it looks as though Hicks might try to face down the vehicle. But with the RV rumbling toward him, Hicks loses his nerve and scampers awkwardly behind another motor home, defeated. Jerral Johnson peeks out from behind his motor home to see what's going on.

"They have a fuckin' squabble every year," he says with an easy shrug. "They think we ain't got enough sense to park these things."

A short while later, Skipper and Donnie walk by, on their way toward the stadium to watch Louisiana Tech's Friday walk-through. I invite myself along. It's customary in college football for the home team to make its stadium and field available to the visitors for a couple of hours on the day before a kickoff, so they can get a feel for the place. The sessions are sometimes open to the public and sometimes not—it depends on the team and the stadium policy—but the end zone gates to Legion Field are wide open, and the three of us walk in unchallenged. I imagine the view from the grass at Legion Field—a canyon of aluminum bleachers so steep it blocks the early afternoon sun—must seem awesome to visiting players, but the Bulldogs don't seem particularly intimidated. They're running through their workouts in sweats and helmets, no pads, and at the end of each drill, the players bark furiously.

"They don't seem too scared," I say.

Skipper shoots me a look. "They may not be scared, but I'll tell you one thing," he says. "They're the ugliest football team I ever saw."

Tech has reason not to be intimidated by Alabama. They won the last meeting 26-20 in 1997. The irony is that La. Tech had been added to Alabama's schedule for the purpose of offering the Tide an easy win early in the season. The benefit of the arrangement for La. Tech was that a game against a big national opponent—even a blowout loss—earned them money and, theoretically at least, helped recruiting. The lopsidedness of the deal is underscored by a single simple detail: La. Tech has signed on to play Alabama twice in a row at Alabama. Alabama never has to play at Tech's home stadium. The implication is, it's not worthy of us, and anyway few Alabama fans could even tell you where it is. This is a common trick of big-name schools—it allows them to bank the revenue of another home game without putting their records at risk—but it carries a hidden downside, one summed up by the coaching cliché "If you don't think the little games matter, try losing one." A loss to a so-called "small" team could destroy a name team's confidence and throw an entire season into a spin. After losing to La. Tech in 1997, for example, the Tide lost its next three games.

The Bulldogs play a death-by-a-thousand-cuts kind of offense built around the short pass, a scheme that neatly squares with Alabama's weakness—pass defense. In 1997, La. Tech quarterback Tim Rattay, a sophomore with a hair-trigger release, dissected the Alabama secondary and threw for 361 yards. Rattay is back, this time as a senior, and Alabama's pass defense is untested. After forty-five minutes of watching the Bulldogs practice, Skipper, Donnie, and I walk from the stadium in silence. They seemed a little too confident for our tastes. Something feels funny.

In the evening, Johnson slices a baloney stick in half and throws it on the grill. There's not much to cooking a baloney stick, it turns out. You simply apply heat until the thing starts hissing, then slice. Bobby and Bobbie produce a cafeteria-sized smorgasbord of artery-clogging casseroles, barbecue platters, and pies from their RV—a kind of Brinks truck for Tupperware—and we gorge ourselves. After dinner, a WIAT-TV news truck pulls up to do a live feed, and a rumor quickly spreads that Paul Finebaum is on board. Some fans try to recruit a heckling force, but the truck's driver grumbles that Finebaum has better things to do than show up at Legion Field on a Friday night. The gathering crowd disperses. I stick around long enough to greet the Bices, who pull in at around 11:00 P.M. For a few minutes, Chris and I chat about the rosters for tomorrow's game. He predicts another rout. In the distance, Skipper's karaoke set is blaring. The tune is Hank Williams Jr.'s "Family Tradition."

* * *

On Saturday, after a dose of Bama Bombs for good luck, I head into the stadium with the Bices. We scan the upper bleachers to find a block of empty seats so we can sit together. La. Tech is just the sort of game skipped by the small coterie of Alabamians who go to football games for entertainment, rather than to fulfill psychological needs, and though we can't empathize with these people, we are happy to sit in their seats when they stay home. We have no problem locating space for three high in the West Stand, at the twenty. The temperature is eighty-five and the sun fierce. By the time we reach our seats we are shellacked with sweat. There's a long, swelling chant of "Roll Tide, Roll," and kickoff.

On the first few plays there is a troubling sign. Alabama's quarterback, Andrew Zow, is misfiring. He has a tendency to be either spot on or terribly off—when he's off he throws with a quick stabbing motion, like someone trying to swat a fly, and his passes either go wildly long or whistle straight into the ground several yards in front of the receiver. On his first few attempts, Zow swats flies. The balls aren't catchable. Alabama has to punt.

Tech quarterback Tim Rattay starts out hurling passes downfield: a bomb to the Alabama forty-two, a ten-yard throw for a first down, then another to the Alabama twenty-three. Then with the nonchalance of someone playing a backyard game of touch, Rattay rolls to the left and flips the ball toward the underneath receiver in the end zone: touchdown.

The crowd is just settling in—many are not yet to their seats—and we're more baffled by the turn of events than scared. But on Alabama's next drive, things get worse: Alabama fumbles and Tech recovers. There's a colossal groan from the crowd, as if everyone had simultaneously bitten into a batch of spoiled stadium hot dogs. The Bulldogs throw an interception, and Alabama fumbles the ball right back. The sloppy play works to Tech's advantage. They're supposed to play ugly—they're 1-2 coming in to the game. In short order, they've brought Alabama to their level.

In the second quarter, Alabama manages a short drive, but it fizzles and the Tide has to kick a field goal. When Rattay gets the ball back, he again goes to the air. The Bulldogs are down to the Alabama twenty-seven. With just over four minutes to go in the half, Rattay drops back and lofts a ball to the near right corner of the end zone and a six-foot-four beanpole of a receiver named Sean Cangelosi. Cangelosi, who's covered by three much shorter defenders, leaps into the air—a full head higher than any of the cornerbacks—and catches the ball softly in his abdomen, as if it were an egg. Another Tech touchdown.

Approaching the half Tech leads 12-3, and their game plan has become clear enough. Tech's receivers are taller than the Alabama defenders—none of whom are over six feet, and one of whom is a mere five foot seven. Rattay is simply floating the ball up high and letting his receivers do the rest. Since it's unlikely that the Alabama defensive backfield is going to grow significantly during halftime, the Tide coaches will have to find a creative solution. They need to blitz, and put Rattay on his back before he has the chance to find the tall guys.

More disturbing though than Tech's play is our own. Our players look lost, and on the sideline, they stand around dopily, as though waiting idly for a bus. DuBose wanders the sideline in strange isolation, sealed inside his headphones and hardly making eye contact with his players. As the teams head to the locker rooms, boos trickle out of the stands. The crowd is turning on its team.

Alabama kicks off in the second half, and Rattay begins bushwhacking his way down the field just as he'd done in the first half. Tech kicks a field goal and goes up 15-3. Rather than going for the end zone on kickoffs, the Bulldogs have been pooching the ball high and short, in hope of causing a turnover or just preventing a gain by the Tide's speedy kick returners. After the field goal, the Alabama coaches make an adjustment; they send Shaun Alexander in at an up position on the return team. Alexander doesn't run back kickoffs, but he has sure hands and is elusive if space opens up for him to get speed. If it's possible to sneak onto a football field in front of eighty thousand people and a television audience in the hundreds of thousands, that's what Alexander does, sauntering into the lineup with the head-down, humdrum gait of someone checking the backyard for weeds. The Tech kicker doesn't see him and lofts the ball high to the far sideline—right at Alexander, who takes a quick step to the left, makes a slithery moonwalk move to the right, then a quick step backward that makes it look as though someone on high has quickly punched stop, rewind, and play on the VCR of Life. The Tech defenders overpursue, and an alley opens up diagonally across the field. Alexander spots it and slingshots through. Once in the clear, he jogs into the end zone for the score.

Three series later, Alabama scores again, on a gliding sweep by Alexander. The crowd is like a groggy fish released into the water—stunned, oxygenated back to life. Alabama makes a two-point conversion and in just ten minutes has gone from trailing 15-3 to leading 18-15.

The mood in the stadium has lightened, as much because of the score as because of the effect of the bourbon wafting in a bracing barroom stench from the bleachers around us. Empty miniatures of

Jack Daniels lay around our feet like spent cartridges at a firing range. Evening is falling; the stadium lights are now on, casting a luminous blue tint onto the playing field and the stands. The party is beginning as the game winds toward its foregone end. On the next series, though, Zow fly-swats a pass directly into the hands of a Tech defender, and three plays later Rattay throws another touchdown. Two minutes into the fourth quarter, Tech leads again, 22-18. The Tide responds with a touchdown and, after its defense holds, another field goal, so that with two minutes, thirty-eight seconds to go, Alabama leads 28-22. Eighty thousand of us do the simple but nevertheless problematic math. We lead by six; with a touchdown and an extra point, Tech can win it.

The Bulldogs, though, have to go seventy-eight yards. Alabama drops back into a "prevent" defense, rushing only three linemen, which gives Rattay an extra moment to search downfield for an open receiver. He flings the ball downfield, high above the Lilliputs in the Tide secondary: a leaping catch, twenty-five yards and a first down. A minute forty left. This time Alabama rushes five linemen. Rattay pumps his arm as the pocket collapses on top of him. As he stumbles backward, his cleats bite the turf awkwardly, violently torquing his right ankle. A hulking two-hundred-forty-pound mass of red in the form of linebacker Darius Gilbert smothers Rattay at the thirty-five. He gets up limping. Tech calls time.

I have an unsporting feeling: I'm happy he's limping.

Rattay, though, limps back in, for a third and twenty-two. Again, Alabama drops back into its prevent defense, and Rattay arcs one downfield. A giraffelike receiver named James Jordan extends an arm and catches the ball with one hand, like a frog snatching a fly from midair.

La. Tech is now at the Alabama thirty-nine. Rattay lines up in the shotgun and takes the snap—another completion to Cangelosi. Alabama is rushing only three men, and Rattay has all day. Tech is now at the Alabama sixteen. I sense the crowd trying to make noise, but even we are on our heels and can barely muster the energy to shout. The thing is getting away from us. Our cheers aren't forceful and throaty. They're caterwauling whines.

Rattay takes the snap again. This time Alabama rushes five. Rattay is surrounded. He finds himself extended between two Alabama linemen; one, on the ground, has his ankle—that tender ankle—and the other has Rattay up high, around the shoulder pads. They twist him, as though they were trying to wring water from a large mop. Then the defender on top, a Volkswagen-sized lineman named Kenny King, drives Rattay headfirst into the ground. Rattay is badly hurt. His ankle has been horribly wrenched, and it's all he can do to hop off the field on one foot and collapse on the bench. He has thrown for 368 yards and three touchdowns, and now he's finished. Hallelujah and amen.

Rattay's backup is a sophomore named Brian Stallworth, who in the final minutes of the game has become as much of a spectator as anyone in the stands behind him. He is so certain he won't be seeing action against Alabama that he has thrown just two warm-up passes all afternoon. He is ice cold. Stallworth sprints onto the field with the confounded enthusiasm of someone who has just been selected to play *The Price Is Right.* He takes the snap from the shotgun, rolls right, and is immediately sacked. Twenty-eight seconds left. The clock is running. Tech has no time-outs. On fourth down, with nine seconds to go, Stallworth has to throw into the end zone. Alabama again lines up in its prevent defense. Stallworth will have plenty of time. He takes the snap and waits, bouncing anxiously on his toes as three lanky Tech receivers pogo down the field into a pack of Alabama pass defenders. It's the same play Tech scored on near the end of the first half—Cangelosi to the near right corner of the end zone. Stallworth will throw it up high and let the six-foot-four receiver leap for it. He cocks his arm and heaves a high, arcing spiral, as Cangelosi and three Alabama defenders converge. For a few century-long seconds the balls wobbles in the blue mist of a humid Alabama night. The crowd is frozen. It feels like leaning back in a chair, when you've lost your balance and are teetering between disaster and a mere thrill. The ball is falling now . . . toward a nest of outstretched hands. Hirschel Bolden, the Alabama cornerback, extends his right arm just as Cangelosi leaps into the air. The ball falls just beyond Bolden's reach, and Cangelosi cradles it delicately into his ribs. Touchdown. Tech wins 29-28.

Once I came across the word *depersonalized* on a medical questionnaire. I asked the doctor's assistant what it meant, and she said I'd know if I experienced it. Now I know. Feeling depersonalized isn't just the feeling of being cut off from your surroundings but the feeling of being cut off from yourself. It's akin to physical shock, not an out-of-body experience, but a no-body-at-all experience, a dull existential numbness. With the exception of the few Tech fans in the corner, everyone else in the crowd seems to have been converted into shades; they're lifeless, opaque, and wearing the dazed expressions you sometimes see on the TV news when a film crew shows up immediately after a tornado has vacuumed a small town off the earth and the residents are wandering about disoriented, the entire architecture of their lives collapsed. It may sound melodramatic or insensitive to compare a loss in sports to an actual tragedy—in fact, it's both—but the point is, at the moment of a loss, a fan is incapable of making such distinctions. A loss *feels* like an actual tragedy.

If despair were gravity, the solar system might be slurped over the rim of Legion Field, to form a new black hole just west of downtown Birmingham. The crowd is silent, but the silence isn't peaceful; it's menacing, foreboding. A murmuring of boos begins in a corner to my right and surges into a full-scale verbal revolt.

"There goes DuBose!" a woman behind me screams as the coach leaves the field.

We've just seen a classic coaching loss—watching the videotape later will only confirm, infuriatingly, that fact—and my anger, like the woman's, is directed at DuBose. The team showed up not just flat but nearly catatonic; the coach hadn't even seemed to try to get the team's collective head in the game. And I can't help but think that if we'd been blitzing from the start, we might have hobbled Rattay two quarters earlier.

While the Tech fans edge together in an ever tighter clump, the loss fractures any semblance of togetherness among the Alabama fans. The university president, a bow-tied dandy named Dr. Andrew Sorensen, walks across the field and is roundly hooted by the crowd. He backed the athletic director's decision to keep DuBose after the scandal, and the crowd is letting him have it. "What do you think about *that*, Dr. *Bow Tie*?" a man behind me shouts. In nine seconds Sorensen's bow tie has been transformed from a symbol of erudition and fastidiousness to a symbol of his ignorance about football and detachment from the fans. This is not a bow-tie-wearing crowd.

The crowd sets upon itself as well. In the far right corner of the stadium, a brawl erupts—bodies tumble and drinks arc into the sky over the crowd, like flares off the sun. Some frat boys have decided to vent their anger on some other frat boys, and the fight has spread through the student section. Blue lines of police officers shoot up and across aisleways, spraying pepper gas onto everyone they encounter, even each other. The melee is quelled, but perhaps a dozen cops are incapacitated, bent over with their hands on their faces, fanning their eyes with their hats as they sit on the bleachers beside a dozen or so sorority belles whom they've gassed as well. There's a strange irony to the scene; the white police department that firehosed blacks in the 1960s is now predominantly black and gassing white fraternity and sorority preps. In thirty-five years the Birmingham Police Department hasn't figured out how to spray a crowd without having it blow up in their faces.

The Bices and I tread down the stadium steps in silence. Even the preternaturally positive Chris is at a loss to find the silver lining to this debacle. Instead, he forlornly wanders back and forth along the emptying bleachers, collecting discarded plastic Alabama cups with the innocent, melancholic look of a lonely teenager skipping stones at an isolated pond someplace. I'm in the early stages of an accelerated run-through of the stages of grief. In my funk, I question why I ever bothered to set myself up for such a letdown by getting involved with a sports team. Somewhere between the stadium exit and Jerral Johnson's RV (where a baloney stick is already sizzling on the grill), I have the thought that maybe I should just quit my reporting now before I am too far in. The season is shot. Alabama has lost to a nobody, and that only means plenty of upcoming losses to the somebodies. On some level I know this is absurd—that losing is an integral part of being a fan, perhaps more so than winning, and that I should stick it out, take lots of notes and try to make sense of it later. But I'm wallowing in an overwhelming tide of self-pity and in a weird, utterly frustrating headspace where being aware of an emotion isn't enough to turn it off. Winning never causes the fan to question the pursuit of being a fan, but losing almost always does.

At Jerral Johnson's RV, a group stands in a collective stupor, listening on the radio to the postgame comments by the coach and players. I get a baloney sandwich and a Solo cup full of sweet tea. A reporter on the radio asks DuBose if he might quit.

"I haven't considered it," DuBose says unconvincingly.

"Think he'll resign?" I ask a fellow baloney eater, a burly man with a lumberjack beard and cold red eyes.

"Resign?" the man sneers. "He ain't gone *resign*, son. He's gone *GIT . . . HIS . . . ASS . . . FARRED!"*

In 1994, a psychologist named James Dabbs took saliva samples from twenty-one Brazilian and Italian men before and after Brazil's World Cup soccer victory over the Italians. He found that in the Brazilians, testosterone levels shot up 28 percent after their win, while in the Italians, testosterone levels plummeted 27 percent. Scientists say the reaction is similar in male animals after a fight over a mate, and theorize we've evolved this way to ensure the peace soon after battle; it's our bodies' way of telling us to accept the result. Whatever the reason, the mood in the Alabama lot certainly backs Dr. Dabbs's findings. The place is positively flaccid. The Toad is shuttered; cousin Ron is presumably inside getting his sulking out of the way as well. I spot Donnie ghosting across the lot and try to flag him down, but he refuses to acknowledge me. I come upon a friend of Donnie's named Bill Prescott sitting in a folding chair in a dark, narrow passage between two RVs, his face against the side of one of the vehicles. "You okay?" I ask.

"That team ain't worth a donkey shit," Prescott mumbles.

Prescott says he's isolated himself from his friends so that he doesn't say anything to them he'll later regret. He urges me to clear out.

Besides feeling utterly forlorn, I'm beginning to feel somewhat out of place. My custom after losses at Legion Field has always been to get away from the stadium as quickly as possible and into my own private pocket of mourning. Now I'm stuck here, and save a few resiliently social fans like Jerral Johnson, most have retreated to within their motor homes and drawn the blinds. Familiar faces that earlier greeted me with comradely smiles now cast suspicious, or at least diffident, glances. I imagine that if I had a motor home, I'd retreat there myself, but as it is, I wander around in an awkward physical and mental no-place between being a regular fan and one of the RV-ers.

I make my way to the Bices'. We sulk together for a bit, then Chris and I pull up a couple of folding chairs in front of his neighbors' RV, beneath a generator exhaust pipe and in front of television and more football—Florida vs. Tennessee. Even that's hard to watch, since we can't help thinking about the roar that goes up at Florida Field when the Alabama score is announced.

There are any number of very drunk people in the lot, and possibly the drunkest of them all is our host, a short, bearded man named Jimmy, whose sunburned and alcohol-infused skin is roughly the same hue as his crimson Alabama hat, shorts, and T-shirt. When Jimmy gets up to get a beer, he nearly falls to his knees. He so condemns the Alabama team—the coaches, the players, the administration, the fans—that I feel compelled to come to their defense.

"Besides the secondary, I thought the team played fairly well in the second half," I say.

Jimmy looks at me as though I've insulted his mother.

"Oh I got it," he says, his voiced caked with sarcasm. "You'll analyze the fuck out of everything won't you?" Jimmy stands and plods toward me with a leaden gait, like Sasquatch. "Well this . . . is . . . the . . . wrong . . . day . . . *to . . . fuckwithhme!*" he barks.

I'm suddenly face to face with a very angry drunk person, albeit a small one. The muscles in Jimmy's neck twitch. His eyes are glassed over and rolling back in their sockets. Jimmy is either going to pass out on me or take a swing at me. His friend jumps out of his chair and separates us.

"Don't mind him," the friend tells me. "He's a sore loser."

He takes Jimmy by the arm and deposits him in a folding chair in front of the television. "Problem is I'm a short drunk stupid motherfucker and *I* could've knocked that ball down," Jimmy says to no one.

The Florida-Tennessee game brings a modicum of relief. Alabama fans despise both teams, and one of them has to lose. It's Tennessee,

23-21. At least we have company. Jimmy is out cold. The Bices' relatives left right after the game, disgusted, so I'm offered my old berth for the evening. Larry the dog, as always, is glad to see me.

The next morning I wake at 7:00 A.M. The scene is suitably desolate. RVs are pulling out. A few locals scour the lot for empty beer cans. Three mangy-looking stray dogs are scavenging for barbecue scraps. I walk over to Jerral's RV—he's having coffee on board with Bobbie and Bobby. They've been up for hours. The three of them are talking about the only thing worse than enduring a home loss to Louisiana Tech—namely, listening to what Finebaum will have to say about it on Monday's radio show.

"I want to not listen to him," Bobbie says. "But I can't."

"Well," Johnson says with resignation. "They beat the dawg shit out of us."

We say goodbyes, pack up the RV, and Johnson and I climb on board. He puts in a CD of Andy Griffith gospel tunes, cues up "When the Saints Go Marching In," and we roll out of the lot. Neither of us has much to say. The sole excitement of our ride home: about an hour into the trip, a foul odor emanates from the bathroom. Johnson asks me to pour some holding tank deodorant in the toilet and to give it a good flush. The main ingredient in RV holding tank deodorant is formaldehyde—it doesn't deodorize the contents of the tank so much as embalm them. I pour a few globs down the bowl and close the lid.

"It gets to sloshin' around in there and comes alive," Johnson says.

We near Rainsville and I ask Johnson if I can expect to see him next week in Tuscaloosa for the Arkansas game. Johnson says he isn't going. There's a chicken show next week in Macon. He plans to make that run for Exhibitor of the Year after all.

"I'll tell you what," Johnson says as his corrugated-steel hangar comes into sight. "Driving home after a loss—now that there is a pain in your ass."

Chapter Six

Stray Bullets and Snot-Nosed Kids

THE HEADLINES OF THE SUNDAY NEWSPAPERS IN Alabama give a good idea of the local mood toward Alabama's head coach:

> *DuBose:* How Long Can He Last As 'Bama's Coach?
> *Barring a Miracle DuBose Won't Be Back*
> *DuBose Lamest of Ducks*

Predictably, Paul Finebaum uses his column to pile on. "So what is DuBose's future?" he writes in the *Post Herald.* "He has none."

But worse for DuBose, even the nice guys are turning on him. Clyde Bolton, a retiring columnist for the *Birmingham News* and the elder sage of Alabama sports writers, issues what amounts to a formal renunciation of DuBose in his column: "DuBose has yet to prove he is qualified to be the head football coach of the University of Alabama," he writes. "In fact, the results are increasingly leading me to the conclusion that he isn't. He was my choice, and he was the people's choice—but that was then, and this is now."

The fans, too, have had it. Three thousand of them call or write University of Alabama president Andrew Sorensen to demand DuBose's firing. When Sorensen goes to the grocery store, he's accosted in the cereal aisle by an angry fan, and by another when he stops to get gas. Hopes have been demolished, and there's a mounting feeling that someone has to pay.

I actually feel badly for Mike DuBose. He's alone. His "dream job," as he's called it, is well on its way to becoming a nightmare. I imagine long, uncomfortable silences between DuBose and his wife at night in the den. The irony is that the thing that made DuBose's job worth dreaming over—the state's ardor for football—is the very reason it has become nightmarish. What Alabama fans give in adulation after a win, they take back doubly in condemnation after a loss. One gets the feeling that Mike DuBose hadn't figured on that part of the equation. Maybe it's just that he hadn't counted on losing—there's a fine line, after all, between optimism and delusion. But on Monday, at least this much is clear: if DuBose wants to remain Alabama's head coach—or even an Alabama resident, for that matter—he has to beat Arkansas on Saturday.

It won't be easy. The Hogs humiliated Alabama last year, 42-6. Their star quarterback, Clint Stoerner, a mustachioed warrior with the toughness of an iron spike, is returning to face Alabama's clearly feeble defensive backfield. The one thing Mike DuBose has going for him is that the game will be at home, the season's first on campus in Tuscaloosa. Maybe the home crowd will give the team a boost. A columnist for the campus newspaper, the *Crimson White*, sums up DuBose's predicament in these disturbing, if mostly accurate, terms: "Have you ever picked up a date and felt her dad didn't want you taking out his princess?" the student writes. "Mike DuBose has a date Saturday. The University of Alabama alumni waits on its skybox porch like a concerned father with his shotgun. . . . If DuBose fails to bring his team home on time and happy, shells may be flying."

On Monday morning, I turn on a sports talk radio station called WJOX to learn that the fans' desire for vengeance has been at least partially satisfied: Sorensen, perhaps mindful of the public blood-lust, has fired the athletic director, Bob Bockrath. It's a curious move. Bockrath's effect on the outcome of the Tech game was oblique at best—he'd proposed the settlement that kept DuBose at the university after the coach admitted the affair with his secretary—but in the wake of the public outcry over the Tech loss, that's enough to get him canned. If the callers to WJOX are any measure, the firing of the athletic director is well received. The mob has a body and is briefly appeased. I'm ambivalent. As a fan, I certainly understand the desire for revenge, but, revenge delivered, I feel no better. The loss to Tech still stands. We still have the same coach on the sideline. Our defensive backfield still seems beyond hope. A new athletic director can't solve these problems. And unfortunately for me, a sulking fan is a considerably more reluctant interview than a happy one, and you can forget getting invited to join him for a weekend on his RV. Angry fans are also more prone to violence than happy ones. I have to be vigilant. Luckily, there's an easy way to tap the depths of fan Weltanschauung while maintaining a safe distance. I call Paul Finebaum.

Despite his reputation as a crank, Finebaum is happy to meet with me, and in fact encourages me to come down to the studio for his afternoon show. His voice conveys the eagerness of a hungry man about to dig into a perfectly cooked steak. This after all is what he lives for: the Alabama football team in turmoil. DuBose's affair with the secretary was a blessing for Finebaum, coming as it did during the doldrums of August. A loss to La. Tech—now that's something too, an event guaranteed to fill up the phone lines. But on top of all this—the firing of the athletic director? For Finebaum, it's just too perfect.

Finebaum's show begins at 3:00 P.M so with a little time to kill, I stop by a local bookshop in a suburb called Mountain Brook to check out the section on Alabama football. There are shelves of books on Alabama football—more about Alabama football, in fact, than about Alabama, the state. I pick up one called *Crimson Coronation*—a sort of sci-fi sports novel in which various Alabama football teams from the last century play each other in heaven—and attract the attention of the store owner, an Alabama fan. We talk football for a few minutes, and I mention I'm on the way to meet Paul Finebaum.

"Be careful," the man says. "Stray bullets don't have names on them."

On this cheerful note, I strike out for the studios of WERC on Red Mountain, just down the ridge from the television studio where sixteen years before I'd met Bear Bryant. When I enter the sound booth, Finebaum is just climbing into his headphones. He raises his eyebrows impishly, rubs his hands together, and takes his seat at the broadcast table beneath a microphone that hangs off a boom like a ripe grapefruit. The producer cues up the show's intro, a blaring heavy-metal guitar riff followed by: "It's the *Paul Finebaum Show.* Where legends are made . . . and most college football coaches *fired.*"

"Welcome to the show, everybody!" Finebaum barks into the grapefruit. "It's a manic Monday like few we've seen. . . . Bear Bryant is probably *rolling over in his grave.*" The row of lights indicating callers fills instantly, and after a recap of the Bockrath story Finebaum goes to the phones. The first caller is an obstreperous Auburn fan named B.O.B.—short for "Bring on Bama"—who calls to taunt Alabama fans. He screams so loudly that he's nearly unintelligible but gets his point across with a stream of contemptuous guffaws that cause the needles on the sound panel to twitch back and forth like windshield wipers. B.O.B.'s call prompts a response from Phyllis from Mulga—a regular caller and a hardcore Alabama fan with a voice like a tractor at full throttle. At Finebaum's urging, Phyllis reenacts that fateful final play: *"I screamed. I hollered. I'z actin' a fool!"* she says. Every fourth or fifth caller is an Alabama fan who has moved past the game to the Bockrath firing, and who wants to thank Finebaum for "keeping the coals stirred under Bockrath's seat," as one of them put it. This last category of calls seems to please Finebaum exceedingly; Bockrath has been one of his favorite targets. Strange, though, is that Alabama fans—whose football program has been thrown into chaos thanks in part to Finebaum's relentless ridicule of their athletic director—are calling to thank him for ridiculing their athletic director. The fans are so eager for someone to blame that they've readily adopted the position of a man most of them claim to hate. From a Bama fan's perspective, Finebaum is lead in the pipes of public opinion; by the time his listeners realize they've been poisoned, it's too late.

Finebaum's producer cues up a tape of DuBose's comments in the locker room after the Tech game.

"Coach, do you have any plans to resign?" the reporter asks.

"I haven't considered it," DuBose says.

"*Maybe you should,*" Finebaum says to his audience.

Three hours into the show, it's time for one of Finebaum's twice-weekly conversations with former Auburn coach Pat Dye, a man he mocked mercilessly when Dye was an acting coach. Dye is now the spokesman for a local crane rental company that sponsors Finebaum's show, and in the name of economic opportunity, the two men have patched things up at least enough to bicker with each other twice a week on the radio.

"I couldn't wait to git-cho column today, Pawl," Dye says, in a drawl that oozes like lukewarm tar. "I knew you'd get down on Mike. He down on his knees and *you kickin' him in da stomach.*"

Finebaum gives me an exasperated look, then rolls his eyes backward, sticks out his lower lip, and rotates his jaw lazily, like a cow chewing cud: his Pat Dye imitation.

"Coach, Mike DuBose couldn't beat a dog," he says later.

"Paaaaaawl," Dye says, in slow motion. "You da only person I know beats his dawg."

After his show, Finebaum has some time to kill before his night job as the evening sportscaster on WIAT, a local television station that made news recently when an executive there fired the entire staff, anchors and all. Ratings were so bad he'd concluded the only hope was to start with a clean slate. Finebaum is part of the new regime, and to boost ratings, he's had free rein to practice his stock-in-trade—angering Alabama fans. With regular segments like "Loser of the Day," his sportscast is as much a comedy act as sports news. Not that Finebaum thinks the gig is much fun. He calls WIAT "the Alcatraz of TV journalism" and considers himself an inmate. Well maybe, but on top of his column and his radio show, it seems to amount to a decent living, if Finebaum's wheels are any indication. He drives a brand new ink-black Jaguar, which I trail out of the WERC parking lot down Valley Avenue to a desperate-looking strip mall and a dingy Mexican restaurant. The place is empty, which to Finebaum is precisely its charm; it means less chance of an unpleasant encounter with some enraged Alabama fan. He glances around the room nervously and picks a seat facing the door.

"I used to live in total fear," he says. "There were death threats. People would throw things. I didn't trust anybody, so I went underground, quit drinking, and became a recluse at a very young age. Even my fellow columnists hated me. They thought, this guy will flame out or get fired soon, so why waste the time?"

We order a couple of chicken enchiladas.

Finebaum says his radio show may have saved him. "It humanized me," he says. "When people could attack me for a couple of hours every day, it defused the tension."

To my surprise, Finebaum isn't a person who enjoys being despised. I'd assumed that the typical shock jock—a Rush Limbaugh or a Howard Stern—operates on the assumption that to be really liked by a large number of people it's necessary to be hated by some other large number. Finebaum has managed to figure out a way to be despised by almost everyone. This is something he endures more than enjoys—his half of an artistic bargain. "It's a game, of course," Finebaum says, as if reminding himself. "If you take it seriously, you'll go out of your mind."

Finebaum's act isn't playing so well at WIAT, however. The executive who'd brought him in to boost ratings apparently wasn't prepared for the fallout when people actually started watching: a slew of angry letters and calls demanding that Finebaum be fired, threats to boycott station advertisers, and calls to corporate offices demanding the removal of WIAT's management. There's evidence those managers may be getting cold feet. When the DuBose scandal broke, Finebaum angered many viewers by running a graphic of DuBose in a bra.

Alarmed by the negative response, station managers issued an ultimatum to Finebaum: "No more bras. Lay off the women and children." They also commissioned a telephone survey to assess viewer opinion of their sportscaster. The results are due this evening, and Finebaum—no stranger to his own unpopularity—is alarmed at what his bosses will uncover.

So after dinner we drive up Red Mountain to WIAT's studios. I follow Finebaum to the sports department, a dark closet full of video equipment. Inside, an intern is frantically scanning through videotape of the day's sports action, looking for footage Finebaum can use during his sportscast. They won't need much; as part of a new rapid-fire newscast format, Finebaum's sports segment lasts a mere two minutes.

A piece of viewer mail taped to the door catches my eye.

> DEAR SIR:
> Paul Finebaum went over the line. Last night he called a bright, talented handsome three-year-old boy a "snot-nosed kid." Finebaum is a sarcastic, mean-spirited, unkind snot. He has to be sick. I am through watching your station until you come to your senses and get rid of that divisive poor excuse for a sports director.
>
> Sincerely,
> Wayne Smith

"Excuse me," Finebaum says. "I've got to see if I've got a job." When Finebaum returns a few minutes later, he looks grim. The data from the viewer survey are alarming: Finebaum has received the most negative response in the history of the station.

"People just overwhelmingly didn't like me," he says.

But there's a catch: as much as Alabamians dislike Finebaum, the station's Nielsen ratings show they're tuning in in ever greater numbers to watch him. The disconnect between the viewers' opinion of Finebaum and his ratings has his bosses flummoxed. They've never seen anything like it.

Finebaum disappears into the sports department closet, and for a few anxious minutes he and his assistant put together a short, acerbic bit on Bockrath's firing. Finebaum then digs into a small, clear plastic pouch on his desk and fishes out a makeup sponge, which he dabs miserably on his cheeks, nose, and bald head, snuffing out the glare. We head upstairs to the studio.

"Paul Finebaum!" the weather lady says cheerily, as we walk on to the set. "See those negative ratings? You're like a song people can't get out of their heads. People hate you, but they're watching!"

The weather lady is right, of course, but as an Alabama fan, I don't see the contradiction. Good news on the team is easy to come by—I just log on to one of the fan sites or read the local news coverage of the team, most of which is unfailingly complimentary. Finebaum provides the other view. And what's more interesting—all the good things people think about you, or all the bad? Put another way, if you could eavesdrop on the conversations of people you know, would you rather hear your friends praising you, or your enemies deriding you? Alabama fans listen to Finebaum the way liberals listen to Rush Limbaugh—as a painful but practical exercise in self-awareness. From a business standpoint, this is the genius of Paul Finebaum. Early on he recognized the appeal of negativity and quickly cornered the market. To remain negative—and to keep people listening—Finebaum sometimes contradicts himself and remakes his arguments on the fly. If he's harping on a quarterback controversy and one of the competing quarterbacks is lost for the season with an injury, he'll simply turn his attention to a rift—real or imagined—in the coaching staff. He's a kind of rhetorical retrovirus that morphs and replicates to remain contrarian. Finebaum's style makes him a nightmare for any college administrator, football coach, or university public relations officer who comes under assault from him—you can't turn Finebaum's listenership against him because they already hate him. Finebaum, and perhaps by extension, the sports press, don't have to be right—they just have to *be*, and the fans will come running. As Jerral Johnson's friend Bobbie said after the Tech game, they can't not listen.

* * *

I work the phones for a day, trying to find someone else out there generous or just foolish enough to invite a stranger on their RV for the weekend, but it's hopeless. In retrospect, I'm amazed that I'd been invited by anyone at all. The Bices' sense of adventure, or at least their lack of caution, has turned out to be more unusual than I realized. There's a simple solution to being RV-less, of course, and that's to buy my own, and each day that passes without a berth on someone's else's RV, the more seriously I consider purchasing one. On the advice of that helpful Burton Campers salesman, I look in the classifieds of the *Birmingham News* to see what's available. There are plenty of listings, many for under $6,000, which I've set as my limit. RVs are apparently like boats; when you want to sell one, you want to sell it very badly. I figure that if I lowball someone and get a good deal, I can buy an RV, use it for the rest of the season, and then flip it without taking too much of a hit. By late Tuesday morning I have appointments to view three RVs, each one located in far corner of the *News*'s coverage area. I have a lot of driving to do. I set out at lunchtime.

My first appointment is in Trussville, with a man named Robert Prater, who tells me to stop by his church, where he says he'll be doing a little landscaping work. I picture him with a spade and pruners, but I find him on a backhoe, digging a drainage gully the size of a small canal. Prater eases up on the throttle and shouts directions to his house—just a mile up the next road, the one with two RVs in the front yard. They're both open and both for sale, he says. I wave at Prater, and he throttles up on the backhoe before quickly easing off the gas again.

"Oh, yeah," he yells over the din. "Don't mind them dogs!"

Dogs or hyenas, I can't tell which. The animals are brown and mangy, and they greet me by barking furiously as I ease my car across the yard. The smaller of the RVs—a diminutive Winnebago model called a Mini-Winnie—is easily written off. It doesn't have a full complement of tires. I know enough about motor homes to know that I want one with tires. The other one is bigger and possibly, it seems, functional. It's a Champion, like Ron St. John's Toad. A bumper sticker on the back reads: IF YOU FOLLOW TOO CLOSELY, I'LL FLIP A BOOGER ON YOU.

I make nice with the dogs through the window before getting out of the car. They don't want to attack me, it turns out, just to sniff me in inappropriate places, so I scamper across the yard and climb inside the Champion. Its interior is threadbare—exposed wiring, discombobulated cabinets, a dark brown shag carpet that is unraveling into furry clumps that look like decomposing gophers. The interior is coated in years-old cooking grease. There's no need for a test drive.

Back at the Clay Baptist Church, Prater doesn't seem the least bit surprised when I tell him his RVs aren't for me. I get the feeling I'm not the first person to pass on them. Prater, though, is all smiles. From atop his backhoe he invites me to stop by the church on Sunday for the annual homecoming. "They'll be gospel bluegrass and a potluck dinner," he shouts over the engine. "More food'n you'll know what to do with."

I tell him I'll have to miss out because I'm heading to Tuscaloosa for the Bama game. Prater nods and gives me an affirming smile that suggests I've hit on the one possibly valid excuse for missing services at the Clay Baptist Church.

My next appointment is with an elderly man named W. H. Smith, who's selling a 1969 Bluebird school bus that he and his son converted into an RV. Smith is "asking $2,500," according to his ad in the *News*, which means he'll take much less, which in turn means that the thing has to be very nearly undrivable, since nothing that big can actually function without being worth at least a few thousand dollars. When I press Smith on the issue of drivability, he insists the bus is worth seeing. He gives me directions: once off the main road, turn right at the goose pen, go to the second house on the right, and ring the doorbell. I do as told and when I make the right at the goose pen, I see a disheartening site—a grime-caked school bus completely overgrown with brush. Smith is wearing a flannel shirt and overalls when he emerges from his house, and he greets me enthusiastically and tells me not to worry about the cosmetic issues—that he and his son customized the bus themselves for trips to the beach, and he's certain that everything on board works and needs only to be cleaned. Entering the bus first requires that we hack our way through five feet or so of thick vegetation and pry open a door that is frozen shut with rust.

The interior resembles less an RV than a greenhouse. The floor is covered in a crust of compost. There are animal droppings everywhere—from raccoons that must have gained access to the bus through any number of broken windows. A tangle of wires and frayed electrical cables lies like a net across the floor—no threat to us, since the vehicle's batteries are long since dead. Mr. Smith doesn't remember the last time he cranked the engine, but again he's confident it works perfectly. The interior has been built out with particleboard and plywood that is now badly warped and stained from water damage. We walk toward the rear. There are banquettes on either side.

"Now these here are your holding tanks," Mr. Smith says, lifting the lid of one of the banquettes. "This 'un's for your gray water"—the soapy water from the shower and sink drains. He turns around and lifts the lid of the opposite banquette. "An this 'un's for your shit."

I've seen enough. I tell Mr. Smith I'm looking for something that might require a little less attention. He purses his lips, as if he were contemplating some sort of counterargument, then his face slackens.

"Lemme ask you sumpin'," he says. "You like model trains?"

"Sure."

"Come with me."

I follow Smith to a garage-sized outbuilding behind his house. He flips on the lights to reveal a model train set that spirals endlessly around the room like unraveled yarn. Smith throws a switch. The diorama flickers to life, and half a dozen trains slither into motion. We play contentedly with trains for an hour—first Smith at the controls, then me—and high-five once when two trains barely miss each other at a crossing. Smith gives me a tour of his train memorabilia collection, introduces me to his belligerent pet geese (he keeps them for security purposes, he says; they make a racket when strangers show up), and he makes a halfhearted attempt to sell me his late mother's Dodge Dart, which Smith has garaged for thirty-five years. Two hours after my arrival, Smith and I say our goodbyes. I've found a friend but not a ride.

My next appointment is in a town called Montevallo, south of

Birmingham; another Winnebago. The address I'm given takes me to a mobile home off a country highway and . . . more dogs. The Winnebago's owner is a sullen, wiry character with a smudge of facial hair on his upper lip and matted black hair on his head. He's disturbingly quiet and communicates primarily by moving his head. Eventually, the explanation for his mood comes out: he's selling the rig reluctantly, under orders from his wife.

I take the driver's seat and negotiate the vehicle over the ruts in his dirt driveway toward the main road. We drive a couple of miles out, in silence, and back toward his home . . . in silence. The Winnebago runs well and is in decent shape, but it doesn't have a shower, the one amenity besides an engine that differentiates an RV from a ten-dollar camping tent, in my opinion. Back at the mobile home, I try to crank the generator, but the machine responds with a deadened click. The owner marches into his house, comes out wielding a large screwdriver, and disappears into the dark confines of the generator compartment. I hear a few grunts, the sound of metal clanging against metal, then a loud snap: a bright blue arc of electricity fires through the air from the tip of the screwdriver to somewhere deep inside the RV. The man is knocked several feet backward. His hat and the screwdriver fly in different directions, but he hops quickly to his feet. "Don't worry about me," he says reassuringly. "I work for the power company."

The man is preparing to climb back into the generator compartment when I tell him not to worry—I'm interested and I'll be in touch. I make sure I have his correct telephone number, and as we shake hands, he gives me a soul-piercing look that says, more or less: Bullshitter.

That leaves one more: a 1978 Allegro motor home parked clear across the county in Trussville, where I'd started my day. The asking price is $7,500, out of my range, but there's a chance something that costs so much might actually function, so I decide to have a look. The Allegro is owned by a friendly sounding character named Mr. Watts, who appears from behind a screen door as soon as I pull into the driveway. He's a silver-haired fireplug of a man and is accompanied by an overweight brown dachshund that resembles a football with feet. Watts is originally from the mountains of southwest Virginia and speaks with an accent that still bears the Scottish inflections of his forebears—he says the words *out* and *about* so that they rhyme with *boot*. A few years back, Watts says, he and his wife retired to South Florida, only to have their house vacuumed off the earth by Hurricane Andrew. They bought the Allegro, parked it on their empty lot, and lived in it for a year. When their insurance settlement came through, they bought the house in Birmingham and hightailed it out of Hurricane Alley. Since settling down, Watts and his wife have used the Allegro to go to a few square dancing conventions, but that's it. It's time to sell, he says.

The Allegro is twenty-eight feet long, beige with brown and orange stripes, and has a nearly concave nose, two aluminum bars for bumpers, and large mag wheels—two in the front, four in the back—like the ones you see on a big Ryder truck. It has an Alabama Crimson Tide spare tire cover that Watts, a Virginia Tech Hokies fan, left on for years—partly for the practical reason of having something to cover his spare tire, and partly for the reason that he kind of liked the logo. This predisposes me both to the Allegro and to Mr. Watts. But there is an even more powerful pull: Allegro motor homes have close ties to Alabama football. They're built in Red Bay, Alabama, near the Mississippi line, by Bob Tiffin, affectionately known around the state as "Old Man Tiffin," not so much because he is old as to distinguish him from his son, the Alabama football hero Van Tiffin, whose last-second, fifty-two-yard field goal—"The Kick"—beat Auburn in 1985. The mere memory of it—rendered with digital clarity in my brain, complete with a soundtrack of two Alabama radio announcers in an ecstatic duet of "It's good! / It's good! It's good! / It's good!" followed by a blast of crowd noise that rattled the radio speakers—still prompts a pleasing gush of endorphins in my frontal lobes. Though this particular Allegro was built nine years before that miraculous moment, it's related—sired of the same loins as Van Tiffin himself.

I follow Watts inside, and the football with feet waddles aboard as well. The interior of the Allegro is . . . *interesting*. It's carpeted in pinkish-orange shag, with rust-colored furniture, curtains, and banquettes; green simulated-wood-grain paneling; and a snot-green, puffy-vinyl dashboard. There's a double stainless steel sink, a large refrigerator, a working four-burner propane stove, and a self-contained shower stall made of mustard-colored plastic. The RV is clean and obviously well maintained, even if the color scheme lacks a certain something. The engine is an eight-cylinder Dodge 440 that Watts says manages just four miles to the gallon. There are a few problems I should know about, Watts says—a slight oil leak on the engine block that sometimes causes the interior to fill with smoke; bald tires; a leak in the sewage holding tank that causes its contents to dribble into a puddle beneath the RV; a carburetor quirk that makes the engine impossible to start when hot, which means that in midjourney the Allegro has to be refueled with the engine running, which in turn means occasionally exposing oneself to the risk of explosion. Otherwise, he says, the Allegro is in fine shape.

"How's the generator?" I ask.

"Just had it tuned."

"Air conditioner?"

"It'll run you outta here," Watts said. *Ootta here.*

Watts gives me the keys. The engine is big and impressive. At idle, it sounds like a ski boat's—*glug glug glug*—and with just a little gas, like a New York City garbage truck. I back the RV out of his driveway and strike out on a drive around the neighborhood. The Allegro seems responsive, for a house anyway. It requires the braking room of a freight train, and in tight turns, a curious, metal-on-metal sound emanates from the wheel well, but the radio works, on AM anyway. I turn it on, spin the dial a few times, and find the *Finebaum Show: "I mean, how many times can you call for a guy's resignation?"*

Watts and his dog are waiting for me in the yard when I get back. I manage to get the Allegro into the driveway without incident.

"I'd like to get a mechanic to look it over," I tell Watts. "And if it checks out, I'll give you fifty-five hundred for it."

Watts jams his hands deep into the pockets of his brown polyester slacks, purses his lips, and rocks back and forth on his heels. He looks up at the Allegro, then at me, at his pet football, then back at the Allegro.

"I could do that," he says.

We shake. A funny sort of smile creeps across Watts's face. It's a mysterious look I won't fully understand for some months: the look of someone who has just unloaded a used RV. It's a look that says: *Now it's your problem.*

"You'll enjoy it," he says. For a brief moment it looks as though Watts is about to collapse into a fit of laughter.

The next day I pick up the Allegro and drive it to the Saab Tire and Automotive in downtown Birmingham. The people at Saab—no relation to the Scandinavian car maker—have a reputation for being able to fix anything with wheels and an engine, and I've been told they're straight dealers. I pull into the garage there, and the shop boss—a girthy, bearded chain smoker named Jack (his shirt says so)—takes a slow turn around the vehicle.

"How much you pay for it?" he asks.

"Fifty-five hundred."

Jack takes a deep tug on his cigarette and exhales.

"Shit," he says, apparently impressed. "How many miles?"

"Forty-eight thousand."

Jack takes another tug on his smoke. The ember brightens. He exhales lazily.

"Shiiiit," he says.

"Generator work?"

"Runs great," I say. "Guy said he just had it tuned."

He shakes his head wondrously.

"*Shiiiiiiit,*" Jack says. I follow him on board. "Air conditioner?" he asks.

"It'll run you outta here."

Jack sits in the driver's seat and turns the key: *glug*, *glug*, *glug*.

"How much you say you paid?" he asks.

"Fifty-five."

"Tell you sump'm," Jack says. "When you ready to get rid of it—gimme a call."

Buoyed by Jack's endorsement, I deliver a check for $5,500 to Mr. Watts, who still has that smile on his face. We shake and say goodbye, and I take the RV back to Saab to get a few things fixed. The next morning Jack calls with an estimate for repairs. The Allegro needs new tires, a new head gasket, and an alignment. The brake lights, headlights, and windshield wipers don't work—an electrician will have to be called in to do some rewiring. The ominous sounds from the wheel well involve something called the ball joint, which is apparently vital to the safe operation of all motor vehicles and needs to be replaced. In all, the Allegro needs $1,500 worth of repairs. Parts have to be ordered. The work will take about ten days.

"Them motor homes' a bitch," Jack says.

The next day I strike out for Tuscaloosa by car.

Chapter Seven

The Man I Hold So Near

TUSCALOOSA, ALABAMA, IS ABOUT FORTY-FIVE MINUTES west of Birmingham, and from the interstate, it's a town easily missed. It appears as little more than a depression in the forested landscape to the north, and only two structures in town rise above the trees: a nine-story brick building with a flashing clock and thermometer on the roof—the AmSouth Bank—and Bryant-Denny Stadium, where Alabama plays. During night games, the stadium lights throw a luminous pillar high enough into the sky to be seen throughout the county. During the day, though, it merely peeks over the trees, like a porcelain bowl set in high grass. Anyone adventuresome enough to leave the interstate at Tuscaloosa will first have to run a gauntlet of strip malls—fast-food restaurants, a yogurt stand, a fried-catfish joint called Ezell's Catfish Cabin, and a bait shop called The Worm Shack—before encountering any structure that looks more than a few months old. The campus, though, is of another era. The president's mansion has massive white columns and sweeping staircases, and even the fraternity and sorority houses look like the architectural offspring of Tara. A stately bell tower called Denny Chimes provides a soothing soundtrack for campus strolls, and the central Quad is shaded by ancient oaks. A mile or so past the school is downtown Tuscaloosa, which has the forlorn charm of an old river port town. The buildings, many of them old cotton warehouses, are brick with wooden awnings, and seldom over two stories tall. On some, faded murals advertise merchandise long obsolete, and businesses that long ago closed their doors. The side of town away from campus peers down on the Black Warrior River, which oozes silently by between seemingly endless curtains of willows. As long ago as 1580, there has been a village on this knoll. Creeks and Choctaws lived here alternately until white settlers moved in and forced them west in the 1830s on the Trail of Tears. Those settlers set up a port to ship their cotton south toward Mobile. From 1826 to 1846 Tuscaloosa served as the capital of Alabama; the university was founded there in 1831. During the Civil War, the school was converted into a military college for the training of Confederate officers, a change of curriculum that in 1865 attracted the attention of a pyromaniacal Union Army brigade called Croxton's Raiders. Croxton was particularly good at his job, and as a result, there are just four antebellum buildings on campus now; the most beautiful of them is a small brick columned structure off the Quad known as the Gorgas House. It overlooks a large grassy mound—the ashes of the original campus library—which is now a semisacred place where fraternities and sororities perform their secret rites.

The first football game in Tuscaloosa was played in 1893—Alabama lost 4-0 to the Birmingham Athletic Club—and with a few ignominious exceptions, like George Wallace's "stand in the schoolhouse door," almost every subsequent dispatch from Tuscaloosa to the outside world has mentioned the sport. Local T-shirts now proclaim Tuscaloosa a "Drinking Town with a Football Problem," which is meant as a boast. Perhaps in spite of itself, Tuscaloosa isn't completely behind the times. Mercedes recently built a huge factory outside of town to produce SUVs, and as a result it's now possible to watch German news on the local cable TV and to walk into bars downtown and see squads of baseball-capped fraternity boys slugging beers next to tables of men with mustaches, wearing sandals with socks and shouting "Prosit!" Some transplants—particularly professors—take offense at the notion that their new home is hopelessly monomaniacal. They'll tell you that not everything in Tuscaloosa revolves around football, that there's a health food store, a yoga studio, and a whole throng of folks who go to the mall during games because they know the parking lot will be empty—that there is a mass of people in town who just don't care. And imams have overrun Opp.

When I was a kid, Tuscaloosa was on par with the North Pole as a magical destination. Instead of Santa Claus, Tuscaloosa had Bear Bryant. Even the town's name—which derives from the name of an old Choctaw chief—suggested someplace remote and magical. Despite growing up just forty-five minutes from Tuscaloosa, I'd only been there on football Saturdays. On a Wednesday, traffic slips along at an easy pace. The roads aren't crammed. There's no crowd noise, no plumes of barbecue smoke curling over the grassy clearings. A languid silence hangs over campus, broken only by the occasional shriek of a train whistle and the distant pistol-pops of snare drums at marching band practice.

On Friday morning, all that changes. By 8:00 A.M., a line of fifty RVs has formed on Bryant Drive in front of the Law Library parking lot. They're prohibited from entering before noon because until then the lot is supposed to be used by . . . well, the sort of people who frequent law libraries—professors and law students. The idea that a few tweeds get precedence over the RV corps strikes the RV-ers as ludicrous. This isn't as irrational as it first sounds. The lot is about 90 percent empty—just a few cars parked on the gravelly perimeter. Perhaps three times as many RVs wait to get in the lot as there are cars parked there. Every now and then, as the RV-ers wait impatiently to get in, a student walks lackadaisically from the Law Library and climbs into his car, then rolls out of the lot in unhurried defiance. After a while a few of the RV-ers begin to gesture at the exiting drivers, urging them to hurry up and get out of the way. The scene starts to resemble a picket line. Eventually, it's too much for the man driving the lead RV. A few minutes after ten o'clock, he puts his RV in gear, swerves past a dazed law student, and rips into the lot. The land grab is on. A few bold sooners try to save places for friends—they claim turf by setting out lawn chairs—and are set upon by their peers. In the confusion, someone—an RV-er or somebody at the Law School, it's never determined—calls the cops. A squad car pulls into the lot, as RV-ers are dropping their jacks, unfurling their awnings, deploying grills and picnic tables and big Astroturf carpets. A few ambitious bon vivants have cracked open the day's first beers. The police officers don't even bother to get out of the car. The RV corps is here. There's no undoing it.

In the evening I do my own informal RV census: two hundred and fifty in the Law Library parking lot; a hundred more in the parking lot behind the Ferguson Student Center; fifty in the parking lot behind Tutwiler, the women's dorm; twenty-five downtown, in a lot overlooking the river; twenty-five in a private lot near the Druid City Hospital, a bus ride from the stadium; and perhaps a hundred more scattered all over town as haphazardly as Matchbox cars on a playroom floor. People are outside. The evening is filled with voices and music and horns and skeins of barbecue smoke. There's a pep rally, and fireworks crackle in the sky. Crowds spill out the front doors of the fraternity houses. The melancholy induced by the Tech game has dissipated as quickly as morning mist off the Black Warrior River. The cure for football-induced melancholy is clearly more football.

I come upon a curious scene near the Strip—a line of people standing sock-footed in front of the largest RV I've seen yet: a Liberty Prevost—a $1.4 million job, the sort of thing you'd expect a country music star to travel in. The owner is giving tours to everyone willing to take off their shoes before boarding—he doesn't want red Tuscaloosa County clay getting tracked throughout his million-dollar bus. I add my shoes to the pile and get in line.

The owner is a fleshy, gray-haired man who works the line with the practiced reserve of a clergyman greeting parishioners at the front door of a church. He introduces himself as Sherrell Smith. The name rattles around in my head for a minute before I put it together. It's the Chicken Man, aforementioned by Donnie.

To make any vehicle worth $1.4 million, a manufacturer has to cram it with an excess of gadgetry. Smith's model has a global positioning system, two phone systems, a fax machine, a fifty-inch projection television, a VCR, twin satellite dishes, a trash compactor, a microwave, a convection oven, twin washers and dryers, four air conditioners, a ceiling fan, a twenty-five-cubic-foot refrigerator—"all that crap," in Smith's words. An onboard computer allows the owner to do everything but drive from the queen-sized bed in the back. The decor is equally excessive: mood lights; pastel-colored banquettes; a spaceship *Enterprise*–style retractable door that swooshes open and closed at the touch of a button; a marble bath; a reflective stainless-steel ceiling that makes the interior shimmer like a casino; and, in the bedroom, a glass wall etched with an image of galloping horses. Taken as a whole, the interior looks like Graceland jammed into a closet.

Ironically, Mr. Smith couldn't seem less like Elvis. He's almost catatonically subdued. He speaks in a whisper and seems not so much to walk as to tiptoe. Everything about his manner suggests caution and reserve, and yet what could be less reserved than the purchase of a million-dollar motor home? No one seems more puzzled by the contradiction than Smith himself. "I just broke down and bought it," he tells me, as if explaining how he came to own some new fifty-dollar handheld gizmo.

Smith started out as a chicken farmer, raising an average of a million birds every seven weeks for the Tyson Corporation, before getting into the much cleaner business of building chicken houses in north Alabama and Tennessee, a part of the world that just happened to have no end of need for new chicken houses. Smith then had the idea to open big hardware stores in areas where he'd built those chicken houses, and to act as the farmers' main supplier. He eventually opened four. The whole operation, known as Smith Poultry & Hardware, is now a $20 million-a-year business.

Smith's wife pokes her head in the door. "Hey, Sherrell—how do you turn on the neon lights?"

Smith hits a button on a switch panel. There's a smattering of applause from outside as the lights come on.

Smith got his first RV in 1986 and traded up every couple of years, but it wasn't until 1997, after he was diagnosed with prostate cancer, that Smith went in for his million-dollar job. Smith's doctors told him the cancer had spread to his kidneys and lungs, and they gave him six months to live. So, figuring he should enjoy his final months on earth, Smith sold his chicken farm and sank the cash into the Prevost, as a final act of indulgence. He and his family drove together to football games and took trips, preparing for his demise. But on a ski trip out west, Smith ran into a man who told him about an experimental oxygen-tent therapy some doctors were using to treat cancer. The therapy wasn't approved in the United States, but it was available in Mexico. With a million-dollar RV, Smith was nothing if not mobile, so feeling he had nothing to lose, he climbed in his Prevost and drove from Alabama to a clinic near Tijuana. He spent several weeks in an oxygen tent, and his cancer went away.

"My doctor's impressed," Smith says with a shrug.

Surviving cancer has changed Smith's relationship with his RV. The Prevost was no longer a final act of indulgence—it is an ongoing act of indulgence that has consequences both for Smith's bank account and for his dealings with fellow fans. It's hard not to seem uppity pulling in the lot in an RV that costs as much as ten or fifteen of the RVs around it, and seeming uppity is probably the worst offense a member of the RV corps could commit. The fan hierarchy, such as it is, values ticket stubs more than dollar bills. For Smith, being thought of as rich was the *downside* of owning a million-dollar RV. "It's nothing to brag about," Smith tells me. "The others know whatever I drive, I'm a chicken farmer. I'm just who I am. All my life I've never tried to be bigger than I was. I still consider myself a lower-type person."

The paradox is that for Smith to enjoy his own RV, he has to let others parade through it all weekend. He seems at ease with the bargain. Fellow fans get to marvel at the interior of a million-dollar RV, and Smith gets to make clear that he sees himself as one of the crowd. A weekend-long stream of visitors is just one of life's necessary inconveniences, like working eighteen-hour days in a chicken house or sitting in an oxygen tent in Mexico for a month, or, for that matter, just filling the thing up with gas. Smith is happy to do it, and asks only that guests take off their shoes.

* * *

My first task on Saturday morning is to get a ticket to the game. I've never worried much about getting tickets to Alabama games—in part because scalping is legal in the state, and you can almost always pick up a last-minute single outside the stadium. The RV-ers, though, take a different view; tickets are a basic provision, up there with food, water, and beer, and few would ever think of driving all the way to a stadium without a guaranteed seat. I ask some RV-ers I recognize if they happen to have a spare, and they react as if I've declared a medical emergency. A man tells me to stay put, and he and two pals strike out across the lot with business-like haste. A few minutes later, I hear my name yelled. A Mobile pharmaceutical company employee named Frances has been stood up by a friend and so now has a spare. Frances is in her mid-thirties with a lustrous wave of black hair and a big friendly smile. I anticipate some haggling over the price, but Frances only wants to grill me about my team allegiance. The extra seat is in the Alabama section next to her own, and she has no intention of sitting beside an Arkansas fan. I give a "Roll Tide," and Frances parts with the ticket for face value.

There's one more stop before kickoff—the Bear Bryant Namesake Reunion at the Bryant Museum. The namesake reunion is exactly what it sounds like—a gathering of people named after Paul William "Bear" Bryant. The museum keeps a registry of such people—they fill out a form headed "I was named for Coach Bryant" and are invited once a year to a pregame barbecue at the museum. The list is, of course, voluntary and only modestly publicized, so it can't account for everyone named after the Bear—or those who'd been named Paul, Bryant, or Bear for reasons that remain a mystery even to them. But these limitations notwithstanding, the current tally of registered Bear Bryant namesakes stands just shy of six hundred.

The Bryant Museum is just across Bryant Drive from the main RV lot; a mere quarter mile from Bryant-Denny Stadium; not too far from Bryant Hall, the dorm; and a short drive from Paul William Bryant High School in Cottondale. A quick drive around Tuscaloosa puts the idea of naming your kid after the Bear Bryant in a new light. Why not do it? Everyone else is.

A red and white tent has been set up on the lawn out front of the museum, just to the left of the life-sized bronze statue of the Bear at the entrance. Two guitar-strumming fraternity types are singing "Brown-Eyed Girl," and people are milling about eating hot dogs, hamburgers, and Golden Flake potato chips (the Bear's favorite). The paper nametags tell the story: Bryant Adam Paris, Bryant Christopher Carrol, Bryant Marshall Lambert, Bryant Atkins, Paul Bryant Mitchell, Katherine Bryant Hawks . . .

The Bryant Museum's director and the event emcee is a man named Ken Gaddy. He's a slight, professorial-looking man in a coat, tie, and glasses. I find him between raffle drawings in the big tent, giving away houndstooth hats—part of the Bear's uniform—to a few lucky namesakes. The reunion, he says, was the idea of the original Bear Bryant namesake, Paul Bryant Jr., a quiet, highly successful business man who made a fortune owning dog tracks. Bryant Jr. is on the University's Board of Trustees and is a major booster of the football program—he donated $10 million to the expansion of Bryant-Denny Stadium, for example. Over the years he received dozens of letters from fans saying that they, like him, had been named after the Bear, so in 1996, Bryant Jr. urged the museum to try to get the group together. Gaddy drafted a press release calling for the namesakes to declare themselves that was picked up by local newspapers and the Associated Press. After that, Gaddy says, "Namesakes started ringing the museum's telephone off the hook."

The museum is packed. A crowd of Bryants stands mesmerized in front of a television, watching a documentary about the late coach. Another group of Bryants stares confoundedly at the suit Tony Brandino wore to his five-hundredth game (apparently five hundred games in a row seems excessive even to people named after Bear Bryant). I walk over to a bulletin board in the lobby where the father of one Connor Bryant Hajek has posted a poem.

My saddest day thus far
Was the day Coach Bryant died.
It hit your dad so hard.
I hurt so bad I cried.
I wish I could have played for this

Man I hold so near.
But at least his name shall live
In the son I love so dear.

The poem suggests that naming a child after a favorite football coach is the fan equivalent of a baptism or a bris, a way of putting the cultural marks on your children before they've had a chance to survey the offerings of the cultural smorgasbord and build their own meal. The biggest fear most parents have is that their children will grow up to become something totally different from themselves, and the key to avoiding this fate is to start indoctrination early. As an act of preemption, naming seems to work. There aren't a lot of Baptists out there named Mohammed, and there aren't a lot of Auburn fans named Bryant.

Actually, the religious comparison is apt. In a paper titled "Meanings and Interpretations of Paul 'Bear' Bryant," a group of anthropology students at Alabama polled hardcore Crimson Tide fans and locals on their opinions of the late coach and found that fully 26 percent associated the Bear with "godlike qualities." The default explanation for Bryant's exalted status in Alabama is that he won and gave Alabamians something to be proud about at a time when the rest of the country and world looked down on the South. He was a kind of redeemer. I suppose the theory makes sense for a certain generation, but I liked the Bear long before I was old enough to understand that people outside of Alabama held my home state in exceedingly low regard—long before I felt a need to be redeemed. I became an Alabama fan and Bryant fan the way most people come to their teams and their heroes—because my father liked Alabama.* He went to school at Alabama—his fraternity, Sigma Alpha Epsilon, occupies a monstrous antebellum knockoff just around the corner from the Bryant Museum.

It could have easily been otherwise. My father considered going to Georgia Tech in Atlanta to study engineering, but went to Alabama

---

*** In a study of sports fans done in the mid-seventies, a Canadian sociologist named Barry D. McPherson found that over half of fans cited family members as the source of their team allegiance, with 35 percent attributing their team selection to their father, more than any other single source.**

to be closer to his parents, who lived nearby and were divorcing, largely because my grandfather, a country lawyer and politician, was an alcoholic. So it's fair to say that the ultimate reason I like Alabama is because my grandfather drank too much. (It's not so grim—he stopped drinking and remarried my grandmother twenty-five years after their divorce, but that's another story.) My granddad might have known that he was screwing up his marriage by drinking, but he couldn't possibly have imagined the effect it would have on his yet unborn grandson's autumn Saturdays fifty years later. I doubt the thought would've deterred him, but I like to think it might have caused him to pause contemplatively mid-Bourbon.

There are some practical benefits to liking the same team as your parents—not getting disinherited, for example; or avoiding years of arguments at the dinner table—but that's probably not why it happens so often. I imagine people follow their parents because continuity is reassuring, and because it takes a lot of energy to break with the past. It's a threatening notion to a lot of fans that we don't like our teams for all the reasons we say we do (the colors, the tradition, the fight song, the style of play) but rather because of the random process of imprinting. I find the thought liberating. It's a lot harder to hate the other side when you allow that your arguments for liking your team are just as contrived as the other guy's are for liking his. The way we find teams isn't so unlike the way we find wives or husbands—through happy accidents—and with sports it matters little if, as with myself and young Connor Bryant Hajek, the marriages are arranged.

I make my way back through the throng of Bryant's unofficial heirs, and head to another one of them, Bryant-Denny. "Sweet Home, Alabama" is playing over the PA system. The sky is a vivid blue, the air a clean and cool 66°F—perfect football weather. Mike DuBose paces the field watchfully during warm-ups. He's wearing an unreadably bland expression, a look either of resignation or of confidence—I can't tell which. The mood of the crowd is just as difficult to gauge. It's a mixture of anticipation and unsettled anxiety, the lingering effects of the Tech loss and Bockrath's firing and the unresolved doubts about the coach's competence.

I sit down next to Frances during warm-ups, and manage to learn a little bit about her. She describes herself as a "*major* Bama fan," the exact phrase, in fact, she had used to introduce herself to potential mates in a personals ad on Match.com. Frances hasn't missed an Alabama game since 1994, when her then-husband had a heart attack. They've since divorced; he got the season tickets, but the two are on friendly terms and have worked out a kind of custody arrangement that allows her to attend a lot of home games in their old seats. Otherwise, she has to scrounge.

"I don't miss a game," she says. "If I watch it on TV I get sick—literally throw up." Frances opens her mouth and pokes her finger in and shakes her head in disgust. "If we lose, I want to crawl up and die."

A clarion blares from the loudspeakers. The stadium grows hushed and the crowd turns its attention to the Sony JumboTron above the south end zone. I haven't been to Tuscaloosa for a game since the JumboTron was installed, and it feels strange that before the sacred entry of the team, we're all going to kick back and watch a little TV. The crowd hardly seems to mind; fans are comfortable nowhere if not in front of a television. What follows is essentially an infomercial for Alabama football. The buzzword at Alabama is "tradition"—12 national championships, 20 conference championships, 49 bowl appearances over more than a century. Constantly invoking our tradition doesn't help us win football games exactly, but it's an implicit defense of our obsession. Tradition provides consolation for our losses, and it's the moral force behind our victories. The infomercial starts with a few black-and-white stills from the old days—including a picture of the Bear when he played tight end—grainy footage from the 1926 Rose Bowl, then moves on to color shots of the goal line stand in the 1979 Sugar Bowl against Penn State that led to a championship. The crowd roars as if the play is happening in real time. Bear Bryant's face appears, craggy, MacArthur-like, and his thundering voice rattles the girders: "I ain't ever been *called* nothin' but a winner," the old man intones, "because I ain't ever *been* nothin' but a winner." More cheers. I look at Frances; her eyes are glassed with tears. Next, the replay of George Teague's miraculous, come-from-behind ball-jacking of a Miami receiver in the '93 Sugar Bowl. I get goose bumps and let out a howl myself. The Bama logo appears on the screen. The stadium rumbles with the piped-in sound of stampeding elephants; after an elephant's trumpet, the stadium announcer proclaims, "This . . . is . . . *Alabama football!*" and the team shoots out of the tunnel. It's utter show biz, but I'm won over—another hapless victim of the JumboTron.

It doesn't take long, though, before we're back to reality and the mood is spoiled. On Alabama's first drive, just two and a half minutes into the game, Zow drops back to throw a screen toward the left flats. The ball is tipped, and Arkansas intercepts and goes on to score. We've picked up right where we left off last week, and the crowd is plunged into a brooding funk. Zow, though, responds with a touchdown drive of his own, and Alabama ties. A few minutes later, he throws another interception, and the crowd begins to boo. Tyler Watts, the backup quarterback, is brought in—to cheers—and throws an interception—to boos. It goes back and forth like this—Bama fumble, Arkansas interception—and at the half, miraculously, Alabama leads, 14-13. Frances and I agree we'll take it.

In the third quarter, the Tide starts off with a confident drive for a touchdown. The defense holds and we get the ball back. We're driving when Shaun Alexander is crossed up and drilled, jarring the ball out of his hands. It hits the turf on its nose, bounces into the air, and is snatched by an Arkansas linebacker who sprints into the end zone: touchdown Hogs. But before the depression can sink in, Zow heaves a forty-three-yard pass. We're cheering again. Two plays later Alexander knifes his way through the Arkansas defense for a touchdown. Frances and I high-five, and Bryant-Denny froths over. We score, on a sixty-six-yard throw from Zow, and nearing the end of the game, Alabama is up 35-28.

With fifty-eight seconds to go, the Hogs have a fourth and fifteen from their own fifteen-yard-line. Stoerner, the Arkansas quarterback, lofts a pass over the middle for fifteen yards and a first down. On the next play, he drops back again—and this time hurls a thirty-yard completion to the Alabama thirty-one. The Hogs scurry upfield to the line. There are six seconds to go. It's happening again, just like last week. One more play. Stoerner has to go for the end zone. I look at DuBose on the sideline. He's clapping awkwardly—he always claps in a pinch—and wears a deep, innocent look of dejection on his face, like a child who has let go a helium balloon. His dream job is floating out of reach . . .

Arkansas snaps the ball, then, something eerie: it's the same play as the week before. Stoerner drops back, his receivers sprint for the near right corner of the end zone, and he throws the ball high. There's a paralyzing sense of déjà vu, then here it comes . . . an arcing spiral into the end zone as the clock hits zero . . . another jump ball. A cluster of red and white jerseys leaps upward like bridesmaids to a bouquet. The ball disappears into a bundle of groping hands and after a moment squirts out at ankle level, falling to the turf. It's incomplete. We've won.

In such moments, a very strange image crosses my mind. I imagine that somewhere deep in my brain there is a little cheerleader, perhaps no bigger than a sea monkey, leaping and kicking ecstatically. How else to explain the percolating, giddy tickle to the psyche that follows a win? With each footfall and herkie, some pleasure-giving cocktail of serotonin, testosterone, adrenaline, and god knows what else is extruded from my brain cells, and goes trickling across my frontal lobes. In fact, it's amazing what doesn't matter after a win. Anxiety is soothed. Life's quotidian concerns become insignificant and utterly manageable. To take a simple example, I have $7,000 locked up in an RV that isn't even roadworthy—and I don't mind at all. My new friend Frances is recently divorced and lovelorn enough to be buying personals on Match.com; does she feel the slightest bit lonely or lovelorn at this particular moment, as her squad jogs off the field, pumping their helmets in the air? Not a chance. Chris Bice has to wake up at dawn tomorrow to drive all the way back to South Carolina to go to work guiding airplanes safely to earth. Does this obligation weigh on him in any way? Of course not. He's heading back to the RV lot to "pitch a bitch"—his term for a parking lot hoedown. Even Mike DuBose is able to put aside the question of his job security long enough for hugs and high fives from his team. He's scampering off the field when a CBS reporter intercepts him. "Coach I have to ask you—Do you feel like this win is important in terms of taking the focus off you and putting it back on your football team?"

"I don't know about all that," DuBose says. "This football team is a good football team. The other stuff—we don't have any control over."

Fatalism is the right attitude, I think. In *Moby Dick,* Ishmael says that the secret to enjoying time on a whale ship is just to assume from the outset that you won't survive the journey. After that, every subsequent experience—every moment of not dying—is gravy. The same might be said of the Alabama coaching job. Last week, DuBose was gone. This week, he came within one play of losing his job. But he's still alive, in a sense, with nothing to lose.

The question of DuBose's job is one every Alabama fan is content to put off, at least for an evening. It's time to hit the bars. I follow Frances to a place called Harry's—a rat hole of a pub covered in rusty, bullet-pocked road signs, with a ten-foot-tall mural of Bear Bryant overlooking the bar. The place is overrun by college kids enjoying the house drink—a bucket of red punch and pure grain alcohol. The bar is a swirling olfactory kaleidoscope of cigarettes, whiskey fumes, and the stale smell of wet, beer-soaked wood. A band rips Pearl Jam covers at an eardrum-searing volume. Everyone, especially Frances, is dancing. There's a lake of vomit in the men's bathroom, which the patrons walk around blithely, as if it were supposed to be there, like a piece of furniture. No one seems to mind. Life in Tuscaloosa has returned to normal.

Chapter Eight

Fighting Gators, Crash Landings, and Fireman Mike

DESPITE THE FACT THAT SPORTS FANS ARE EVERYWHERE—among men and women, in all classes, in nearly every nation and society—very little real research has been done to understand them. Maybe the abundance of fans is precisely what makes them so hard to study, since doing so would require confronting a tangle of contradictions. The studies that have been done are piecemeal—dots of color on a far-from-finished portrait—but even so, they show that many of the basic assumptions about fans are wrong. Take the common assumption that fans are lazy and passive. While the Bices—with their incredible outlay of energy each weekend—provided anecdotal evidence that fans aren't all couch potatoes, research goes much further, suggesting that fans are on average much more likely to be athletic and to play sports themselves than nonfans.

Studies done in Europe consistently show that two-thirds of soccer fans in Denmark and Germany also play soccer and remain athletically active at a higher rate than the nonfans in those countries. In the late seventies, the historian Allen Guttmann writes, surveys taken at Yankee Stadium and Fenway Park found that just under two-thirds of the fans there described themselves as athletically active; more than double the percentage of those in the general population who made the same claim. As Guttmann and others have pointed out, the charge that fans are lazy says perhaps more about the sort of person making the claim than about fans themselves. No one would suggest that to enjoy the ballet one needs to dance, or to enjoy the opera that one needs to be able to sing a high C. Just as a person can enjoy a Renoir without knowing how to paint, it seems reasonable that a fan should be able to appreciate Ray Lewis without knowing how to blitz.

Nevertheless, fans, it's safe to say, don't enjoy a reputation for their intellect. And yet there's even evidence to suggest that fans may actually be smarter on average than nonfans. In 1993, a group of researchers compared the graduation rates and grade point averages of hardcore college basketball fans to students who didn't care about basketball. Lo and behold, they found that 64 percent of the hardcore fans graduated in six years or less, compared with just 48 percent of the nonfans. The average GPA for the hardcore fan was 2.55, compared with 2.46 for the nonfan. Unresolved is whether watching sports makes people smarter, or whether smart people are drawn to sports; but you might want to think twice next time you assume you're someone's intellectual better just because he's wearing face paint and screaming like a maniac.

Another assumption: fans are depressed, unfulfilled people who turn to sports to fill the void in their lives. Again, if the science is to be believed, it's quite the opposite. Nonfans are the depressed and unfulfilled ones. A 1991 study by a Murray State University professor named Daniel Wann showed that hardcore basketball and baseball fans at the University of Kansas had *higher* self-esteem and suffered *lower* rates of depression than nonfans. The research may not refute the notion that some people are driven to fandom by some sort of internal emptiness, but it certainly suggests that in the face of such feelings, becoming a fan might be a fairly reliable antidote. (Consult your doctor before tossing out your anti-depressant meds for season tickets.)

There's also a commonly held belief that large numbers of men imperil their marriages by abandoning their spouses on weekends to watch sports, creating legions of so-called "football widows." Leaving aside the obvious point that plenty of women like sports as well, and that those who don't might not equate three hours of free time on Saturdays or Sundays with being "widowed," scientists say that there's simply no evidence that the phenomenon of the football widow is real. In 1995, a group of sociologists conducted a telephone poll of several hundred people in urban areas and asked them to characterize the effect of spectator sports on their relationships.[†] Ninety-three percent said their partner's interest in watching sports on the tube actually had a *positive* or neutral effect. The study raised the startling possibility that televised sports actually *helped* relationships.

What about aggressiveness? Isn't it obvious that sports fans are more violent than everyone else—more likely to riot or to beat up strangers for no reason? Not even, say scientists. Study after study has failed to show that hardcore fans exhibit any more aggressiveness than the rest of the population.[‡] Individual fans certainly get rowdy from time to time, but research suggests that alcohol is more likely than sports to trigger such behavior. What about all those soccer riots? you might ask. While it's true that fan riots can be horrific, their violence gives a mistaken impression that obscures the real probability of encountering violence at a sporting match, not unlike the way the trauma of plane crashes obscures the statistical reality of flight safety. I've been going to games since I was six, and I've never seen anything beyond a fistfight or the occasional fraternity scrum. A sports fan is simply not any more dangerous than anyone else.

This is useful information to keep in mind as I prepare for my

---

[†] **Gantz, W., Wenner, L. A., Carrico, C., & Knorr, M. (1995). "Assessing the 'Football Widow Hypothesis': A Co-orientation Study of the Role of Televised Sports in Long-standing Relationships."** ***Journal of Sport & Social Sciences,*** **19, 352–376.**

[‡] **A discussion of such research, along with a comprehensive look at the psychological and sociological research on sports spectators, can be found in the excellent book** ***Sport Fans: the Psychological and Social Impact of Spectators,*** **which was edited by four social psychologists, Daniel L. Wann, Merrill J. Melnick, Gordon W. Russell, and Dale G. Paese, and published in 2001 by Routledge.**

trip to Gainesville to watch Alabama play the Florida Gators. After Saturday's Florida-Tennessee game there, two fans had been killed in postgame fights. Both incidents occurred at apartment complexes near the stadium, and in both, police said, alcohol was a factor. In a story about the deaths, the *Gainesville Sun* succinctly noted, "Drunkenness was a Gainesville problem over the weekend, much of it attributed to drinking before, during, and after the football game." Well, when else, right? But it is true that Gainesville is possibly the drinkingest football town in America. Florida is one of only a few schools that allow spectators to leave and reenter the stadium during the game, a policy that results in a halftime exodus of students to a row of bars across from the stadium—notably a dive called the Purple Porpoise—to replenish their waning buzzes. The situation complicates life for the visitors. Fans may not be violent by nature, but drunk people often are, which has a lot to do with why the Bices aren't making the trip. Gainesville is where Chris fears he "might kill somebody." He and Paula have plans to accompany some friends to a Clemson game close to home. They'll watch the Bama game on television.

It goes unsaid, but there's another reason to skip the Florida game: Alabama's dismal chance of winning. The Gators are undefeated. They enjoy a five-year, thirty-game winning streak on their home field, the Swamp and, in fact, in the last decade have lost there only twice. Their average margin of victory at home in that period is twenty-seven points. There is almost no category in which Alabama matches up against the Gators. They pass—we can't stop the pass. Bama runs—the Gators stop the run. Alabama is a seventeen-point underdog. Few people in America give the Tide a chance.

To me, though, this is all the more reason to make the trip. No win is as satisfying as an unexpected win, and on the off chance one is to occur, I plan to be there to experience it. I call Frances on Wednesday to inquire about a ticket; she has an extra. Singles are going for two hundred bucks from scalpers, but Frances wants only face value; I'd brought her good luck against Arkansas. We'll be sitting in the upper corner of the stadium, in the nosebleeds, along with ten thousand of our fellow Bama fans.

In the afternoon I stop by Saab Tire and Automotive to check on my RV. They're making progress, in the sense that taking the top end off an engine and scattering small pieces of it about the interior of the RV constitutes progress. A mechanic named Jason tells me that he's removed a coffee can's worth of goop from the engine, which should result in a significant improvement in gas mileage.

"How much improvement?" I ask.

"What do you get now?"

"Four miles to the gallon."

"Might get four and half," he says.

Not for a while, though. Jason says he needs another week to get the RV running. I'll be driving to Gainesville by car. I console myself with the thought that breaking down and spending large sums on mechanics are as much a part of the authentic RV experience as nights under the stars in stadium parking lots. Before I leave, Jason promises I'll have the RV next week for the drive to Oxford and the Ole Miss game.

* * *

The drive from Birmingham to Gainesville takes about nine hours, most of it over narrow two-lane roads through the red clay flats of south Alabama and the sandy piney woods of northern Florida. I arrive in the late afternoon driving headlong into an after-school traffic jam. My first view of the University of Florida campus is from its perimeter, amid a frozen river of SUVs, pickups, and convertibles and a thumping cacophony of hip-hop beats. The campus looks like a corporate office park—big empty parking lots around a cluster of boxy modern towers of steel and glass that reflect the setting sun in wavy orange ribbons. There's no pretense of longevity here, no attempt to justify the present with the past. Florida football is much the same. The team's pass-happy offense is the shiny new version of the game, an affront to football traditionalists on its face, but even more so because it works so well. Florida makes an interesting contrast to

Alabama. Everything about Alabama evokes nostalgia—the emphasis on tradition, the campus architecture that harkens back to bygone days of southern glory. It's an old school that aspires to look even older. Bama plays old-school football—conservative, bang-it-up-the-gut ball that favors strength over flash. Even the uniforms, simple red and white with the numbers on the helmets, are throwbacks. Florida has a new campus, a new style of play, even cursive on their helmets. If football allegiances were fluid and changed to fit one's ideology, I should pull for the more modern team, the Gators. I'm not nostalgic. I like progress. But allegiances aren't fluid. However accidental or random their beginnings, once they get locked in to the psyche, they take ferocious hold, as if our brains are programmed to pick sides and never look back. Most wars might be attributed to this instinct. In the face of conflict, the reflex isn't to contemplate the competing arguments before choosing sides, but to react first and then construct a rationale around one's allegiance. Whatever sympathies I feel for what Florida represents are trumped by the fact that in my childhood orientation, they are them and we are us.

I check into the University Centre Hotel, a mirthless concrete highrise just off campus. Despite being perfectly dismal and smelling like a freshly opened drum of fruit-scented chemical air freshener, the hotel is charging $185 a night. The game-weekend gouge is on, and every other hotel room in town is booked. On football weekends, the population of Gainesville nearly doubles. There are only five or six home games a year, so there's little economic incentive to build the thousands of hotel rooms needed for those few occasions when the town is overrun. Hotels fill up, prices shoot through the roof. It all amounts to an elaborate argument for owning an RV.

I have an invitation, thanks to Finebaum, to attend the weekly meeting of a Florida booster group called the Fightin' Gator Touchdown Club. Finebaum speaks to the group every couple of years, and he likes them for the simple reasons that they are rowdy and that, unlike most of the booster clubs in Alabama, they don't boo him off the stage. Gainesville is loaded with booster clubs—besides the Fightin' Gator Touchdown Club, there's the Quarterback Club, the Gator City Gators, a women's group called the Goal-liners, and probably a couple of dozen "lunch bunches" and "pub clubs"—groups of eight or ten friends who gather weekly at the same diner, barbecue joint, or bar to talk about their team. The clubs are arranged in a hierarchy, according to size, exclusivity, and how much money they raise for charity or for the university. At one end of the scale is the Quarterback Club—they meet at lunch, in suits, and have country club–like admissions policies—and at the other, those lunch bunches. The Fightin' Gators are squarely in the middle. The club was started by twenty-five men who thought the Quarterback Club hopelessly stiff. Instead of meeting at lunch and sipping Sanka, they decided to meet at night and kick things off with happy hour. They dispensed with exclusivity and opened their new club to anyone willing to pay the annual membership fee. They didn't exclude by race or gender—rare for a booster club. The result of this vision is the largest booster club in town, with over seven hundred members. The Fightin' Gators are meeting at a local convention center, and Kenny Stabler, the former Alabama and Oakland Raider quarterback, is the speaker. My contact, care of Finebaum, is the club's president, a north Florida fertilizer dealer named Marty.

The lobby of the convention center is crammed with burly bodies—nearly all in khakis, dock shoes, and blue or orange golf shirts—and when I walk in I feel briefly like an undersized tailback trying to squeeze through the defensive front of the Florida Gators themselves. I've entered at the bar, and a hundred or so Fightin' Gators are pressed together in a desperate attempt to get a final round before the meeting starts. Ken Stabler—the Snake—is in the middle of the throng, easily singled out by his swoosh of white hair and his houndstooth blazer, a nod to his old coach. He's holding a plastic cup of beer high in the air and trying to scooch his way back from the bar without spilling his drink. A voice shouts that the meeting is starting, and I'm swept along in the horde as it shuffles toward the main hall.

A short, lubberly man in a blue checkered golf shirt, glasses, and a Fightin' Gator Touchdown Club cap walks to the front of the room and calls the meeting to order: it's Marty. As he waits for the crowd to come to order, Marty stands in place, his head cocked back, peering impassively at the rabble through his glasses, like a schoolmaster.

When the Fightin' Gators have found their seats and quieted, he moves to the first order of business, an upcoming road trip to the LSU game in Baton Rouge. The club has chartered buses and plans to stay at a casino for two nights. Anyone interested in going needs to pony up their $480.

"Thank God they moved the game back to 3:30 P.M.," Marty tells the room, "because if it was a night game I'd need the horns of Jericho to get your asses out of bed Sunday morning."

Marty's expression suddenly darkens. In the wake of the deaths after last week's game, the cops are going to be cracking down on public drinking, he says. He encourages the Fightin' Gators to be careful. And something else: the tabloid show *Inside Edition* has sent a crew to Gainesville for a story on hard-drinking Gators fans.

"Stay away from 'em," Marty bullhorns. "They're sneaky. They'll lead you one way and when you see where they're going, they'll turn it around on you. They can make a silk purse out of a sow's ear."

Eventually, Marty introduces the Snake, and the Gators pounce to their feet. There aren't many former Alabama quarterbacks who could command this kind of reception from the Fightin' Gators, but it's the Snake's time with the Oakland Raiders, a team that partied and kicked ass—a neat summation of the Fightin' Gators' ethic—that endears him to this crowd. The Fightin' Gators are more interested in stories about getting drunk and thrown in jail than paeans to Bear Bryant, and Stabler, mindful of his audience, happily obliges. He tells the one about the Raiders linebacker who was so broke he had to sleep in his car, a couple of stories about having guns pointed at him by drunk teammates, and one about showing up to bail a teammate out of jail for a weapons charge, only to find him standing naked in his cell except for a pair of blue cowboy boots and his Super Bowl ring.

"We were the only pro team that traveled with its own bail bondsman," Snake says.

The crowd eats it up; for half an hour, they're sitting on the edge of their seats, slapping knees and laughing in a beer-soaked baritone that vibrates the metal legs of the chair I'm sitting in. Then someone blurts, "Hey, Snake, who's going to win tomorrow?"

The room grows ominously quiet. The Snake gives a nod to the crowd—the Gators are tough, he says, no doubt about that. But he says he sees something in his own team, too—talent, a desire to avenge their coach, a potential on the verge of bursting free. The Tide will pull it out, he says. The Snake is engulfed in boos. He's unmoved though. As he's done so many times before, the Snake stands in the pocket and takes it.

Afterward Marty invites me to join him and a group of Fightin' Gators at the bar of a local Applebee's. Marty has the scarlet skin tones of someone who drinks more than occasionally, but here another fan stereotype is undone: Marty doesn't drink at all. I ask if that's how he got elected president of the Fightin' Gators—as the only member sober enough to run meetings. Marty doesn't laugh. Turns out, I've hit on a sensitive subject—not the drinking, but Marty's election as president. He grew up in Georgia and during a confused period of his youth had been what he calls an "adamant, radical Georgia fan." He changed his ways when he moved to Florida, but when he ran for president of the club, word of his early dalliance with the Bulldogs got out, nearly dooming his chances. I press Marty for details of the election controversy, but he won't go there. "It was an issue," is all he'll say.

I ask Marty about the fights after the Tennessee game. He rolls his eyes dismissively. It was all blown out of proportion, he says. "We got some pockets of obnoxious, asshole people," he says, "But overall we're pretty nice." I ask Marty if he's ever behaved like an obnoxious, asshole person. He furrows his brow thoughtfully.

"There was the time I went around my section at the Auburn game asking all the Auburn fans for their names and writing them down," he says guiltily. "They asked me what I was doing, and I said, 'I'm kicking ass and taking names.' "

"We lost that one," Marty's friend says.

"What did the Auburn fans do?"

"They come back to give him shit," the man says.

Marty shrugs. "Helps to personalize the enemy," he says.

A friend of Marty's wants to set me straight about something.

The measure of a fan, he says, isn't how obnoxious he is, but what he's willing to sacrifice for his team.

"Take the Fightin' Gator Touchdown Club," he says. "We got people who drive seventy miles for a meeting. Jerry Fisher from Tampa—that's a hundred fifty miles away—flies his plane in. Makes 50 percent of the meetings."

"Wow," I say.

"That's nothing," Marty says. "He flew it to Mississippi State, crash-landed in a tree—still made the game."

* * *

On Friday, the Alabama RVs come rolling into Gainesville. The problem, though, is that once they've rolled in, the Alabama fans have no idea where to go. Florida isn't a regular season rival—Alabama and the Gators more often meet in the postseason, in the conference championship in Atlanta—so even long-standing members of the RV corps don't know the Gators' hometown the way they know Knoxville, Oxford, and Auburn—places they visit every other year. By midafternoon, the lost and wandering Alabama RVs are causing such a traffic problem that the local police take to heading them off on motorcycles outside of town and escorting them to the visitors' lot in small groups. The arrangement is perfectly fine with the RV-ers, a good many of whom think they deserve a full-time police escort wherever they go. By lunchtime there are about fifty RVs—a low number, it seems—in a desolate-looking lot off 34th Street, surrounded by busy four-lane streets and guarded by a lone Gainesville policeman. I ask one of the RV-ers where everyone is. Fearing vandalism in town, he tells me, a lot of the RV-ers have decided to stay outside the Gainesville city limits, at a campground in Alachua, half an hour up the interstate.

The Alachua campground is a scenic little bog beneath a canopy of moss-covered pines not far from the highway. A hundred and seventy-five Alabama RVs have overrun the place along with a smattering of deeply confused Canadians—snowbirds who'd never thought to check the American college football schedule before choosing their

RV campground. The woman who runs the campground is a Gators fan but is so thrilled with the onslaught of business that she has donned an Alabama cap and T-shirt and greets each newcomer with a seemingly heartfelt "Roll Tide!"

Inside the lot the usual laid-back Friday afternoon scene of beer drinkers in folding chairs has been displaced by a flurry of activity. On the way from Alabama to Florida, the RV-ers have had to drive through clouds of black insects called "love bugs," which hover over the byways in the Deep South in autumn and which detonate upon impact into quarter-sized splotches the color of mustard. The bug guts supposedly eat through paint, so new arrivals work with the urgency of Indy 500 pit crews to get the goo off their rigs before it leaves a permanent mark. I spot RVs I recognize: Donnie, Skipper, and Bill Prescott are all parked together in the back of the bog. I run into Frances and get my ticket. Jerral Johnson, the Show Chicken Man, is standing over a grill that leaks wisps of smoke. He seems genuinely happy to see me.

"My birds won best variety last week," he says with obvious pride. I ask him if he missed being at the game.

"Naw," says Johnson. "I'z jus' concentratin' on my chickens."

Johnson offers me dinner—potato salad, iced tea, and a succulent filet mignon, which he has slow-cooked in tinfoil—and I pull up a folding chair in front of the television in one of his side compartments to watch the Braves game. The steak's perfect. I ask Johnson how long he cooked it.

"*Ire*," he says.

* * *

Saturday morning the lobby of University Centre Hotel is full of orange- and blue-clad Gators fans. Simply passing through is unsettling: I am a visiting fan, an outsider, and I feel intensely unwelcome, as though I've crashed a wedding of a rival tribe. It's not easy being a visitor in Gainesville. Two reporters for the *Gainesville Sun* gaudily adorn themselves in Alabama gear and spend the day traipsing around town for a story on how locals treat their guests; the experience is so unpleasant and the response so hostile that the reporters abandon the project midway and change back into their civilian clothes. I'm embarking on the inverse of their mission: I want to blend in. I'm not wearing red—superstition, to say nothing of safety, forbids it—so I'm free to wander into the deep reaches of Gatordom without calling attention to myself.

I head to a large commuter lot off North-South Drive, the street that bisects campus and leads to the stadium. The demographic in the Florida lot is subtly different from the one I'm used to. Florida's success on the field has been more recent, and perhaps as a result, their fan base is younger. Probably because young people have less money to spend on RVs than middle-aged professionals, the motor homes are different, too, with more so-called C class models—the kind with a separate cab up front, like a pickup truck, and a boxy living space in the rear, and which cost less than the models that look like buses.

I strike up a conversation with a chatty, sunburned man in a white pith helmet affixed with a solar-powered fan. He introduces himself as Fireman Mike and claims to be a local celebrity, owing to his frequent calls to sports talk radio shows. Fireman Mike is engaged in the impressive task of playing two drinking games at once: quarters, and a game in which contestants challenge each other to match the names and numbers of Florida players, or else to drink. For good measure, Fireman Mike also has a beer in his hand. Despite the threat of a crackdown on public drinking after the deaths last weekend, there are no cops in the inner reaches of the Florida RV lot, and drinking proceeds apace. A folding table beneath the awning of Mike's RV is covered in orange and blue Jell-O shots, half a dozen brands of beer, a saloon's worth of hard alcohol, and a dozen shots of something white and frothy in small plastic pill-cups—a nutmeg-spiced shooter Mike calls "gator come."

Fireman Mike is actually a paramedic. He says he's happy not to be working the game. The humidity and heat will fell any number of people in the Swamp today, and getting them out, he says, is hell on the medics.

"I got a pal who was trying to work a heart attack victim in the stands, and people yelled at him to sit down," he says.

Fireman Mike is friendly and easygoing, enough so that I feel comfortable revealing that I'm actually an Alabama fan. Far from being upset, Mike now seems intrigued. He offers me access to the bar and to a smorgasbord of chips, sandwiches, and pound cakes oozing like lava in the heat. Alabama, he says, is a team he'd always respected. Likewise, I tell him, I have a grudging admiration for Florida as well—as every real football fan must. Well, how could any real football fan not give credit to Alabama for their ten national championships? he asks. True enough, I say, though it's twelve National Championships. Our conversation goes on like this—forced and careful, but oddly intense. We seem to connect not despite our differing allegiances but because of them. There's an intimacy between enemies. When I mention that I might wander into the Florida student section to watch some of the game, Fireman Mike offers to let me borrow a Gators cap, "so you don't get killed," he says.

Then: sirens. The Alabama team buses are approaching. Everyone in the lot, including Mike and his gang, drop what they're doing and sprint like bandits from a bank toward North-South Drive. I follow along, quickly losing Mike in the rush. As the sirens grow louder, perhaps two thousand Gator fans line the curb. A motorcycle cop speeds past, shouting, "Get out of the way, you assholes!" to everyone in his path. As the buses approach, the Florida fans begin to clap, extending their arms horizontally to mimic the snapping jaws of a bull gator. The buses slow through the encroaching crowd, which seems almost Nurembergian: long, regimented lines of people clapping as though hypnotized. It's an intimidating sight, and also deeply annoying. The Gators fans are being rude to my team. The buses pass in front of me as hundreds of faces, purple from exertion, blare insults at full volume. I look to my left: Fireman Mike, screaming as loudly as anyone. Our eyes meet. The buses slip past, and the mob lining the curb breaks into an exhilarated and self-congratulatory round of applause before dispersing. I can't go back to Mike's RV. A schism has opened between us that we don't have the history to overcome.

The crackdown on public drinking takes effect as I approach the stadium, though by normal law enforcement standards it isn't much of a crackdown. The operation consists mostly of cops telling fans either to pour out or to finish their drinks before entering. The result is a series of police-supervised chugging contests up North-South Drive, leading to the main entrance of the stadium. Once inside, I ascend to my seat and find Frances, who is not happy. She'd sold her extra ticket to me at face value so she didn't risk sitting next to a Gators fan, and yet directly behind us is a deranged-looking college student wearing blue face paint, a Florida hat and T-shirt, and holding an orange and blue shaker. He's shouting as I take my seat:

> *Cmongatorswegonebeatdesedumbrednecksgator-baitgatorbaitgatorBAIT!*

Despite the soggy Florida heat, the cluster of Alabama fans in the end zone huddle together. There are about four thousand of us in this corner—the biggest concentration of red in the stadium—and with blue all around us, there's a need to compress and close ranks. The sun blazes, the turf glows green, and the helmets of both teams reflect the sun like gemstones. The teams come out to a blast of brass and the pop and sizzle of the toms and snares. Then, that Nurembergian clapping routine again—*Clap . . . . . . clap . . . . . . clap . . . . . . clap . . . clap . . . clap . . . clapclapclapclap*—and kickoff.

In the early minutes, the Gators javelin-toss the ball down the field, but their first drive ends with a fumble, and Alabama recovers. We eke our way downfield, close enough for a field goal, and go up 3-0. The Bama fans in the corner are still celebrating when on Florida's next play, the Gators quarterback flings a long parabola into the center of the field and into the hands of a receiver whose legs are churning like a whirligig in a stiff breeze. An Alabama defender dives for the ball and misses, and there's no one else between the Florida player and the goal line. Amid the thunderous release in the Swamp, a single voice cuts through—that of the Gators fan behind us, who in the process of celebrating the score also manages a fusillade of insults, at machine-gun pace: Alabama fans are dumb rednecks, assholes, cheaters, scumbags, morons—redneck moron cheater asshole scumbags—as well as every conceivable derisive term for homosexuals. Frances and I trade forlorn looks. He is the one Florida fan in a corner of the stadium jammed with Alabama supporters, and it's as though his isolation has awakened a primal defiance in him. I'm beginning to understand why the Bices aren't here.

There's hope though. Andrew Zow, the Alabama quarterback, is on. His passes are taut and linear, his delivery deceptive—the ball seems to accelerate toward his receiver's hands, as though sucked toward a vacuum. Zow is young, a sophomore, but in the pocket, he has a calm that belies his age. Bodies are airborne all around him, like gymnasts on trampolines, and yet Zow stands impassively firing strike after strike, as if he were casually throwing darts in a booth at the local fair. He leads Alabama to the Florida one, with a first down. Three times we slam the ball up the middle, and three times we are stopped. On fourth and goal, Zow hands off to Alexander, who knifes through a hole on the left side: touchdown.

Before the half, we manage another field goal and when the teams leave for the locker room, we're ahead 13-7—hardly a safe margin against a team like Florida, but then the score doesn't tell the full story. Alabama has held the ball over twenty-one minutes to the Gators' eight and a half. We've run forty-one plays to their seventeen. The Florida defense was on the field in the unforgiving Florida sun nearly three times longer than Alabama's. If we keep it up, there's a chance we could wear them down.

At the half, there's a scramble to get out of the sun and beneath the bleachers. I run into Donnie, trying to buy a bottle of water but stuck toward the back of a line he describes as "longer than a line in a whore's dream." I skip the water and try to get out of the stadium to see what's happening across University Avenue at the Purple Porpoise. A throng of students pours out of the stadium with me, many of them doused in sweat and with the desperate look of junkies in the throes of inadvertent detox. The ritual of reupping one's buzz at the Purple Porpoise, though, takes on a less menacing aura when I find the bar too packed to enter. I'm stuck outside with a mob of testy students, frustrated over their inability to get a drink. There's a commotion inside, and shouting—it's impossible to see it for all the bodies, but word leaks out that a couple of women are engaged in a fist fight, brought on when one of the women whacked the other in the face with a plastic beer pitcher. The police are called. (A police spokesman later attributes the fight to the fact that the women had been "drinking all day.") No sooner is the fight quelled than is it time to head back to the stadium for the second half. The crowd outside the Porpoise quickly divides into three distinct groups: those hurrying to the stadium for the kickoff of the second half, those staying behind to drink at the bar, and those paralyzed with indecision over which of their two addictions will win out, alcohol or football.

In the second half, the game seesaws; Zow throws an interception, which the Gators return for a touchdown. But then two minutes later Zow floats a delicate ball over the shoulder of a wide-open Alexander, who goes forty-seven yards for a score. Florida answers, on a slashing nine-yard slant pattern, and then Zow fires a series of laser-guided passes downfield before making a scalding throw to a leaping receiver in the back of the end zone: Alabama leads, 26-22. The Gators score a field goal, and then with six minutes to go they score again on a long pass over the middle. Alabama trails by a touchdown, 33-26. The game comes down to a final fourth and two, deep in Florida territory. An apocalyptic roar rises from the Swamp, led by Blue Face behind me, who's yammering in a kind of shamanic drone *cmongatorscmond-cmongatorscmond!* Zow hands off to Alexander, who rips through the line and gallops toward the end zone, a single blue jersey in his way. There's a collision, and the blue jersey slides off Alexander like a droplet of water down a speeding fuselage. Touchdown Alabama. In the exothermic burst of joy that follows, I feel myself lost in a tangle of arms and bodies, a throbbing mosh pit of celebration. . . . The game is tied. We're heading for overtime.

Overtime in college football is exquisitely fair and simple. The teams get an equal number of possessions from their opponent's twenty-five-yard line and play until one team comes out ahead. If the first team scores a touchdown and an extra point, the other team will have to answer with the same. If the first team manages only a field goal, a touchdown by the other wins. And so on. The advantage lies with the team that plays defense first—they know how many points they need to survive. Alabama wins the coin toss, and chooses to let Florida play offense.

A solemn silence falls over the stadium. The notion of finality is intimidatingly awesome, and when the Florida offense and Alabama defense jog onto the field, they're met not with a roar but with a gentle cascade of applause, as at a golf match.

And then the first snap: a run up the middle for a yard. The Gators chip their way toward the goal—a quick throw to a wide out for four, another short pass—all the way to the Alabama five. Johnson takes the snap from the shotgun, takes a half-dozen short, jittery steps to his left, and throws toward the left corner of the end zone. A sprinting receiver leaps and makes the grab, and again the stadium shakes. The Gators are up 39-33.

The field goal kicker jogs lazily onto the field and takes his spot seven yards behind the center. This is the easy part—the Florida kicker has missed a single extra point all year. He waits head down. The center rifles the ball to the holder. The ball leaves the kicker's foot at an angle, toward the right. It's still rising when it flies past the outside of the post: no good. We jump to our feet. We can win the game on a single possession.

The missed extra point heightens the burden on the Florida fans, and they respond. When the Tide jogs onto the field, it sounds as though the Gates of Hell have blown open. Seventy-five thousand human beings scream so forcefully that it seems possible their mouths might open back over their heads and swallow them in reverse. Alabama, in their grass-stained whites, breaks the huddle, and the crowd noise escalates to a searing pitch. Zow bobs his head as he calls the signals, with Alexander behind him, hands on knees. He takes the snap, hands off to Alexander, who cuts through the left side of the line untouched, then slashes left where a Tide blocker is driving a Florida player backward like a tank with an oil drum stuck beneath its treads. Alexander rolls around the blocker into the open, accelerates, and gambols into the end zone. Touchdown.

To win, all we need now is the extra point. Our starting kicker is injured, so the backup comes onto the field and takes his position behind the center, head down, arms dangling pendulously at his side. The holder calls the signals. Two Florida defenders on the left side of the line jump. The ball is snapped, set, contact. Wide right. He missed it.

The Gates of Hell are again blown open, but quickly slam shut, as one by one the Florida fans make out a small yellow rag on the turf, signifying a penalty. The referee has flagged Florida for jumping before the snap, and Alabama will get another try. The kicker jogs back onto the field. The ball is snapped and set, up it goes, carving left just inside the upright. The cheerleader in my brain begins bouncing madly across my frontal lobes and tumbling through my consciousness. She's shouting, "We won! We won!"

Winning always feels good, but winning away has the additional quality of feeling illicit. With so many people opposing you, it feels as though you've gotten away with something. I feel less like a fan and more like a looter. The mob coalesces into an intimate pack—only victors can connect so deeply. Losers are consigned to the dolor of their cocoons. I turn around to look at Blue Face. He seems to be crying, though it's hard to tell for his face paint. For a brief moment, I feel the stick of pity. Misery up close is an ugly thing. When Blue Face sees me looking at him, his eyes narrow into a gaze of utter hatefulness. Pity fades, and I sing:

Hey Gators!
Hey Gators!
We just beat the hellouttayou!
Rammer Jammer Yellowhammer!
Give 'em hell Alabama!

We're still singing as we parade down the ramp out of the stadium, further energized by the compactness forced upon us by the narrow passageways beneath the bleachers. We're shuffling along, our arms pumping, singing our song, when we emerge from beneath a concrete beam to find ourselves facing an oncoming ramp from the Florida section: a column of blue-clad misery gazing at us with malevolence. They're close—no longer an anonymous blue thing out there in the distance, but rather individuals. The enemy has been personalized. On that stretch of the ramp where the two sides converge, no Alabama fans sing. There's a steady patch of quiet at the bottom of the ramp, a glassy sluice in a stream of emotional whitewater. The two ramps turn away from each other, and the crowd separates, blue one way, red another. When we make the corner and can no longer see our rivals eye to eye, we pick up the tune again in midverse . . . *Jammer Yellow hammer . . . Give 'em hell Alabama!*

* * *

After the game, I drive Frances back to the Alachua campground, where we find the RV-ers strewn slumberously about in hammocks and folding chairs. One man dozes on a picnic table. Crowd noise is displaced by the relentless ratchet of crickets. The sun, the suspense, and the intense release of the win have left us depleted. The camaraderie forged inside the stadium has solidified into something calmer and deeper. A group of RV-ers at the back of the lot have taken on the task of feeding the whole campground; they invite me and everyone else over for dinner, so we gather around a grill and picnic table jammed with Tupperware and casseroles and gorge ourselves.

There's a final pleasure: watching ESPN's *GameDay*, the highlight show. The highlights themselves are secondary—we'd seen the game, after all—but there's something validating and deeply satisfying about having an objective entity like ESPN single us out and recount our triumph. We gather around a television in the underneath compartment of our hosts' RV. The Alabama logo appears on the screen, and everyone falls silent as one of the hosts nearly injures himself diving to turn up the volume. What would they show—Zow's long pass to

Alexander? Alexander's overtime gallop? The missed extra points? But what's this? A close-up shot of Shamari Buchanan, the Alabama receiver, a black senior with a graceful physique and chiseled good looks? He didn't even play.

In fact the ESPN story isn't about the game at all. It's about a scandal that has broken at home while we have been away. A story in today's *Birmingham News* has uncovered a scheme in which a Crimson Tide–friendly Alabama state trooper has been "fixing" Alabama players' speeding tickets—in other words, making them disappear. Buchanan, the story says, was a beneficiary. This sort of thing is illegal, of course, but worse to Alabama fans, the ESPN commentator points out that Buchanan could get kicked off the team and games might have to be forfeited.

"It's the stupid niggers," a woman snarls.

What?

"Stupid niggers are always getting us into trouble."

Silence, then:

"She's got a point," a man at her side says. "Them niggers always doin' sumpin' stupid."

Needless to say, it feels as though someone has yanked the emergency brake of life. It's not a surprise to me, unfortunately, to learn that a few vicious racists exist among the thousands of Alabama football fans, or fans of any team for that matter, but the brazen expression of such hatefulness is as jarring as it is depressing. I find it bizarre on many levels. First is the strange contradiction that two people brought an afternoon of joy by a black quarterback and a black running back running behind a black star lineman could flip so quickly and absolutely on the entire race. Second is the question of how the couple seized on Buchanan's race as an explanation for his having done something wrong, if in fact he has; there is a long list of much better explanations—he is basically a kid; he's a football player in a state where football players are treated as demigods and could easily succumb to an inordinate sense of entitlement. (These contradictions are further exposed when we learn days later that the ticket erasures are the handiwork of a white assistant coach, working with a white state trooper who, it turns out, has been working the trick for years, a perk of that whitest of social phenomena, the Ol' Boy network. Shamari Buchanan had been a dupe.)

Finally, the episode is so unnerving because *I thought we were on the same team.* A couple of hours back, I might well have been hugging and high-fiving these two in the stadium. After the game, they'd kindly taken me in and turned me loose on their buffet table and given me free run of their Igloo cooler and their pecan pie, on the assumption that I was one of them. And, then, just as quickly as our bond formed, it falls apart. And not just that: I despise them. They're the enemy.

The incident in the campground gets me thinking about the connections between fans in the first place: they're as fleeting as they are intense. The Marxist critique of spectator sports holds that sports are a means the wealthy use to mask class divisions and to distract the disenfranchised from the realities of their lot. You don't have to subscribe to this theory completely to see that sports can serve as a temporary salve for deeper divisions—political, economic, social, perhaps even religious—but that's less a function of sports per se than a peril of neatly dividing the world in terms of "us and them." The problem with such a Manichean view is that the dividing lines are always changing. Someone shouts "Roll Tide": I think, "Us." He breaks into a line in front of me: he's "Them." Someone nearly runs me off the road: Them. I see an Alabama bumper sticker on his car as he passes: Us. A man wears a red shirt and cheers with me when Alabama beats Florida in the Swamp: Us. Then turns out to be a virulent racist: Them. Why had the couple felt free to voice such hateful opinions to a perfect stranger? Because I was a white. (*Us,* They must've thought.) But I don't share their views on race: Them indeed.

I leave the campground immediately, feeling more let down by my fellow fans than I'd felt uplifted by my team. I'm gliding atop the long, flat tarmac of I–75 heading back toward Gainesville when my cell phone rings: the Bices. Chris and Paula have been trying to get through for hours, they say. They're desperate for details: Was it loud? What did the Florida fans do afterward? What were the expressions on their faces? I recount as much as I can. The Bices had drove the Hurricane to the Clemson game with friends, as planned, but when kickoff came around, they couldn't pry themselves from the TV broadcast of the Alabama game. They spent the afternoon cuddled together in the RV (with Larry, of course) watching the game and regretting their decision to stay away. I mention to Chris what happened at the campground, hoping that he'll share my outrage, but he's able to muster only resignation. He's spent enough time at football games that he can't be surprised when a few obnoxious, asshole people, as Marty would've put it, embarrass themselves in front of the bunch. His response is interesting: he gets defensive—not about the couple's comments, but rather about the idea that they're representative of Alabama fans. He's not a racist, he says, and he doesn't want to be painted with a broad brush or for Alabama to look bad. He's worried about how "we" will look; I'm still struggling to understand who exactly "we" are.

I hang up and turn on the radio, scan the dials, and land on a local sports talk radio show where Florida fans are expressing their collective grief. With slurred speech and the kind of belligerence you hear only in a drunk's voice, one caller notes grimly what for him is the worst part of the loss: that Florida has been outcoached by Mike DuBose. As he slogs on in a lugubrious diatribe, my mood is salvaged by a satisfying thought: perhaps it's Blue Face on the line, or Fireman Mike.

Chapter Nine

Hawgs and Lost Causes

THERE'S PERHAPS ONLY ONE PLEASURE FOR ALABAMA football fans that approaches the ecstasy of a Crimson Tide win, and that's picking up a copy of Paul Finebaum's column after he has mistakenly predicted the Tide would lose. No one is more acutely aware of this fact than Finebaum himself. Eating crow is good for newsstand sales and ratings for his radio show—what Alabama fan doesn't want to tune in to hear a chastened Paul Finebaum?—and the act carries the additional benefit of placating the ire of any number of people who might otherwise be inclined to sneak up on Finebaum in public and whack at his kneecaps with a tire iron. Finebaum has a talent for turning contrition into theater. After blowing a call against Auburn, he once rode a tractor into downtown Auburn as penance. After another errant call, he'd had to milk a cow at a county fair. Milking a cow might not sound like the height of daring, but given the self-consciously nerdy persona he cultivates, the image of a suited Paul Finebaum tugging at a swollen udder, his bald head peeking out from beneath a heifer's loins, was at least as jarring as the sight of him in drag. The local press showed up for these gags—which Finebaum publicized zealously on his own show—and all the good-natured coverage was enough to give the impression that Finebaum's running critique of local sports teams was just a friendly joke that everyone was in on. The hardcores didn't buy it though. Going along with Finebaum is out of the question for them. But there was always the chance that if Finebaum managed not just to eat crow, but to gorge himself on it, and publicly, he might at least claw his way back to even in the public consciousness. From where Finebaum spends most of his time, even looks pretty good.

So in his *Post-Herald* column, Finebaum gets to work, calling the Florida game "*Field of Dreams*, *Rocky*, and *Rudy* wrapped into one."

"You really have to hand it to Alabama's embattled coach," he writes. "Somehow, some way, against the most incredible odds and suffocating pressure I have ever seen a coach face, DuBose has led Alabama back from oblivion. . . . It would be easy to snicker (and some people already have) at the fact that in his postgame comments, he gave credit to God. . . . However, until someone comes up with a better explanation of what happened—I'll defer to DuBose."

Finebaum isn't about to let the Alabama football program off the hook, though. In his view, every silver lining has its cloud, and in this case the cloud has blown from over Mike DuBose's head to cast a darkening shadow over Andrew Sorensen, the school president. At the beginning of the season, Sorensen found himself in a near-hopeless pinch. If he had fired DuBose for the secretary scandal—the week before the start of a season of promise—he would've had to shoulder the blame for any catastrophes on the field, which in turn could've imperiled his job. But if he kept DuBose, Sorensen stood the chance of being accused of sacrificing the moral and academic standing of a university for a few gridiron wins. So he'd tried to finesse it, by keeping DuBose but docking his pay and forcing him to apologize in public. That took the heat off Sorensen for a bad season—that would be DuBose's problem—but the ploy didn't shield Sorensen from the charge—levied most prominently in the *Atlanta-Constitution*, but by plenty of other sports columnists, including, of course, Finebaum—that he'd opted for the politically expedient solution rather than the morally sound one. The loss at home to Tech, though, provided the hint of a solution. A couple more disasters like that and Sorensen could fire DuBose midseason, claiming that the football program wasn't going in the right direction, or some such ambiguous phrase that obliquely suggested that the thing with the secretary had as much to do with the dismissal as had the team's record. That would satisfy all camps—the hardcore football fans who wanted DuBose gone for losing, and the moralists in the press who wanted DuBose fired for lying. And Sorensen would have plenty of time to locate a new coach for next season.

The win over Florida, though, screws up the whole plan, such as it is, and in the process inspires a lot of sports columnists to once again wonder in print what DuBose is still doing as head coach in the first place. More wins will only provoke more coverage of Alabama in the national press, which in turn will only increase the scrutiny of Sorensen and his decision to keep a coach who had lied to him and to the public. Among Alabamians, only Finebaum possesses the peculiar mental equipment that allows a person to see how a winning football team might have a downside for a University of Alabama administrator, and he's the first to point out Sorensen's dilemma. "Until now, this story primarily has been a local and regional story," he writes in his post-Florida column. "The national media has paid scant attention. Now that has changed. Should Alabama continue to win—and DuBose somehow manage to keep his job—the 'football factory' label will be cemented on the side of Denny Chimes. Sorensen will be stamped as the academician who sold out principles for bowl trips."

"At the rate Alabama coach Mike DuBose is going," Finebaum concludes, "he'll be firing University of Alabama president Andrew Sorensen shortly instead of the other way around."

Sorensen himself must wonder. Just three weeks after the Tech game, his office is again inundated by calls, e-mails, and letters from people demanding not only that he not fire DuBose but that he extend the man's contract. "After the Tech game I heard from three thousand people who wanted him fired, and after the Florida game I heard from three thousand people who wanted me to give him a contract extension," a befuddled Sorensen tells me in his office one afternoon. "What still puzzles me—they were the same three thousand people."

* * *

On Monday a triumphant DuBose is due to speak to the Monday Morning Quarterback Club in Birmingham, so I wangle an invitation to see how he plays. The Monday Morning Quarterbackers in Birmingham are at the opposite end of the booster club spectrum from the Fightin' Gators in Gainesville. They're bankers, lawyers, and stockbrokers, Chamber of Commerce types in navy blue Brooks Brothers suits who, for all their boosterism, wouldn't be caught dead in any piece of apparel with a team logo on it. The Fightin' Gators whoop and holler and shout; the Quarterbackers stand quietly in a buffet line, their conversation clipped and manly and mostly about golf. They're hardened football fans who seem to go to great lengths to appear as though they haven't the slightest interest in the game. The difference between the two types of clubs is more than just one of style. The Fightin' Gators managed a $25,000 donation to the University of Florida the previous year; the Birmingham Quarterback Club donated $860,000 to its chosen charities. Some of the Quarterbackers are actually trustees of the University of Alabama—the kind who hobnob at the President's Mansion before kickoff, sit in the President's Box during the game, and vote on whether or not to, say, fire the head coach during the week. It's a crowd any head coach would want on his side. Where the Fightin' Gators feel lucky if the head coach speaks to them every third year, the Quarterback Club grants an audience to the head coaches of both Auburn and Alabama every year without fail. As someone who grew up in Opp and spent his entire professional career on the sideline of a football field, Mike DuBose has nothing in common with this crowd, but he'd be well served to get them on his side. The timing is certainly good. After the big win, DuBose has earned a reevaluation of sorts. He doesn't have to give the Gettysburg Address, but if he can connect with the Quarterbackers, flash a human side, show a little charisma and maybe a dash of humility, he might go a long way toward winning back the support of the elites who more or less run the Alabama football program.

News crews have staked out the Harbert Center, the gray granite box where Birmingham's elite civic groups meet, and when DuBose arrives, little halogen quasars atop the television cameras fire to life. As he approaches the front door, DuBose is bathed in white light, like an arriving movie star. Stunned slightly, he jerks upright, straightening his spine and adjusting into a conqueror's pose. He doesn't lope dodderingly as is his custom; he fairly strides. There's a commotion in the lobby—an Auburn women's club is meeting downstairs, and several of the dames step back, smile, and nod at DuBose respectfully; they know as well as anyone what it means that their rival has beaten Florida in the Swamp. The news crews catch up with DuBose upstairs, where the Quarterbackers lunch, and he gives a few interviews, exuding a confidence I haven't seen all season. While DuBose works the press, his hosts form a line at a large wooden cabinet to pick up nametags the size of hubcaps. An officer opens the meeting with an invocation ("Oh Lord, we gather here to celebrate football . . ."), and a few minutes later the emcee stands to introduce DuBose.

"Coach, I'll tell you what I like about you," he tells the room. "You treat your players like men: you let 'em wear earrings." DuBose gets a standing ovation, and with the audience in the palm of his hand, he quickly sets about alienating them. His speech is a halfhearted recitation of his favorite football clichés: "I like 'is football team. It's a good football team"; "It's a tremendous challenge and tremendous opportunity"; and his favorite verse from Ecclesiastes, about what he calls the "team concept"—"Two are better than one because they have a good reward for their labor. For if they fall the one will lift up his fellow but woe to him that is alone when he falleth for he hath not another to help him up." The word of the Lord delivered with the rhythmic staccato of a rap lyric. If DuBose stopped here, the speech would merely be odd and a bit deflating. Instead, he decides to improvise a line. While he's sure his players believe in the "team concept," DuBose says, he's afraid that "others in the Alabama community may not."

The Birmingham Monday Morning Quarterback Club is not the

sort of crowd that takes well to being lectured to by anyone, but especially not by a man who had thumbed his nose at the dignity of their beloved university, to say nothing of the team concept, by giving his secretary the business in the sanctum sanctorum of the football building. In the empty silence that follows, a fork clangs on a plate and all that Brooks Brothers wool rustles like an oak tree in a breeze. Watching DuBose stumble at the lectern—misjudging his audience and the thickness of the cushion the Florida win has given him—is painful. He's clearly in over his head. For the football coaches of most other teams it would be enough to win, but at Alabama, where the soul of every coach is weighed against the awesome legacy of Bear Bryant, DuBose has to charm, inspire, dominate, and comfort the anxious souls of a state. He's not capable of it, and judging from how uncomfortable he seems in a sport jacket and tie at a lectern, it seems he knows this about himself. If he's going to keep his job as Alabama's head coach, he'll have to be something close to perfect on the field. It's a tall order. Even Bear Bryant wasn't perfect.

* * *

Two days later, a miracle: Jack from Saab Tire calls. My RV is ready. The news, though, brings a new anxiety: now I have to drive it. There's still a kink to work out: the sewage holding tank has a slow leak; a new tank is on order but could take weeks to arrive. Jack says if the leak bothers me or my fellow RV-ers, I could always try to patch it temporarily with some waterproof epoxy. In the name of neighborly relations I decide to go ahead and apply the patch, and spend an hour on my back beneath the vehicle smearing a substance with the consistency of cookie dough along the bottom of the tank. The crack isn't easily visible, so I don't know if I've managed to seal it off completely, but I've done all I can. I take the RV for a test drive—more a test of my driving ability than of the RV—and to fill it up with gas. The attendant at a local filling station watches me curiously as I rack up a seventy-dollar tab at one of his pumps.

"What kind of mileage you get?" he asks eventually.

"Four, four and a half," I say.

"Dang," the attendant says. "She's a *hawg.*"

And like that, my RV has a name.

In August the University of Mississippi sent a sternly worded letter to its visiting opponents saying that because of construction on campus, motor homes will be banned from university grounds until noon on Fridays. University of Alabama officials pass out copies of the letter to the RV crowd, who upon receiving it, decide to show up on Wednesday. By the time I get an Ole Miss public relations officer named Mike on the phone midweek, the RV-ers are already arriving.

"You're going to be inundated," I tell him.

"More than you know," he says.

"Where are you going to put them?" I ask, meaning "us."

"We've got a pretty good-sized clay lot off campus—call it the Mud Hole," Mike says. "I've been telling them to park down there."

So Thursday afternoon I strike out for Oxford and the Mud Hole. The roads from Birmingham to Oxford are exactly the kind a neophyte RV driver would hope to avoid—no interstate, just narrow state highways, some of them two-laners with crumbly shoulders that encourage oncoming vehicles to play chicken for the good pavement in the middle. I pick up Highway 78 out of Birmingham near a cluster of rusted-out steel mills on the west side of town, and head toward Jasper, through some dreary scenery—mobile homes, strip malls, satellite dishes, junkyards, and, every few miles, a souvenir stand or convenience store that sells Confederate battle flags. The road between Jasper and Tupelo treads over a series of long, parallel ridges, the rippling aftereffect of the Smoky Mountains; the Hawg slows pitifully on the inclines and caroms frightfully down the slopes. I pass signs for Red Bay, Alabama, where Allegro motor homes are built, and feel a strange connection to the place; twenty-one years ago the Hawg rolled off an assembly line here. In retrospect I might have paid a visit to the service department, because a few miles down the road, a thrashing sound begins in the ceiling of the RV, then slowly moves down the left side all the way to the back. I pull onto the shoulder to have a look; a piece of thick brown rubber molding has blown loose from the top edge of the RV and dangles down the side of the Hawg in a large U, like a necklace. Parked on the roadside, it merely looks ridiculous, but at seventy miles per hour, it threatens to bang holes in the aluminum siding and to bash in the portside windows. It has to be dealt with, so I flip on the hazards and drive slowly down the highway toward the imperial glow of a Wal-Mart. Inside, I invest three dollars in the miracle of modern engineering that is a roll of duct tape. I then climb the aluminum ladder at the back of the rig to the rooftop and set to taping my RV back together.

When I get back on the road, the sun is setting and a fingernail of a moon has appeared behind the darkening scrim of loblolly pines on the horizon. I pull the clumsy rubber knob that turns on the headlights, as other Alabama RVs blow past, honking their horns in recognition of my Crimson Tide wheel cover. I honk and wave back, though the horn on my Allegro produces an only barely audible hum at the frequency of a didgeridoo. Oncoming cars flash their lights, a kind of welcome, it seems, from locals who must be enthralled at the sight of the oncoming flotilla. Concurrent with this outpouring of enthusiasm—more flashing lights, frantic waving, blaring horns—is the growing impression that night in Mississippi is a shade or two darker than night everywhere else. There are no streetlamps along the highway or reflective strips on the pavement, and the countryside is concealed in inky shadows. The headlights of oncoming cars burn through the darkness like oil wells flickering in the night—flash, flash, flash—and the horns from passing cars and RVs punctuate the steely silence with increasing urgency. Only when I pull off the road for gas do I realize the reason for all the commotion: my headlights don't work.

I spend the next hour at a seedy truck stop taking apart and putting back together the headlamp button-switch in the floorboard, which gets the lights working on the bright setting only. Back on the road, oncoming drivers still flash their lights, only now because I'm blinding them. I forge on, and in just over an hour make the Oxford city limit.

The Mud Hole, unfortunately, is on no local map and there are no signs for it. I pull into a convenience store parking lot to ask for directions, and just as I do, a line of four Alabama RVs races by me in tight formation, like the cars of a model train. On the assumption that they know more than I do, I hit the gas and latch on as the caboose. Oxford is organized around a central square with an old courthouse at the center and a perimeter of balconied two-story buildings from the late 1800's—old seed and tack stores now turned into restaurants and bars, boutiques, and the great bookstore Square Books. The square is the central meeting place in the daytime for the remaining of the squinty-eyed, leather-complected "square squatters" who populate Faulkner's novels, and at night, from cocktail hour until the bars close, for the homogeneous clump of SEC kids—boys in white oxfords and khakis, girls in gauzy sliplike sundresses in flowery prints in maroon and fuchsia. The square focuses everyone's attention inward, almost like a stadium, so that it's impossible to walk its perimeter and not feel that you're on display. This is never more the case than when you show up at cocktail hour at the rear of five gaudily turned-out RVs covered with the logos of the visiting team. Around we go, choking the square with exhaust and the loud rattle of diesel engines, while a few hundred intoxicated students laugh and point at us as though we're a comedy act—a parade of clowns on funny bicycles. The situation underscores a simple fact of motor-homing: try as one might, it's impossible to look cool in an RV.

Eventually we make our way out of the square toward camp, onto Coliseum Drive, down a gentle slope to the left, and to a large, freshly graded dirt lot: the Mud Hole. Save a lonely spiral of tire tracks—entering, then exiting—the Mud Hole is empty. This is a head scratcher; the fleet has disappeared. The four of us throw our RVs in park and get out to plot our next move. Just as we've resolved to give up our search and set up camp where we are, a red Saturn with a tow bar on the front bumper appears on the hill above us, lights flashing and horn blowing: friendlies. A rubber-faced man named Dan, a member of Donnie's pack, has been sent to rescue us. He waves for us to follow, so we do, down a narrow campus drive past the Ole Miss soccer field. There they are, a sparkling city of motor homes, flags flying resolutely overhead, tightly configured like the well-defended outpost of an outnumbered occupying army. Our fellow fans stand to greet us, beer cans in the air, and several wobbly figures direct us into place. A full day at the wheel has paid off; I back into my parking spot with the skill of a veteran. Seven and a half hours after leaving on a four-hour trip, I've arrived.

Arriving feels good. I'm not only at my destination, but with my people, and I can't remember a time in my life when I've been so enthusiastically welcomed by so many. Or so it seems. I open the door of my RV to find Skipper slumped in a folding chair, a drink in hand, his legs spread indecorously. He looks up at me and his face darkens.

"Not *you*," he says.

Well, buying a Harley doesn't make you a member of the Hells Angels, just as showing up in an Allegro motor home doesn't qualify you as a made guy in the Bama RV entourage, at least not among the hardcores like Skipper—and who else shows up on a Thursday for a Saturday but the hardest of the hardcores? I might've overreached, or assumed too much by showing up on a Thursday instead of Friday, when the bulk of the motor homes arrive. But I'm here, so I resolve to make the best of it. Step one is to level the Hawg on some plastic shims I picked up at Wal-Mart; I put the shims in place, put the Hawg in gear and ease onto them with surprising aplomb. I draw the curtains, and drift to sleep to the muffled sounds of laughter and voices, and the trill of crickets.

* * *

At noon on Friday the main lot near the stadium opens to RVs, so we wake up early to get in line for the bum rush for weekend spots. The first step is breaking down camp; not long after dawn and with coffee mugs still in hand, the RV-ers set about repacking their outdoor living rooms and lowering their rigs from their jacks onto solid ground. With all the shouting and the bustle, the move has the energy of a cattle drive. I roll the Hawg forward off its shims, gather them up, and toss them inside, and soon I'm part of the caravan snaking through campus and toward the main lot in front of the Tad Smith Coliseum. Once in line, engines are quelled, coffee pots are once again engaged, and everyone gets out of their rigs to socialize and walk the line to view each other's rides. By 11:00 A.M., the line stretches a mile. The campus cops give us access to the parking lot, and I manage to claim two spots for myself, one for me and one for the Bices, who are arriving from South Carolina shortly. Our spots are just behind an RV with an incredible collection of Alabama pennants and flags flying wispily on a pole connected to its rear bumper. When the Bices make it inside, I pull up toward the flag man to make room for them right behind me. We're just across the street from a fraternity house, Pi Kappa Alpha—the Pikes—and as we set up our outdoor living rooms, the brothers watch us quietly from the shade beneath the columned porch of their mansion. It's clear from the smirks on their faces that they plan a night of mischief.

Game day in Oxford centers around the Grove, Ole Miss's holy place, an oval-shaped ten-acre lawn beneath a canopy of regal oaks on the oldest part of campus, a ten-minute walk from the stadium. It sits at the doorstep of the Lyceum, a stately administration building with six three-story ionic columns supporting a frieze, the center piece of which is a clock with Roman numerals. In the early 1980s, Ole Miss's head coach at the time, Billy Brewer, began taking his team through the Grove on its way to the stadium on Saturdays. Fans turned out to cheer them on, and not knowing exactly when the team would show, some of them brought lunch and drinks and made a picnic of the waiting. The scene caught on the way RVs had at Alabama, only with a much lower barrier for entry. All a person needed to join was an appetite, a blanket, and perhaps a sandwich—someone would always give you a beer.

Over time, as with the motor home scene, picnics in the Grove became more extravagant. Ole Miss fans began to truck in tables and linens, then crystalware and candelabras, tents, and La-Z-Boy recliners, until the Grove turned into a grand spectacle—a kind of Kentucky Derby without the horses. For many Ole Miss fans, the Grove has come to take precedence over the games themselves. Perhaps it's just as well—the school's last National Championship came in 1962; against Alabama, Ole Miss is 7—47. Perhaps in response to their record, Ole Miss fans have redirected their competitive instincts; if they can't outplay visiting teams, they'll outhost them. "We may not win every game," the Ole Miss faithful are fond of saying, "But we've never lost a party." The Grove is a bit worse for wear from all that partying. A few years back, the locals say, one of the old oaks there began to look sickly, and a team of arborists was called in to have a look. They collected samples of dirt, wood, and leaves, and after some time returned their diagnosis: alcohol poisoning. Before heading to the stadium for kickoff, the picnickers were pouring the bottoms of their cocktails onto the lawn. It was killing the trees.

As evening falls, all of Oxford, from the RV lot to Fraternity Row to the square downtown, begins to sparkle. The remoteness of the town in the Mississippi wilds gives it the feeling of an exquisite summer camp, a resort even. Sorority girls cruise by in gleaming SUVs with rush slogans—"Hillary for Queen," "Missy for Queen"—scrawled on the rear windshields in shoe polish. The Pikes lurk in the shadows of their house sipping cocktails and keg beer from Solo cups. I head downtown to a cramped, sweltering hangar of a bar called, with irony, the Library, where a blues band pounds out coital swamp rhythms and where a handwritten sign in the men's room pleads, "Pls. Do not clog the toilet. It gets real nasty." In defiance, the urinals overflow with beer bottles. Outside, near the alley exit, there's a spectacular sight: a Dumpster with a mountain of empty brown beer bottles protruding six feet over the rim. A bar back heaves a few more bottles on the top of the stack and tells me, not without a little pride, that it's only a day's worth of drinking.

I go to sleep just after 1:00 A.M., my ears still throbbing with the gnarly blues beat of the Library, my hair and clothes reeking of smoke. A short time later, I'm awakened by a commotion outside. I look out the front window of the Hawg and see my neighbor standing beside his RV in a T-shirt and pajama bottoms, holding a pistol in the air. He's yelling in the direction of the Pike House and threatening to shoot someone. I look up above his rig; the flagpole has been picked clean.

The Grove is off limits to tailgaiters until 6:00 A.M. on game day, and at dawn on Saturday morning, a crowd waits around the perimeter for the all clear to rush in and claim their spots. The Grove is surrounded by cars and pickups; there's a U-Haul truck crammed with a rug, chairs, and a proper dining room table. At 6:00 A.M. sharp, a university official gives the signal, and the resulting rush looks like a cross between an Easter egg hunt and a jailbreak. Bleary-eyed Ole Miss fans sprint into the morning mist to stake their claims. They unfold their tents, unload their dining room tables, unpack bars, and unfurl flags, so that before most in the state have had time to heat their skillets for the breakfast bacon, the Grove is transformed into a mock-up of a Confederate bivouac. The first Bloody Mary is poured before nine.

The fans in the RV encampment are slower to rise, and they wake irascibly when word of the previous night's looting spreads through the lot. A dozen RV-ers, all men, gather nearby for a morning powwow. They're holding coffee mugs and, with their free hands, pointing to various locations around the lot: two chairs taken from over there; a flag stolen from there; RVs over there have been egged. Everyone seems determined to be outraged, but despite our best efforts, there is an unmistakable undercurrent of giddiness. Our worthiness as fans can be gauged by how much our hosts resent our presence, so the vandalism suggests we measure up. A recovery mission is contemplated, then indefinitely postponed for lack of leadership. My neighbor vows to keep watch on Saturday night—with his pistol—and the group disbands.

The vandals passed me by, but I have a different problem: the Hawg is leaking. The epoxy cookie dough on the holding tank has failed and now a puddle has formed on the pavement underneath and is seeping toward my neighbor—specifically, the one with the pistol. I get my wash bucket and tread across the road to the Pike house to look for a spigot. The fraternity brothers are still asleep, so I fill the bucket without incident and walk back across the road, cool water sloshing on the back of my pants leg. The idea is to disguise the origin of the puddle and to make the water look like the byproduct of some sort of early morning cleaning project. I discreetly empty the bucket on the tarmac and toss it inside. No one seems to have noticed.

By late morning a stream of people courses from the RV lot to the Grove, now an electric emporium of smells, colors, and noise bustling beneath a clear blue sky. It's a measure of the Grove's allure that the RV-ers prefer to tailgate there, rather than in their own outdoor living rooms. Tubas and trombones reflect the sunlight in blinding bursts. Smog from barbecue grills rolls across the Grove in soft white puffs, like cannon smoke. The Ole Miss cheerleaders percolate on a center stage, the little frenzied tufts of the pom-poms shimmering with the late morning sun. For food there is the delicate—tiny crustless pockets of cucumber and mayonnaise, shrimp, crackers, and neat cubes of cheese—and the bulk—trays piled high with barbecue, steaming hot, brown, and fibrous; troughs of fried chicken; tables tumbling with sandwiches and pickles and pies and mountainous bowls of potato chips, softening in the humid air. The most astonishing feature of the Grove is the women, a legion of perfectly coiffed belles that make the campus look as though it has been overrun by Miss America contestants. They present an intriguing contrast: With their perfect lipstick and perfect hair, perfect figures and perfectly flattering sundresses, everything about them suggests propriety and primness. But each is as likely as not slugging a can of beer, or shouting and hee-hawing with all the fervor of the males. It's the ideal of the southern woman on display—beauty and toughness, formality with a casual twist, the sort of date a man can take proudly to the pregame cocktails and postgame dinner, while still relying on her to scream bloody murder on the third and longs in between.

As a visitor, I'm passed around the Grove like a chalice and in two hours offered a week's worth of food, and a month's worth of drink. I make a conscious effort to pace myself, a sip here and nibble there, but my hosts seem less concerned with my intake than with how impressed I am with the spectacle in the Grove. "Have you ever seen anything like it?" a local lawyer asks me. I assure him I haven't. "Y'all don't have anything like this in Tuscaloosa, do you?" Indeed we don't. "We may not win the games, but we never lose a party." Amen to that. Forty-five minutes before kickoff, there's a flurry of activity as men repack their coolers and cover their grills and the women reapply their makeup and tousle their hair. Then we're all off to the stadium in a single sprawling herd. I find myself walking next to two rowdy Ole Miss students named Eric Kimbrough and Chris Lancaster.

"What happens in the Grove after the game?" I ask.

"We come back here and get *drunk as hail,*" Chris says.

Vaught-Hemingway Stadium, one of the smallest in the league, is overflowing, both with people and with pride: CBS is broadcasting its first-ever game from Oxford, and the locals beam over the prospect—new to them—of being validated by national television coverage. The Alabama fans find it all very quaint. My seat is down low, in the far corner of the stadium, with the rest of the Alabama crowd. I sit down next to two identically dressed women with matching sun hats, fans, and the puzzlingly anachronistic look of extras from the set of *Little House on the Prairie*. It's a mother-daughter team from Birmingham—Alycia and Renee Bowers—who introduce themselves as the Huggers, a name they earned for all the affection they're known to heap on Alabama players whenever they see them—outside the locker room after games, in the lobby of the team hotel beforehand.

"It's 'cause we love on 'em on all the time," the elder Ms. Bowers tells me.

The Bowers sit fanning themselves in the heat and snapping at anyone who stands in front of them to impede their view. They're old-schoolers who expect the same decorum from their fellow fans as they might from fellow opera-goers, only whenever Alabama scores, their inner girls melt through their prim exteriors, and they lose it like everyone else. It happens twice in the first quarter, on a field goal and late on an Alexander touchdown, then again in the second quarter. At the half Alabama is up 17-7. The Tide scores twice more in the third—Alexander will rack up 214 yards by day's end—and though Ole Miss makes a run in the fourth, the Tide holds them off to win, 30-24. The Huggers are exceedingly pleased—enough so to hug me. The crowd unspools from the stadium and wanders back into the Grove, groggy and sun-wearied, but only marginally more subdued than before the game. David Cutcliffe, the Rebels' coach, appears for a postgame radio interview on the stage at the back of the Grove and gets an ovation. A single loss and the state of Alabama wants its coach's head; a loss to Ole Miss fans barely dampens the party.

I find the Bices, who along with Larry the dog have laid claim to a postage stamp of grass in the middle of the Grove. Chris has his go-cup; I scavenge a couple of beers for Paula and myself, and we relax on a picnic blanket. As dusk falls, the Ole Miss band plays a dirgefully slow rendition of "Dixie," and all around, the tents come down and snap shut amid a relentless clanging of bottles and cans. The cheerleader in my head isn't jumping about so much as swaying playfully to Oxford's easy rhythms. As we sip our drinks, someone lights a forest of tiki torches, which burn gold under the arbors while all around silhouettes ghost by in the purple shadows. The hubbub of the afternoon subsides, and the Grove transforms into a peaceful, exquisitely beautiful place. Ole Miss fans have found a way to make losing nearly pleasant, which is somehow in line with the school's Confederate fixation: theirs is the Lost Cause indeed, and so they've learned to cope.

Chapter Ten

John AY-ud

WHAT EXACTLY *IS* THE CHEERLEADER IN MY BRAIN? A number of neuroscientists in recent years have been trying to answer that very question by studying the brain activity of monkeys (close cousins to fans), along with compulsive gamblers and others prone to the obsessive pursuit of highs. Those scientists believe that the secret of the cheerleader lies at least partly in the brain's production of the pleasure-giving chemical dopamine. Several years ago a Cambridge University neuroscientist named Dr. Wolfram Schultz studied the production of dopamine in the midbrains of monkeys when the animals were given a reward, usually a squirt of apple juice, and discovered something most fans would have been delighted to tell him for a cold can of beer: that the amount of dopamine dispensed by the brain is proportional to the amount of surprise experienced at the reward. When a monkey got more juice than it was expecting, its brain produced a glut of dopamine. When a monkey got the amount of juice that it expected to get, based on the previous squirts, dopamine production remained the same. And when the monkey expected juice and didn't get any, dopamine production plummeted.[§]

Other scientists have found similar results in humans; using brain-scanning technology to study dopamine production in a tiny part of the human forebrain called the anterior cingulum, they found that when humans were given surprises of money in experiments, they reacted much the way the monkeys had when they got juice. The scientists theorized that some people have hyperactive dopamine systems, and that when these people experience the sudden high of, say, winning at slots, their brains latch on to the memory of the experience, and crave it, a condition that can lead to addiction and compulsive behavior. (In fact, cocaine addiction works on the brain in much the same way.) Again, fans know these phenomena intuitively, if not by their exact medical description; if I had access to some tool or drug that provided the high-voltage ecstasy of, say, Van Tiffin's last-minute fifty-two-yard game winner over Auburn, I'd probably have wrecked myself for it. But sports, and college football especially, have built-in protections. There are only twelve or thirteen games a year, evenly spaced a week apart (give or take a couple of days, depending on the choice of the producers of ESPN's Thursday night broadcast). Our drug is doled out according to a strict schedule, our highs carefully rationed. Try as we might, we're rarely given enough to overdose.

* * *

The RV-ers arrive in Tuscaloosa after the Ole Miss game to deeply unpleasant news: the chaos at the Law Library parking lot before the Arkansas game three weeks back has compelled university officials to institute a formal motor home parking policy. They have made . . . rules. The university is selling a limited number of parking permits for $25 each, and even for those with permits, they've made the lot off-limits to RVs until 8:00 A.M. Thursday morning.

[§] **Sandra Blakeslee, "Highjacking the Brain's Circuits with a Nickel Slot Machine,"** ***New York Times,*** **Feb. 19, 2002.**

Word of the new rules trickles out, but the first many hear of it comes on Wednesday night, when they show up at the lot to park. A university cop stationed at the entrance turns them away and tells them to come back at 7:00 A.M. the next morning. The cop's presence is jarring; RV-ers are used to being told to go away by rival schools—this they enjoy even—but it's an altogether new and unpleasant thing to be told to go away by your own side. Most of those turned away simply drive across the street and join the end of a long, growing line of motor homes that stretches up the hill toward the soccer fields overlooking campus. Banned from one lot, they simply create another.

I stop by the line to see what's going on. The RV at the front, a forty-foot Foretravel, belongs to an Albuquerque, New Mexico, man named Willis Horton, a tubby character with glassy eyes, in blue jeans, a cowboy hat, and a red, white, and blue pinstriped shirt, with a white toy poodle named Sassy in his lap. Horton and a couple of traveling buddies—Dwight and Jackie—are having cocktails and flipping through the ninety-nine-channel satellite television system Horton has installed; they invite me aboard for a beer. Horton has the longest commute of anyone I've met. He drives back and forth between New Mexico and Alabama several times a season. In the past two years, he's driven 85,000 miles, 1,100 of them on a single day two weeks ago, to get to Gainesville for the Florida game.

"We go to Alabama games out our ass," Jackie tells me.

Horton and Dwight nod.

"Few years ago they's a rumor we was gonna play Notre Dame in Russia and the next day I was on the phone with a travel agent. I done sat through two fuckin' tornado warnings at Alabama-Auburn games."

"So what's going to happen tomorrow morning when they start selling permits?" I ask.

The three men exchange rueful glances.

"In the military," Dwight says, "they call it a clusterfuck."

I've made a deal with the minister of a local Methodist church to park the Hawg in the church parking lot during the week in exchange for a $200 donation to their general fund, so the next morning I show up there to claim my RV, then putter through Tuscaloosa toward the Law Library lot. It's obvious from a distance that the new parking policy isn't going over well; through the gauzy morning haze I can clearly make out a stroboscopic bouquet of red and blue lights in the distance at the lot entrance. The barricade of police cars gives the lot the appearance less of a tailgate party than of an accident scene. A line of motor homes stretches nearly a mile down Bryant Drive, from the Law Library lot all the way back to McFarland Boulevard. The system seems intentionally designed to provoke a riot; it requires that everyone seeking to obtain a parking pass line up in person at the lot, so anyone unfortunate enough to have parked a mile away has to walk or thumb a ride up to the lot to get in line, and then wait. I park the Hawg near the stately, beer-glazed mansions on fraternity row, walk over, and get in the line. A group of university officials sits at a card table at the front of the lot, outnumbered fifty to one by dyspeptic RV-ers; they've obviously called the cops to keep order. Tempers are already flaring.

"Y'all 'bout taken all the fun out of it," a man shouts at the officials.

"Shit, if this is the way it's gonna be, we might as well go on back to Legion Field," a man in a velour crimson jumpsuit chimes in. He takes a sip of coffee from a Styrofoam cup and glares at the university cop who's directing traffic. "That guy's gonna look funny with a motor home up his ass," he mumbles to no one.

No one is happy about this new process, but there is one person who is unhappier than most: Skipper. He's at the front of the line, gesticulating before a beleaguered-looking university official wearing a red blazer and a world-weary expression: the wizard who came up with the idea of parking permits in the first place. As Skipper orates on the absurdity of the parking policy, the official stands impassively, his arms crossed and chin tucked deep into his neck, like a baseball umpire facing down an angry manager. Skipper doesn't get anywhere, so he does what any self-respecting southerner would do when confronted by an authority he considers illegitimate: he secedes.

With a single furious gesture, Skipper motions to his gang, who loyally fall out of line and follow him toward their respective RVs.

"What's he doin'?" the man in front of me asks.

"He's leavin'," comes a voice from the front of the line.

"Where to?"

"Downtown."

The city has recently opened an empty lot to RVs on a bluff overlooking the river in downtown Tuscaloosa. No one much thought to take the city up on the offer—it's a good deal farther from the stadium than the Law Library lot, is surrounded on two sides by raucous bars, and is far removed from the communal atmosphere of the established RV lots around campus—but Skipper now does so in grand fashion. He casts a condemning look at those of us in line who are too weak to join his cause, then gets in his RV and leads his caravan into the lot, where they turn around theatrically, in a kind of victory lap, and roar past us, a cloud of dust and diesel smoke in their wake.

"God Almighty," an older man in line behind me says. "I haven't seen anything this screwed up since World War II."

There are more RVs than usual in Tuscaloosa this weekend; the Tennessee game is the most anticipated home game of the year. Alabama's rivalry with Tennessee is as intense as any, even Auburn. This is the game that Freeman and Betty Reese skipped their daughter's wedding for, and it usually prompts a day-long work stoppage across Alabama, along with numerous brawls across the South in the sports bars of the fan diaspora. The 1901 matchup set the tone of rivalry for the years to come. "The game was tied 6-6 when an official made a controversial ruling," the *Birmingham News* wrote of the game. "Fans from both sides rushed onto the playing field to voice objections. The contest was called off and 2,000 supporters engaged in fisticuffs until police restored order." Since then, things have gotten only marginally more civil. At least some of the animosity can be explained by a peculiar feature of the Alabama-Tennessee series: its streakiness. A team rarely wins just a single game in the series; instead, it dominates for years. Tennessee has won the last four in a row. Before that, Alabama won seven. Ill will toward a rival accrues exponentially with each consecutive loss, so after Alabama's losing four in a row there's plenty of ill will toward Tennessee on reserve among the Bama faithful. Add to the mix that Tennessee won the National Championship last year, and the Bama Nation is practically ready to take up arms. Overall, Alabama fans are optimistic. The win at Florida and the easy go of it at Oxford suggest that the team has hit stride, and anyway, Tennessee is due for a loss.

There's an easy way to quantify how optimistic Alabama fans are and that's to find out how much they're willing to pay for tickets. The games are technically sold out, but there's a bustling gray market for tickets, some sold by individual fans who happen to have to come into extras, and others by a professional class of scalpers. Unlike many places, in Alabama scalping is legal, so long as the scalper has a business license and pays taxes on his gains. I get a tip from one of the RV-ers that if I want to follow the ticket market, I should track down a locally famous ticket broker named John Ed Belvin. Belvin runs a scalping operation out of a storefront in downtown Tuscaloosa, and he's one of the few people in town who can be counted on to have tickets to the most sought-after games. Belvin seems none too pleased when I call and identify myself as a reporter—"In my business it's important to keep a low profile," he tells me without explaining why, as a phone rings impatiently in the background. Then inexplicably, he changes tack and tells me to come by later in the day, when things slow down.

"How late will you be there?" I ask.

"I get off work at six, then me and my happy ass go home," Belvin says, and hangs up.

Belvin's operation is called Need One Ticket, and it shares a front door with the Downtown Gallery, a framing store that specializes in Alabama football–themed prints and commemorative gear, especially the works of Daniel A. Moore, a former power company employee who made millions by painting famous moments in Alabama football history. Together Need One Ticket and the Downtown Gallery constitute a one-stop shop for the Crimson Tide obsessed: tickets to the left, framed gewgaws to the right. Belvin's side is spare—a pinkish, low-pile industrial-grade carpet; two metal desks; white peg-board walls; and but a single decorative element: a large framed edition of Daniel Moore's *The Sack*, a painting of that famous play (to Alabama fans) in

1986 in which a charging Cornelius Bennett nearly decapitated Notre Dame quarterback Steve Beuerlein in Birmingham. Belvin is on the phone middeal, pacing the floor in a cordless headset. Without interrupting himself, he points me to a white plastic chair and I sit down. Belvin bears an astonishing resemblance to country singer Kenny Rogers—he has a round face, a white beard, and a perfectly combed wave of silver hair laps over his head. He wears the intense expression of a mission control operator during a space launch. In short order it becomes apparent how money is made in the ticket trade.

"What do you have?" Belvin says into his headset. "Where are they? In your hands? You in Centerville? If I get 'em in my hand, I can give you a hundred dollars apiece."

He switches to another line.

"Need One Ticket. Hmm hmm. How many do you want, Mrs. Jackson? Well, you might be the luckiest woman in Tuscaloosa—I've got three together in the upper deck, twenty-two rows up. Two hundred apiece."

During a lull, Belvin stands to introduce himself. When I tell him I'm the reporter who called earlier, he seems briefly disappointed; he'd thought I might be a walk-in customer. We shake hands and Belvin apologizes for having seemed distant earlier; he feared I might be writing an exposé of ticket brokers, he says. The local newspapers do the story about once a year, he explains, and it's rarely flattering. "People don't like ticket brokers," he says by way of explanation. "You got something they want. A local hotel here—they charge $29.95 a night. On a game weekend they'll charge $129, and everyone says, 'Hey, that's business.' But if I try to get $200 a ticket, that's just not right."

Belvin's partner, Tony, a cheerful-looking man with a mustache, a small stack of tickets, and two telephones on his desk, nods in confirmation.

I ask the guys how long they've been scalpers.

John Ed's eyes narrow.

"We're ticket brokers," he says pointedly, "not scalpers."

Conversation is cut short by visitors—a succession of people who've come in to drop off or pick up tickets. There's a fraternity kid who's come to buy, a professor selling his discount faculty tickets at a nice gain, and two fans who just arrived in Tuscaloosa ticketless and are desperate to see the game. Most seem to know Belvin personally, and those who do pronounce his first name the way Belvin himself pronounces it, with three syllables: John AY-ud.

A woman who has come to pick up tickets for her husband introduces herself.

"I'm Terry Terry," she says cheerily, offering her hand.

Terry *Terry*?

"Yep," she says. "There are three other Terry Terrys in town—one of 'em has the same bank as me, the same pediatrician, and we both have dogs named Max."

John Ed raises his eyebrows and gives me a confirming nod. Something about the look suggested a man at peace with the peculiarity of his surroundings.

"John AY-ud knows *ev*erybody," the woman says.

"Well, two out of three," says Belvin. "Thing is, they're all gonna need me sometime or other."

Terry Terry leaves, and a short while later, a man walks in the door with a six-pack of Michelob Light in his right hand

"Whoo Ha! Roll Tide," he says. "Alabama's gonna *kick a little ass*!"

The man introduces himself to me as Ralph, and quickly gets to distributing bottles of beer. Belvin cracks one open and turns his attention to what he says could be the deal of the day: a prominent Birmingham family is willing to trade two sets of four tickets in separate sections for six tickets together. Belvin doesn't have six together—yet—so he works the phones furiously, to try to put together a deal. Ralph, meanwhile, wants to know what I'm writing in my notebook, and when I tell him, he begins to interrogate me on who I've interviewed. Without thinking, I mention Finebaum.

"Yeah?" Ralph asks. "What does Finebaum think of DuBose?"

I try to be diplomatic.

"I'd say he probably doesn't think DuBose has what it takes to win over the long run."

"Yeah?" Ralph says, gently. "Well *fuck* him." Ralph leans toward me. "You wanna hear about class? *Start writin'*."

Belvin, still on the phone, reacts to the outburst by motioning frantically for us to go outside. Reluctantly, I follow Ralph out onto the sidewalk, where with a cigarette in one hand and a Michelob Light in the other, he tells me a story. He'd played football at Alabama in '64 and '65, eventually quitting the team because "Things weren't working out with me and Coach Bryant for whatever reason," he says, in a low, serrated smoker's voice. After he quit, Ralph's mother and stepfather remained involved with the team through the alumni association, and got to know DuBose, then a freshman linebacker just out of Opp. Ralph's mother died of lung cancer on St. Patrick's Day last year, and her funeral coincided with the opening day of spring practice. But despite his commitment on the field, Ralph says, DuBose flew to Gadsden and served as a pallbearer in the funeral.

"Now if any man had a reason not to come to a funeral, it was Coach *Du*Bose," Ralph says, leaning into me so that I can smell the beer on his breath. "And he came anyway. That's class. End of quote. Real class, end of quote. You put *that* in your book." Ralph taps emphatically on my notebook with his cigarette hand for effect, leaving a few flakes of ash on the page. He takes a long drag and tosses his cigarette disgustedly in the street before exhaling.

"That fuckin' Finebaum," he says and walks back inside.

Inside, Belvin is on another call.

"I got four coming in tonight as good as they get," he says. "Listen, the situation is this: The tickets that's not committed in my hands right now is eight. I don't know of any other tickets in Tuscaloosa. It's primo stuff. You have two choices: you can buy the U3s outright or I'll trade your HHs and sell you these others."

While Belvin works his deal, Ralph wanders outside, lurks in front of the building for a bit, then disappears without a goodbye.

"Don't mind him," Belvin says when he hangs up the phone. "He's just bein' a fruit loop."

Around five o'clock there's a lull. Belvin says that by now, most people have either found tickets or given up hope entirely, so market activity is cooling off. Scalping, or rather ticket brokerage, is essentially a futures game, Belvin explains. There are contracts—the tickets—that expire at a certain time—kickoff—the value of which fluctuates according to market conditions. The variables are Alabama's record, the opponent, the weather, TV coverage, and kickoff time, which is frequently changed to accommodate television. Night games are always in high demand—fans like the all-day tailgate party that precedes them—while morning games are softer because the early kickoff limits the amount of time fans have to travel to Tuscaloosa, thus shrinking the pool of potential buyers. All of these factors can change rapidly: A traditionally tough opponent might start to have a disastrous season, so a big game starts to look like a sure thing. The game might be moved to nighttime, making it a hot ticket again. On Wednesday, the weekend forecast comes out and calls for severe thunderstorms; prices fall. And other random events can affect prices; a visiting school might decide to return some of its allotment of tickets if they don't sell; the University of Alabama would put those up for sale two days before the game, glutting the market at the last minute. Belvin is his own Wall Street analyst, constantly looking for any information he can get to stay ahead of the often underinformed retail buyer. For a game like Tennessee, he might hold on to his stash until late in the week, waiting for a spike in prices as fans become more and more desperate. If he sees a possibility of rain coming before the ticket-buying public is paying attention, or gets word from a pal in the athletic department that a kickoff might be moved from 2:30 P.M. to 11:30 A.M. for television, he'll sell early in the week and eagerly cut package deals. Church groups, booster clubs, and charities are favorite customers in such times since they're apt to buy in bulk. Belvin's bread and butter is Alabama football—besides knowing the ins and outs of the market, he is a fan as well, and can make use of any unsold product—but he also dabbles in concert tickets, and big events like this Sunday night's World Series matchup between the Braves and the Yankees. (Tickets are $500 apiece.) For all his research and contacts, Belvin says, nothing tells him more about the market than the phone on his desk.

"When it's ringing, I'm buying tickets," he says. "When it's not ringing—" He shakes his head forlornly.

The Tennessee game has Belvin looking pretty smart. He had a couple hundred tickets to begin with, and when Alabama beat Ole Miss last Saturday, he quietly started buying up tickets while Tide fans were still distracted by the win. He held back until late in the week, and sold the bulk of his holdings at the peak of the market. Now, the night before the game, he has only a few singles he's kept for friends and loyal customers. Belvin won't tell me his profit margin for the week, but it's possible to get an idea. He bought his tickets at somewhere between the face value of $25 and $150 apiece; they're now going for $200. If he averaged a $100 profit per ticket, and sold 250 of them, he would have made slightly over $25,000 on the Tennessee game alone.

Belvin picks up the phone to try to close the deal with the wealthy Birmingham family that wants six tickets in a row. "My life works in streaks," he says as he dials the phone. "If I'm hot, I can't miss. But when I'm cold, I look like a bloomin' idiot.

"It's like a puzzle I'm trying to put together," he says. "You have some missing pieces—" Belvin interrupts himself when his source answers. They sound each other out, haggle a bit, and when Belvin seals the deal, he rubs his hands together excitedly and makes a notation in the three-ring binder on his desk. He calls the customer in Birmingham and tells him it's a go—six tickets together near midfield for the customer's eight, which Belvin will sell later this evening. He's on good terms with the owner of the local Ruby Tuesday's, and says he'll leave the tickets in an envelope there with the hostess for pickup.

"I gotta hide my own tickets, so I don't sell 'em by accident," he says.

At just after six o'clock, Belvin calls it a day. He locks up the Need One Ticket office, and we're off to Ruby Tuesday's to make the drop. Afterward, we make a quick stop at John Ed's house, which is in a subdivision of orange-brick townhouses just across the Black Warrior River from downtown Tuscaloosa, in the village of Northport, a ten-minute drive from Bryant-Denny. The house is moving-day empty, the kitchen barren except for a six-pack of Coors Light in the fridge. Besides a whopping stereo system and a twenty-seven-inch Mitsubishi television tuned to ESPN, the only other signs that John Ed's pad is inhabited are a few framed embroidery odes to Bear Bryant in the entry hall, including one of the Bear's most quoted aphorisms: "If you believe in yourself and have dedication and pride and never quit, you'll be a winner. The price of victory is high but so are the rewards."

"I use that in my ticket business," John Ed says. "When I'm there till 11:00 P.M., that's what I'm thinking about."

John Ed disappears to change, and a few minutes later, we're out the door and off to Innisfree, an Irish-theme bar in downtown Tuscaloosa where there's always a classic Alabama game replaying on a wide-screen television. Over a few beers, John Ed's story trickles out. He's from a town called Lawley, halfway down the winding two-lane highway between Tuscaloosa and Montgomery, where he grew up on a farm raising chickens, cotton, corn, hogs, and a small herd of cattle. His parents were country folk of simple pleasures—one of his father's favorite foods was squirrel brains, for example—and John Ed might never have left Lawley had it not been for the guiding hand and impeccable connections of a neighbor, a local lumber magnate named Olon Belcher. Belcher had been Bear Bryant's teammate at Alabama, and the two had remained close. Belcher hired John Ed to plant pine trees and to drive a dump truck one summer, and was the first to notice that John Ed had street smarts that belied his country upbringing. Belcher also knew John Ed's parents were too poor to send their son to college. One afternoon he called John Ed into his office and told him to wear church clothes to work the next day. John Ed did as he was told, and the next day showed up in his best suit and shoes, and was ordered by Belcher to get into the car and to drive them both to Tuscaloosa. Off they went, up the winding two-lane and through the piney woods to Tuscaloosa and straight to the athletics building and Bear Bryant's office. Belcher explained the situation to Bryant—that John Ed had potential, but no way of paying for college—and asked his old friend if he could arrange a scholarship for John Ed through the athletic department. There was something in it for the coach, too. Belvin, Belcher said, was Charles Cleveland's "best white friend."

Charles Cleveland was one of the most sought-after high school basketball recruits in the South, and one of the first black athletes ever recruited by the University of Alabama. John Ed was a year ahead of Cleveland at Bibb County High, and the two were buddies. Bibb County in those days was a repository of the worst racial attitudes imaginable, but Belvin's father raised his son to think differently from the other kids. Blacks and whites worked side by side with John Ed on the family farm. He'd once said the word *nigger* in front of his father, and was admonished so severely that the word was jarred forever from his vocabulary. At Bibb County High, John Ed hadn't thought twice about striking up a friendship with Cleveland—he'd always idolized talented athletes, and he was more interested in the color of their jerseys than the color of their skin.

In Bryant's office this detail of Belvin's social life took on a new significance. Bryant and the University of Alabama had taken no small amount of grief from the press and the public for maintaining an all-white varsity athletics program. The university had been sued by the school's African American Association, and Bryant deposed about his failure to recruit black athletes (he inartfully repeated the old southern ruse that few blacks had ever applied). Landing Charles Cleveland would do a lot to get the critics off the coach's back, to say nothing of helping the basketball team, which was struggling. Bryant proposed a deal. If John Ed would put in a good word for Alabama with Cleveland, he'd get a partial scholarship as a trainer, taping ankles and retrieving footballs at practice. Without so much as applying, John Ed was on his way to college.

"The strange thing was, I didn't have any say in it," he tells me over a beer at Innisfree. "They didn't say, 'You want to do this?' It was like, 'Here's when you start.' "

John Ed describes working for Bear Bryant, even as a trainer, as the best of times. He seems capable of reciting verbatim everything the Bear ever said to him, but there was one interaction John Ed holds out as the most profound. He and the other trainers usually played a pickup game before practice—the game would end when the first varsity player or coach appeared on the field—and on this particular day, no one noticed as Bryant himself made his way out of the football building and down the sideline, a few minutes earlier than usual. When one of the trainers finally spotted the long shadow of the coach, everyone scattered, fearful of getting in trouble. Bryant, though, yelled at them to keep playing. He took a seat on a bench and watched the game, not critically, as a coach, but as a fan, standing to clap whenever someone made a good catch or block. This was as close as John Ed would ever come to experiencing the game that would largely define his career, and to a degree his life. He shakes a little when he talks about it.

By coincidence, John Ed got his start in the ticket business through his friend Charles Cleveland as well, at least in a roundabout way. During his freshman year at Alabama, John Ed was sent by an assistant coach to Birmingham to give Cleveland four tickets to the Alabama-USC football game as a recruiting perk. The game became famous for the particular way Alabama lost—by being carved to pieces by a black USC running back named Sam Cunningham, a performance it's said that finally persuaded Bryant to recruit black players for the football team. When John Ed finally caught up with his friend Cleveland, he found he'd been beaten to the punch by USC, which was also recruiting Cleveland and had given him tickets to sit on their side. John Ed knew the assistant coach would blame him for not getting to Cleveland before USC, and he didn't relish the thought of returning four unused tickets to the coach, so he wandered out front of Legion Field to try to unload them before kickoff. He expected to get ten or twelve bucks a ticket; the first offer was for fifty dollars apiece. This was John Ed's type of margin. It was the beginning of a life in what John Ed liked to call "the weirdest profession on earth": he is part futures trader, part psychologist, part fan, and part partier. The ticket business isn't without its demands. John Ed always gains a few pounds during the football season, he says, and he's usually exhausted by season's end. But he takes the rest of the year off, recuperating in his beach condo in Florida or on trips out west to Jackson Hole, where he hikes and rides horses.

"I tell everyone I'm like a teacher," he tells me. "In the summer my ass is gone."

I've said hardly a word in the previous two hours, but Belvin feels confident he has a read on me; he pronounces me "an okay Joe," and we make plans to meet up for a beer at the Houndstooth tomorrow after the game.

"You deer hunt?" he asks me. "I've got fifty-five acres in Centerville. We can go down there this week and tell the world to kiss our ass."

In the evening, there's a pep rally on the Strip. DuBose, Shaun Alexander, and Kenny Stabler give speeches, and a local politician reads a proclamation in support of Alabama's effort against Tennessee ("And whereas, nothing sucks like a Big Orange . . ."). The pep rally gives way to a drunken free-for-all. The crowd in the street moths toward the bars, which are too crowded to accommodate everyone, so the party stays outside. Glass from broken beer bottles collects in the gutters like leaves after a storm, and all of Tuscaloosa smells like the bottom of a freshly emptied pint glass. I stumble on perhaps the one place in Tuscaloosa where no one is drinking: an austere storefront nestled between the bars called the University Worship Center, which has the temporary look of a campaign headquarters, the candidate being Jesus, the platform, moral living, abstinence from sex and alcohol. The students who run the center have set up speakers out front and are blasting contemporary Christian music and handing out flyers to the bar goers. A young woman is telling anyone who'll listen that God's love is infinite, while a mere fifteen feet down the sidewalk, another young woman—a partying coed—stands bent over as friends look on, heaving pailsful of pink chunky vomit.

At around 1:00 A.M., a bar called the Booth actually runs out of beer, a local first. God's love may be never ending, but in a hard-drinking town like Tuscaloosa, the supply of Budweiser is finite.

* * *

I never thought it could happen, but I'm beginning to develop an animosity to the Alabama fight song. I managed to sleep soundly through the long freight trains that run just behind Law Library lot during the night, but "Yea Alabama!" blared from the air horns of neighboring RVs starting just after 7:00 A.M., causes me to jerk upright. It's beginning to grate, like an alarm clock with no off switch. I put some coffee on the Hawg's propane stove, and there's a tap at the door. Paula Bice has brought me a breakfast of microwaved Tater Tots and ketchup on a paper plate. After a cup of coffee, I call Paul Finebaum.

Finebaum and I have tentative plans to go to the game together—tentative because Finebaum isn't sure he'll muster the courage he'll need to brave the hostility that awaits him when Alabama plays his alma mater. It's Finebaum's connection to Tennessee, after all, that to many Alabama fans explains his constant harping on the Tide. Showing up at the game might seem like a taunt of sorts. But when I get through to Finebaum later in the morning, he's on the interstate, well on his way to Tuscaloosa. He can't resist the temptation to further inflame Alabama fans. The boldness of his decision doesn't hit me until I see Finebaum scurrying toward me in the lot, head down, shuffling along cautiously like someone dodging sniper fire. His bald dome instantly identifies him, and fans in the crowd begin to shout his name.

"Hey *Paul*," a Tide fan yells as Finebaum approaches. "People in Alabama *hate* you, man!"

Finebaum follows me into the Hawg, and we close the door. Outside, a group of fans gather and point at my RV, which makes us both nervous—Finebaum is worried about his physical safety, and I'm worried about how the hardcores will react toward me when they learn I've harbored the enemy. We decide to make a dash out of the lot and toward the stadium before things get out of hand. I have an invitation to stop by a tailgate party hosted by executives of a local trucking company, and figuring they'll be a more buttoned-down crowd and therefore more likely to tolerate him, Finebaum agrees to come along. On the way to the stadium Finebaum comes in for a steady barrage of taunts—"Who's gonna win today, Paul?" "Hey, Paul—how's Tuscaloosa treatin' you?" "Hey, Paul—thought you'd be in the Tennessee locker room by now." The sphere of Alabama football is so close-knit that even Finebaum's enemies consider themselves to be on a first-name basis with him. Finebaum himself finds all the attention unsettling, so halfway up Bryant Drive, he insists we stop at a souvenir stand, where he buys a red Alabama cap. He hands the woman at the stand a wad of money and doffs the cap, pulling the brim low over his eyes to shield his face and that distinctive bald head from passersby.

"This is an $18 investment in my own security," he says.

A block from the stadium, we come across a massive Prevost motor home, decked in orange and attended by a small pack of photographers. The governor of Tennessee is on board, one of them says. Finebaum may be afraid of the masses, but he's fearless toward celebrities and the well known—people for whom the price of whacking him upside the head is prohibitively high. A moment later, the governor steps outside and Finebaum introduces himself. After a few minutes of small talk, Finebaum has managed to talk the puzzled governor into letting us have a tour of the million-dollar RV, which is owned by one of the governor's supporters.

"I've got one like this at home," Finebaum tells the owner's wife.

"You *do*?" the woman says, taken by the coincidence.

"Yeah," Finebaum deadpans. "I call it my house."

Neither the hostess nor the governor find the remark at all humorous, so we're out of there. We walk across the street to the trucking company reception, in an apartment complex adjacent to Bryant-Denny on Wallace Wade Avenue. The trucking company is Welborn Transport, which runs a fleet of eighteen-wheelers that supply grocery stores around the South. Executives at the company own several apartments in the shadow of the stadium and rent them out to students on the condition that the company can throw parties there on game days. They've run the students out and set up a bar inside and a buffet on the porch, with baskets of corn chips, platters of red sticky barbecue, and piles of white bread and hamburger buns. The guests are well-to-do locals—women with fixed, topiary-like hairdos and bright red lipstick, just so, who wear large knit purses at their sides and perma-smiles. The men are in oxfords, ironed blue jeans, Rockports, and blue baseball caps with the company logo above the brim. I stand in line for a barbecue sandwich and lose Finebaum for a few minutes. When I find him again he's standing in a corner with his hands in his pockets, his eyes wide but flat and black, like someone having a flashback.

"I gotta get outta here," he says. "I'm getting looks."

For a moment, I think Finebaum is joking, but seeing his eyes scan the room as though he were watching a ping-pong match, I realize he's serious. I flip my barbecue sandwich into a garbage can and follow him out the door and across the street into the stadium and to the only place in Tuscaloosa where he might possibly feel comfortable: the press box.

The place is crowded with dozens of newspaper reporters and

local newscasters, all of whom seem to recognize Finebaum, even if he doesn't recognize them. They greet him with bemused smiles that suggest they understand the act of courage it took for Finebaum to come to Tuscaloosa—either that or the irony of his wearing an Alabama cap. Finebaum seems taken aback by the friendly reception.

"Maybe they think I have cancer or something," he says.

The view from inside the press box is new to me, and not altogether pleasant. Looking down into the stadium, effervescing with color and sound—the crowd, the bands, strains of "Sweet Home, Alabama" ricocheting off the bleachers from the cheerleaders' PA system—is like sitting on the rim of a champagne glass and not being allowed to sip. An announcer repeatedly warns us over a loudspeaker that cheering in the press box is prohibited. This ought to be interesting, I tell myself; I've never not cheered at an Alabama game. Cheering in the press box is considered rude, because others are writing or broadcasting live. And anyway, the esprit de corps among sports reporters demands they deny that sports have any power over them, the way soldiers deny fear; they're quite above all the silliness outside. I, on the other hand, am one with that silliness.

My first test comes when Alabama runs onto the field, the band chugging away at the fight song, which is no longer annoying, but rather inspiring and life affirming. I have an urge to sing. But I resist, and instead nod clinically, so as not to give away the feeling that I'm witnessing a near-religious experience. The crowd in Bryant-Denny—at over eighty-six thousand, the largest crowd ever to see a football game in the state of Alabama—is exuberant, and the din is awesomely loud. Finebaum, though, is unimpressed.

"Alabama fans are like middle-aged Jewish wives," he shouts over the roar. "You have to tell them when to be excited." A moment later, he points at my notebook. "For the record, I'm married to a gentile," he says.

For the first five minutes of the game, I manage to keep my cool. A few routine running plays make the effort more bearable. But then: a holding call against Alabama, which reflexively causes me to bark "bullshit" at the top of my lungs. Finebaum gives me a disapproving look, as though I've belched at the dinner table, as do a few of the reporters scribbling dutifully at their desks below. I collect myself; staying quiet is harder than I'd imagined. The Tide starts its second drive on its own one-yard line and then scraps its way across midfield. A quick pass from Zow to Milons and we're on the Tennessee twenty-five. Then Zow drops back and flips a short pass underneath to Alexander, who pauses, as if waiting to be hit, before realizing the Tennessee defenders are nowhere in sight. Alexander lowers his head and starts galloping downfield, and with each step the decibel level rises. When Alexander powers over a lone defensive back at the goal line and tumbles in for the score, the place explodes. I explode with them, letting out a terrific howl of pleasure. Finebaum has slinked away, so that no one knows we're together, and a few seconds later, a white-haired gentleman in a crimson blazer asks me—not rudely and not unsympathetically—to leave. I'm actually relieved; I've got an excuse now to ditch Finebaum and the other clinicians in the press box. I track him down and tell him I'll catch up with him after the game, then head down the elevator to the stands, where I belong.

Later in the second quarter Alabama can't capitalize on its momentum: a penalty on a jumping lineman wrecks a drive, and on the next play, the Vols' quarterback, Tee Martin, blasts up the middle for twenty yards—the beginning of a steady, disturbingly professional drive that ends in the Alabama end zone. The Vols are experienced and calm, alarmingly so, and their poise seems almost to erase Alabama's home-field advantage. The teams play rope-a-dope for the rest of the second quarter, and things settle down. Then just before the half, Zow is hit hard and comes up hopping awkwardly on one leg. Through his face mask, I can see him wincing. The effect of Zow's injury on the crowd is like the music being shut off in the middle of a party. Our backup, Watts, is a freshman, and lacks the experience we'll need to hang with the Vols. We need Zow badly. But at the half, he hops off the field as though he has a thorn in his foot.

The Vols get the ball at the the beginning of the third quarter, and go straight for Alabama's weakness, its secondary. Four minutes in, Martin heaves a pass down the left sideline to a diving receiver: touchdown. The Vols lead 14-7. When Alabama comes back on the field on offense, the question of Zow's status is answered when Watts enters as quarterback. Zow must be too injured to play. The earthmovers on the Tennessee defensive line quickly set to work on Watts, picking him up, dropping him, and smearing him into the ground repeatedly, like a clump of wet clay. Watts is so ineffective that the coaches put the injured Zow back in, but Zow can't plant his weight properly, and his throws are all arm, and all over the place—into the dirt, several stories above the receivers' hands, off toward the benches. With Alabama unable to pass, the Vols now defend the run; their linebackers shoot up the middle every time Alexander gets the ball, shutting down the lanes. Our offense is frozen. Then with eight minutes to go, the Vols' quarterback rolls out on an undefended bootleg and sees nothing but green. He jogs into the end zone untouched, and Tennessee leads by two touchdowns.

As the game wears on, it takes on a pathetic quality; watching Zow pass feels like watching a kid at the fair trying to throw impossibly small rings on impossibly large Coke bottles. The futility is soul rending. On a fourth down with a minute and a half to go, down by two touchdowns, Zow drops back for a final chance, and overthrows his receiver. Tennessee runs out the clock; they've won five in a row. The streak continues, but the misery feels as fresh as ever.

I walk down the stadium steps to the fence next to the field where Finebaum will be doing a live feed for the evening newscast. I quickly locate him; he's abandoned his Alabama cap and his bald head is easily visible among the helmets of the players exiting the field. A woman in the stands is heckling him—"Smile Paul! Smile Paul! Smile Paul!" as he awaits his cue, but Finebaum doesn't seem the least bit intimidated. In fact, he's smirking—a delighted little sore winner's smirk. When the camera goes live, Finebaum picks up on an old theme: "University of Alabama president Andrew Sorensen walked out on the field late in the game and fans started chanting 'We need a new coach!' 'We need a new coach!' " he tells his viewing audience. I'd missed that particular chant, but Finebaum, with his acute ear for scandal, not only heard it but leads with it. After the live feed ends, Finebaum walks over to the fence to say hello. Up close he seems frazzled; perhaps a day's worth of taunting and heckling has taken its toll on his nerves.

"What'd I say?" he asks me. "I feel like I'm in a trance."

To tell the truth, I want to throttle him. The reporter in me—the part of me that can appreciate his ironic distance from the game and Finebaum's role as court jester of the state of Alabama—has been utterly subdued by the fan in me, which has no appreciation whatsoever for irony and can't conceive of detachment. Truth be told, there's not a joke in the world that could make me laugh now, and worse than that, with the fan in control, I feel mocked, alongside DuBose and the rest of the Alabama team. Knowing Finebaum's secret delight as a Tennessee grad only intensifies the hostility. This isn't *funny*, I have an urge to scream—this is *football*!

I'm not alone. Perhaps a dozen Alabama fans are now taunting Finebaum, who, fortunately for himself, is at a safe remove, separated from the pack by a chain-link fence. I wish Finebaum luck getting out of Tuscaloosa with his limbs intact, and suddenly he's the one incapable of ironic detachment; instead of smiling, he winces. Perhaps with tens of thousands of frustrated Alabama fans running around, a good many of them depressively drunk, Finebaum's safety is no laughing matter. We shake and go our separate ways, in our separate moods.

John Ed and I have plans to meet at the Houndstooth, so I mope in that direction. The atmosphere outside the stadium is eerie; thousands are walking away from Bryant-Denny, and yet the only sounds are those of shoes scuffing the concrete, and the occasional clang of a beer can on a garbage drum. The wake proceeds toward the Strip, the bars, and their promise of numbing relief, and even they are spookily quiet. A hundred and fifty sullen fans, mostly men, are slamming beers and pouting in the Houndstooth when I enter. I quickly spot John Ed, in the back sipping a can of Coors Light. As someone acutely attuned to the mood of the Alabama fan base, John Ed has picked up an ominous vibe: there are too many drunk, angry people in one place for his liking. So we quickly make our way outside and walk down the street to

Belvin's crimson Toyota 4Runner, and ride across the river to Ruby Tuesday's, where Belvin makes his ticket drops. Belvin's in tight with the owner, so despite the line of perhaps a hundred forlorn fans waiting outside for tables, we're waved inside and escorted toward a private room in the back. Inside, two hundred or so Alabama fans sit over dinner at their booths and tables as sullenly and quietly as a couple in a quarrel.

In the RV lot, things too are sullen and quiet. I wander over to the Bices' and find them in their outdoor living room with Larry the Dog dozing lazily in his miniature director's chair. Chris and Paula are chatting up the neighbors and going about the business of doling out Bama Bombs and potato chips to strangers with the incongruous air of people who are unaware we've lost. In light of my own depression, it's nerve-wracking to see people on my own side who seem resolute about not being depressed; it's enough to make me suspect them for a brief moment of being double agents, perhaps in league with Finebaum. How else to explain it? Eventually, when things quiet down, I decide to confront them on their good cheer. I find myself being gently admonished by Paula.

"It's not that we don't want them to win as much as everybody else does," she says, "but we can get past a loss. I know it sounds stupid for me of all people to say"—Paula gestures toward the RV—"but it's just a ball game."

I tell Paula that's entirely too reasonable a position for a fan to take.

"I kind of don't like to be called a fan," she tells me, her tone turning slightly philosophical. "When you say I'm a fan—fanatic—some people think I'm some kind of rabid idiot. I always envision those weird people who dress up like dogs in the dog pound in Cleveland"—she's referring to the face painters at Cleveland Browns games—"It's not me and it's not Chris."

"But don't you get the slightest bit down after a loss?" I ask.

"Sure," Chris says. "But it's like when you're on the job—you get ticked off at people all the time, but you get over it. You got to."

"Well, how long does that take?"

"When we get up Sunday morning, we've had time to think about it and put it in perspective," Paula says, "So I'd say we're probably completely over it by lunchtime."

When I met the Bices over the Bama fan e-mail list at the beginning of the season, I certainly didn't anticipate that at some time in the future they'd be lecturing me on how to keep football in perspective—on how to be an enlightened fan. I'd assumed that joyful wins went hand in hand with miserable losses. The Bices somehow manage to enjoy all the upside of winning while limiting the downside of losing. It seems to me that's something akin to the fan's Holy Grail, the equivalent of figuring out how to drink without getting hung over, or to eat to excess without getting sick. Put in pill form, the Bices' unique psychology could earn them billions, but as it is, I'm forced to resort to the only palliative I know—waiting and suffering until the hope of the next game shines through the gloom of the last.

Later in the evening, I tune in the local news for the game recap, entertaining the faintest of hopes that perhaps the replay will show a different result and prove the day just an unpleasant hallucination. I have no such luck; there it is: 21-7 Tennessee. The local station had a reporter at the stadium to gauge fan reaction after the game, and he approaches a glassy-eyed Alabama fan with long hair and a blond mustache who looks as though he walked off the cover of a Lynyrd Skynyrd album. He's obviously drunk, hanging flaccidly on his date's shoulder like a worn trench coat.

"Sir, what's your reaction to the game?" the reporter asks.

The man halts, and tucks his chin into his neck, as if he's about to belch; the drunkard's look of contemplation. He says nothing.

"What about Mike DuBose?" the reporter tries. The man jerks to.

"Oh we just *love* head coach Mike *Du*-Bose," the man says gently. A sinister smile creeps across his face and he leans into the camera.

"Yeah—RIGHT!" he barks.

Chapter Eleven

Getting Some Damn Where

ON TUESDAY AFTERNOON I STOP BY NEED ONE TICKET to see firsthand how the Tennessee loss has affected the collective psyche of Alabama fans. It's a depressing sight—John Ed and Tony, staring at telephones that sit on the simulated-wood-grain tops of their metal desks as silently as stones. The guys are catatonically somber.

"Takes a few days to get over a loss," John Ed says morosely. "Monday it was a ghost town. Today—a little better. But if that thing doesn't start ringing by Wednesday—" He shook his head. "*Man.*"

John Ed is long in the market and the market is tanking. He has 192 tickets to this weekend's game against Southern Mississippi, a weak rival by Alabama standards, and he is desperate to sell. To make matters worse, Alabama's next opponent, LSU—usually a huge draw—is having a terrible year. If the LSU fans don't travel in their usual numbers, the school might release its unsold tickets to the University of Alabama, which would put them up for sale, flooding the market just days before kickoff. Yesterday John Ed got word that the Alabama-LSU game was being moved from an afternoon kickoff to an 11:30 A.M. start for TV—the "kiss of death in the ticket business," he says. John Ed faces the possibility of two dismal weeks.

He has "a few things working," though, he says. A local church group needs a block of tickets, and he's probably their only hope of getting more than a few seats together in the same section. He holds all the cards on that deal. He has a few tickets left to the Shania Twain show in Birmingham this weekend, which he expects to sell for a nice gain; Shania has no win-loss record to batter ticket prices to her shows. For the most part, though, John Ed is exposed in his bread-and-butter game, Alabama football. His face shows his concern; his brow is fixed in permanent furrow, and as he worries, his lips are frozen in a permanent pucker, as though he's sucking on a lozenge. He gets up to pace, pausing every now and then to look out the glass storefront onto Lurleen B. Wallace Boulevard, hopeful, perhaps, that ticket buyers will emerge from the autumn haze. Downtown Tuscaloosa, though, is placidly quiet, save a few chirping birds and the echo of footsteps off old brick facades. John Ed bores his hands deep in his pockets, lets his head drop, and paces again.

"I tell you how we could make a lot of money," he says. "A movie about Bear Bryant."

"What about *The Bear*?" I say. *The Bear* starred Gary Busey and came out a few years after Bryant's death. It was panned by critics and denounced by anyone who'd ever had anything to do with the coach, including his family. Few Alabama fans even admit to having seen it.

"That movie failed because of the arrogance of those Hollywood know-it-alls," John Ed says. "They wouldn't even let them film it here—had to go film it in Georgia. Now, I'm tellin' you—if it's done by the right people—" John Ed raises his eyebrows and taps himself on the sternum "—it can't miss. I'm telling you man, it *can't* miss." John Ed puts his hands on his hips and looks out onto the street at the passing cars.

"What pisses me off is you can make money with some guy who played two plays at Notre Dame—" he's talking about *Rudy*—"and here you have the greatest football coach in history. Shit—he wrestled a *bear*!"

The phone rings.

"Shania Twain? Yeah I've got a few. Ten rows back, one hundred fifty to two hundred. You damn right."

On Thursday morning John Ed sends Tony down to the Southern Mississippi campus in Hattiesburg on the assumption that Golden Eagles fans might be in a buying mood. Southern Miss has rarely beaten Alabama—the series record is 28-5-2—and with the Tide on the ropes, there is a chance Eagles fans might be feeling optimistic, and therefore, free with their money. John Ed says he feels uneasy about selling tickets to opposing fans, but more uneasy about losing his shirt. Tony posts a few flyers on campus and waits in his car to see if he gets any bites.

On Tuesdays and Thursdays at 11:30 A.M., John Ed meets a group of fellow Tide fans for lunch at the Waysider, a meat-and-three joint in a red shack on the edge of downtown Tuscaloosa that serves as a sort of central cafeteria for Alabama faithful. The group has been meeting at the Waysider twice a week since 1982 and calls itself the Hollyhand Sewing Circle, after its ringleader, a contractor named Doug Hollyhand. The walls of the Waysider are a mosaic of memorabilia: Daniel Moore prints, and drawings of the Bear, a former Waysider regular—the waitresses wear red outfits, and earrings of little red and white "A's." On game day the restaurant serves elephant-shaped pancakes to anyone who dares show up in the visiting team's colors. Newspapers are sold from a row of machines out front and are quickly dissected into two piles—sports, and everything else. The air in the Waysider is thick and moist, like a kitchen on Thanksgiving Day. There's always a line for weekend brunch, and during the week at lunch hour the place is uncomfortably full. I shimmy sideways against the backs of chairs to get to my seat, where before me little plastic bowls of biscuits, chicken pot pie, turnip greens, black-eyed peas, and banana pudding are piled high—the southern equivalent of dim sum—next to glistening amber glasses of sweet tea. John Ed pulls up a chair and orders pot roast, mashed potatoes and gravy, green beans, and peach cobbler for dessert. His pals quickly glean his mood.

"Not doin' too good this week, John Ed?"

"Things are pretty slow when they're mad," he says. John Ed introduces me to the group and begins to plow through his lunch joylessly. A jowly, white-haired character named Charlie Horton sits to my right. He's friendly, and takes interest in the fact that I'm a reporter. Horton has been following Alabama football for fifty years, and it's his firm belief that the rest of the world doesn't appreciate how big a thing Alabama football actually is. Horton has a story, he says, that will help me understand, and asks if I want to hear it. I say I do, and Horton briefly stands and adjusts his chair to face me directly, like a man about to conduct an interrogation.

It was after the 1962 Alabama–Georgia Tech in Atlanta, when Bama lost 7-6. Horton was driving back from the game distraught, and desperate to get home, he'd propped his foot on the gas and was blazing toward Tuscaloosa. Just outside of Helena, he shot through a speed trap and was pulled over by a state trooper, who upon learning that Horton was coming from the game, picked up his radio and announced to his colleagues "I've got one." Within a few minutes, every cop in the county had pulled up to the scene, lights flashing, so that anyone passing by would've thought they'd just nabbed one of the FBI's most wanted. The cops ordered Horton out of the car and gathered around him.

"Tell us what happened at the ball game," one of them said.

Horton sticks a forkful of green beans in his mouth, leans back, and crosses his arms proudly, as though he's just convincingly won a very important argument. That's the story, he says. Do I understand it? he asks. I say I understand. Do I *get* it? I say I get it. Was I going to write it down? he asks. I write it down.

The main concern of the Hollyhand Sewing Circle is Andrew Zow's ankle. Zow is listed as questionable for Saturday's game because of the injury he suffered against Tennessee, a severe sprain. The coaches are holding out that he might play, but a quiet middle-aged man at the table says he went to practice yesterday and saw Zow limping badly on the sidelines, a wad of tape around his ankle.

"Ain't no way," he says, through a mouthful of blackeyed peas.

It turns out Shaun Alexander twisted his ankle late in the game, as well. He's not running at full speed and might not play either. John

Ed shakes his head ruefully; word of the injuries will be on the Internet by nightfall and on talk radio tomorrow, dimming enthusiasm for the game. If Alabama fans sense an impending disaster, he says, they'll stay home. John Ed takes a bite of his peach cobbler, closes his eyes, and chews slowly; his mind is working. He's looking for a way out.

After lunch, I follow John Ed back to his office. There are just eight calls on the answering machine, a dismal number given that it's now Thursday. The first message is from a Southern Miss player who needs a pair of tickets for friends and is hoping to connect with Tony on campus. He has to be at practice in an hour, he says; the message is half an hour old. John Ed hurriedly raises Tony by cell phone.

"Tell him you don't know a shittin' thing about the campus and to meet your ass wherever he can," John Ed barks, and hangs up.

The next message is from a woman with a thick French accent who wants a pair. John Ed scribbles her number on his yellow legal pad, with a quizzical look on his face. "I can honestly say she's not from these parts," he says, as much to himself as to me. There are a couple of calls from people who want to sell tickets, which John Ed quickly deletes. The phone rings again—a local mobile home dealer wants three.

"I can work three or I can work four," John Ed says. "I got 'em on the forty for forty apiece and on the fifty for fifty apiece. I can FedEx 'em or you can pick 'em up. Ever how you wanna do it. Hmmm mmm. Well, bring your ass in here!"

I've never heard John Ed sound so amenable. A week ago, having something that everyone wanted gave him a certain swagger; having a lot of something that no one wants has the inverse effect. John Ed slouches into his chair and lets out a long sigh of resignation. He stares at the phone. It doesn't make a sound.

"I don't understand. It's homecoming. There's no TV coverage. And the phone's not ringing," he says. "I tell you, when I'm hot, I'm hot, but when I'm cold, you better watch out because the roof is gonna cave in. I thought people were just mad as hell and that it would pick up Wednesday. I didn't see it coming and now it's too late." At first I think John Ed is narrating his life for my benefit, but I realize it's just a personal quirk. By vocalizing his predicament, he hopes to alter it. He stands up to pace again. "Oh, horse hockey," he says.

I'm beginning to develop an appreciation for John Ed's strange personal lexicon. If he doesn't like someone, that person is likely a "mullet-head," or else a "fruit loop." (Sometimes when his cell phone doesn't work, it too can qualify as a mullet-head.) Someone who is socially awkward is a "weird piece of cheese." John Ed is also fond of citing himself as an authority on a wide range of topics. The setup is always the same: "I made the statement one time that . . ." followed by a prediction that has proven abundantly true in the interim. *I made the statement one time that if Andrew Zow gets hurt and Tyler Watts has to replace him against a team like Tennessee, we're gonna lose the ball game . . .*

"I made the statement one time that if the phone isn't ringing, I'm in trouble," he announces to the walls. "And right now, I'm in trouble."

The phone rings. It's Tony; he made the sale to the Southern Miss football player. John Ed hangs up, and immediately the phone rings again. He quickly sells a pair, then another. John Ed's mood begins to brighten. He still has 150 tickets to Saturday's game, but if he can get the number down to around 100 by game day, he can try to sell what's left at the stadium to the walk-up crowd. It's his least favorite way of doing business: first, because it does nothing for his pregame social life; secondly, because the margins are never as good at the stadium, with dozens of people trying to get rid of tickets at the last minute; and thirdly, because it puts John Ed in the company of a shadier set of scalpers from which he prefers to distinguish himself. In John Ed's view, his customers pay a premium for dealing with him—a clean-cut guy with an office, an actual Alabama fan, no less, who knows good stuff when he sees it. Buying tickets from John Ed is the equivalent of going to a dealer who is also a user. At any rate, as quickly as the phone started ringing, it goes silent, and John Ed's mood quickly darkens again. He expected Alabama fans to sulk for a few days, but usually they perk up by Thursday; perhaps between the losses to Tennessee and La. Tech and the DuBose scandal, the fans are beginning to give up hope entirely.

"If there's not a good walk-up crowd tomorrow," he says, "I'm gonna get my clock cleaned."

I sense John Ed's mood deteriorating, so I clear out, next door to the Downtown Gallery, the framing and memorabilia shop. The Downtown Gallery is owned by a woman in her late-twenties named Sherrill Barnes who has blue eyes and blond hair and who scurries about her shop in running shoes, taking orders by phone, packing paintings for shipping, and dealing with a steady stream of walk-in customers. Sales of memorabilia this week have dropped off, as they have with tickets. Barnes instead busies herself with an unusual task: An angry wife took her revenge on her husband by bashing several thousand dollars' worth of his coveted Alabama prints. Barnes is now trying to extract the prints from the tattered frames without damaging them further.

I pass the time with a gallery tour of Barnes's collection of Daniel Moore prints. They have a strange power. Moore's paintings aren't technical masterpieces, but it hardly matters because their appeal isn't aesthetic so much as mnemonic. They're sort of visual madeleines that in a glance can cause entire autumn afternoons to flash before the eyes. When I look at *The Sack*, for example, I don't see the play from Moore's perspective—at field level, on the Alabama sideline—but from up high in the East Stand at Legion Field, beneath the upper deck, where I watched the game. I can smell the cologne on my uncle sitting next to me—a combination of lime and pepper—along with cigarettes, and the mouthwatering smell of Legion Field hot dogs. As the mental videotape scrolls forward, I see Cornelius Bennett break loose on Beuerlein's blind side, streak toward him as the crowd lurches to their feet in expectation and then—BAM!—Beuerlein is gored. Others clearly experience Moore's paintings the same way. On Fridays, when the fans are in town, you can go the Bryant Museum or the Downtown Gallery and find them standing gape-mouthed before the paintings, entranced. They aren't just looking at the paintings—they are at the games, all over again. The appeal of Moore's paintings is that they help overcome one of the most frustrating things about being a fan—the speed with which the joy of a win fades. Moore's paintings put some of that joy in the bank, for later use. It's also easy to get lost in a Moore painting because they're packed with cryptic references to Bama football lore. The clock in one painting reads 3:23, Bear Bryant's number of career wins. In another, the players behind the Bear wear the numbers 3 and 15; 315 was the number of the win against Auburn by which Bryant broke Amos Alonzo Stagg's career win record. In another, head coach Gene Stallings is on the sideline in the foreground while Mike DuBose—a defensive coach at the time—stands in the background with a golden aura around his head, like the Virgin Mary in a Renaissance fresco. The painting was done with the benefit of hindsight, after DuBose had been named head coach, and the halo was Moore's way of suggesting that even then DuBose had the holy stuff required to be an Alabama head coach. Sometimes, though, history intervened to change the significance of a Daniel Moore painting. After cornerback Antonio Langham's involvement with an agent got Alabama put on probation and resulted in the forfeit of nine games, Moore's depiction of his game-winning interception in the SEC championship against Florida was taken out of circulation by the artist who, at the behest of the university, destroyed his remaining stock. Even that painting of the haloed DuBose is coming in for a reinterpretation of sorts. I'm at a cocktail party at Sherrill's home when the painting comes up. Isn't it taking football a little far, I ask, to put the religious image of a halo over the head of Mike DuBose? "DuBose might'a had a halo on his head in that paintin'," a man says from beer-soaked repose on the sofa. "But he had horns on his head when he was fuckin' that secretary."

I move the Hawg to the Law Library lot early Friday morning, where there is a notable absence of mayhem. The lot is only two-thirds full. The RV-ers who do show up enter the lot at an unhurried, hangdog pace, with none of the usual reckless disregard for pedestrians. No one argues over parking spots or configurations. The lot attendant sits in a folding chair in the sun, calmly reading the *Crimson White* and waving everyone through, so that the new parking policy suddenly looks like the gratuitous bit of bureaucratic meddling the RV-ers had said it was all along. The fact that the policy now seems irrelevant has done nothing to placate Skipper and his gang—they're all parked downtown this week as well.

Late in the afternoon, as the sun is setting and a seemingly endless freight train clatters behind the lot, a man in a pickup truck drives slowly down the row of RVs where I've parked the Hawg. He seems to be looking for someone, or else lost. Over the next half hour, he drives by a half dozen times, always at a creep, before finally pulling to a stop beside a group of us who've gathered around a picnic table for a late-afternoon buffet. The man looks to be in his mid-sixties, with gray hair and an empty, haunted expression in his eyes, which are flat, like pewter.

"You all right?" someone asks.

The man shakes his head. He's an RV-er, he says, and last weekend, he and his wife parked in the Law Library lot for the Tennessee game. They were walking up the sidewalk along Bryant Drive toward the stadium when his wife fell and hit her head on the curb. She lost consciousness and on Tuesday, in the hospital, died from a blood clot in her brain. It's a Friday before a game, and not knowing what to do with himself, the man has taken to simply cruising the lot, perhaps on some vague hope of finding that the episode had been a dream and that his wife is sitting in a folding chair somewhere, sipping iced tea and waving a shaker.

The idea of losing a spouse to such a freak accident is too depressing to comprehend, only the RV-ers don't see it as a freak accident. For them, the cause is obvious, and there is a single undeniable culprit—the university bureaucrat who'd come up with the new parking policy. If the woman hadn't had to walk all the way from the Law Library lot, a roly-poly of a fan with a red beard and sunburned cheeks tells the group, the woman would still be alive. To this, everyone agrees. It's hard for me to see how the absence of the parking policy would've made any difference—the Law Library lot was still a long walk from Bryant-Denny—but apparently parking bureaucrats don't get the benefit of any doubt. They muck up the order of things, I suppose the thinking goes, like missionaries amid an indigenous people, bringing plagues and misfortune to a group that was getting along just fine without them.

By late Friday, John Ed has sold just thirteen tickets to the Southern Mississippi game—five less than he sold in the same period to the Alabama-Auburn game, still three weeks away. Tony is back from

Hattiesburg—the trip yielded just a handful of sales—and now John Ed sends him out to talk to "the brothers," the mostly black squadron of scalpers who sell around the stadium. They're late to the market, and there's a possibility they don't yet realize how bleak things are. John Ed hopes to unload some of his surplus at something close to the face value of $25; he expects that by kickoff, tickets might be going for as little as $10 apiece. There's another potential problem brewing—a bootlegging scalper has parked a van on University Boulevard and hung a sign on it that reads: TICKETS FOR SALE. This development presents John Ed with a choice. Fly-by-night scalpers of the sort that work out of vans are almost certainly operating illegally, without a business license or tax ID number. If John Ed thinks the guy might take a significant piece of his business, he might "send a visitor," as he puts it, by alerting the local revenue commissioner, a good buddy. On the other hand, if the man in the van doesn't realize how soft the market is, he might be willing to take a little product off John Ed's hands, helping John Ed to pare his losses. John Ed wants to sell tickets much more than he wants a pissing match with another broker, so he sends Tony to assess.

In the afternoon, a sullen, doe-eyed blond beauty comes into Need One Ticket, crying. John Ed drops a call to greet her.

"Girl, what's wrong with you?" he asks. He seems genuinely concerned. John Ed set the woman up with a friend of his, a former Alabama football star; the friend dumped her and took back the car he'd given her, all just a few days after the woman's mother had a nervous breakdown. The story comes out in delicate, wet little sobs, which John Ed tries to stifle with a hug. It's interesting to see what awakens John Ed's sympathies; it's hard for him to see being single in Tuscaloosa as a bad thing. On the other hand, not having a car there seems to strike him as beyond misery; it's almost impossible to get to the bars without your own set of wheels. So as the woman sits in a plastic chair weeping away, John Ed works the phones on her behalf. He has a regular customer who runs a local car dealership, and another friend who has an extra truck he doesn't drive very often. He calls both and in exchange for a little help, he dangles the prospect of an upgrade in their tickets to Saturday's game. By the end of the afternoon, John Ed has found the woman a car.

Tony arrives from his mission on University Boulevard—he's sold a handful of tickets to the man in the van. Things are looking up. John Ed rubs his hands together eagerly and picks up the phone. He's going to put some heat on that church group.

"We ain't settin' the woods on fire," he says. "But at least we're gettin some damn where."

There's a bonfire on the Quad in the evening, for homecoming. It's a spectacular sight, long orange curlicues of flame snapping against the black night sky, while on the steps of Gorgas Library, overlooking the ghostly mound that entombs the ashes from the old campus, the band plays exuberantly. Whenever a timber collapses on the fire, a cloud of embers swirls upward in a vortex, and the crowd surges backward slightly, before easing back toward the heat. There's a corollary between the bonfire and the mood of Alabama fans. To keep the passion burning, fans need fuel, in the form of wins, or at least the hope of wins. The crowd around the fire is subdued, surprisingly so for homecoming, because of the loss to Tennessee, but also out of a kind of exhaustion, as if the coaching scandal, the loss to Tech, the win at the Swamp, the loss at home to the Vols have cooled the fire. We're still fans, but the disappointments and controversies have had a muting effect, on homecoming, on ticket and memorabilia sales, on the turnout in the RV lot. Our allegiance isn't in doubt, but our enthusiasm is. We need more fuel.

There are at least two indefatigable fans out there whose moods seem never to wane: Chris and Paula Bice. They arrive late from South Carolina, with Larry, and I spend the next morning grilling out with them under the awning of the Hurricane in the Law Library lot. Game day coincides with the change from daylight savings time back to standard time: "Another hour to party," Chris cheerfully declares. The three of us walk together up Bryant Drive to the stadium before kickoff, on another sparkling day. The weather and the sight of Bryant-Denny seem to reinvigorate the fans: they're whooping and hollering and shouting "Roll Tide!" and "Rammer Jammer Yellow Hammer!" with the holy intensity of a few weeks back. On the way to the stadium Chris freezes, trancelike, at each souvenir stand we pass. He doesn't buy anything, not for the obvious reason that there is no room on his body for another piece of Alabama gear, but because he's saving up for a statue of an elephant he'd seen at the Downtown Gallery, next door to John Ed's office. We part at the stadium—they're up high in their usual seats, section U2 A, row 4, seats 1 and 2. I have a single in the end zone. Chris flips me a walkie-talkie so we can chat during the game.

It's not much of a game, though. Even without Zow and Alexander on the field, the Tide dominates. Freddy Milons, the tide flanker and a bottle rocket with cleats, hisses down the field returns a punt for a touchdown. The once-feeble Alabama defensive backfield manages an interception return for a touchdown. Tyler Watts, the freshman quarterback, performs not spectacularly, but ably, which is enough: The final score is a convincing 35-14. Even so, what's most interesting about the crowd's reaction to the win is the lack of it. Beating Southern Miss is so routine, so mundane, that it's almost beneath Alabama fans to acknowledge. A win over the Eagles is something a Tide fans feels only by its absence. But here it is, and with it, the understated beauty of things-as-they-should-be.

After the game, I set out to find John Ed. I've learned the trick to locating him is to ask bartenders if they've seen anyone who looks like Kenny Rogers; if they don't already know John Ed, the resemblance is striking enough that anyone who comes across him remembers having wondered, for a moment, if indeed it was Kenny Rogers. The bartender at the Houndstooth says she saw Kenny Rogers earlier, but that he'd left. I try the Copper Top, a bar downtown; it's the same story. Eventually I catch up with John Ed at 4th & 23rd , a downtown honky-tonk. He's leaning against the bar, a bottle of Coors Light in his hand, watching a blues band chug away with a thick, throaty sound that seems to summon some primal spirits from the bracken around the Black Warrior. John Ed went into Saturday with ninety-three tickets; he estimates he invested an average of $35 in each one. He sold half at a loss of $10 each, and the rest he took home, unsold—a total loss. Actually, John Ed hadn't sold the tickets at all; Tony had. On Friday night John Ed had simply resigned himself to the catastrophe that was and resolved to go about his usual pregame routine, which involves a lot of barbecue and not a few of those Coors Lights. His reasoning was poetically simple: "I'm a sports fan and I wanna go to the game."

John Ed takes a long slug from his can of Coors Light, and I try to engage him, but he seems distracted. His eyes bounce around the bar. He sees a beautiful belle who, he says, "really cranks my tractor," and another he deems "the baddest bitch in four counties." It's hard, though, to get a bead on John Ed's mood, partly, I imagine, because it's hard for John Ed to figure out his mood. He's lost a wheelbarrow full of money, and yet Alabama has won. In John Ed's mind, two very powerful emotions are at war. I suspect that on his emotional ledger, the deal is a wash, but over the next half hour, another Coors Light, the kicking blues band, and a roomful of pretty girls nudge John Ed back into the black.

"We took a pretty good bath," he says finally, with unexpected cheer. "After losing to Tennessee it's pretty much like the world crumbled. But hey, if I've done everything I can possibly do, I just move on."

With that, John Ed places his empty beer bottle on the bar. The band is pounding out a deep, raucous, soulful sound. A swirl of college students and hardcore football fans presses toward the bar amid a fragrant cloud of whiskey, smoke, beer, and perfume. We elbow our way through the crowd toward the door, which is tended by two hulking, pancake-fed Southern boys who seem none too pleased not to be at the bar themselves. They step aside to let us pass. Once outside in the clean, clear air of a Tuscaloosa night, John Ed turns toward the befuddled bouncers and the line of partyers waiting to get in. He raises his arms in the air, in a V.

"John Ed Belvin," he announces to the world, "has left the building!"

Chapter Twelve

LSU, SAEs, GDIs, and Pink Panty Pulldowns

NO MATTER HOW BAD THINGS GET, WE CAN USUALLY find someone for whom things are worse. This is true even of Mike DuBose. Whatever his problems, at least he isn't Gerry DiNardo.

DiNardo is the head coach of the LSU Tigers—Alabama's next opponent, and the loser of its previous six games. On Saturday, LSU lost at home to Ole Miss, 42-23. According to the *New Orleans Times-Picayune*, DiNardo left the field to a "hail of unprintable taunts and threats from beleaguered and bitter Tiger fans." He has managed to take one of LSU's chief assets—its throng of hell-raising Cajun fans—and to turn it on himself. Tiger fans are so disgusted with DiNardo and his team that they decide to stage an informal boycott of the Alabama-LSU game in Tuscaloosa. Early in the week, LSU officials let Alabama know that the school will be returning some three thousand tickets to Saturday's game. No one in Baton Rouge wants them.

John Ed gets word of the ticket return on Monday afternoon, tipped off by a source in the athletic department. Alabama officials plan to put the leftovers up for sale on Wednesday, giving John Ed exactly two days to sell everything he has, before the price collapses. At Need One Ticket, it's the crash of '29 all over again, with John Ed in a panic sale, working the phones, calling every mad fan and church group he can think of, with offers of package deals, group deals—whatever it takes to reduce his stock. His effort is not without a significant distraction: a reporter from the *Tuscaloosa News* calls to say she is doing an investigative piece about local "ticket scalpers" and wants to interview him.

"Ticket brokers," he growls and hangs up the phone.

It isn't until after the Southern Miss game that Alabama fans wake up to the realization that despite our woes, we are still very much in the hunt for the conference championship. If Alabama wins the rest of its games—LSU, Mississippi State, and Auburn—we win the SEC West, which means we will play the winner of the SEC East—probably Tennessee or Florida—in Atlanta in December. Even a single loss doesn't necessarily put us out of contention, provided Mississippi State loses as well. The fans of most other teams would hardly need to have it pointed out to them that they are contenders for their conference crowns, but the news seems to sneak up on Alabama fans, who seem incapable of knowing where they stand. Tide fans are never quite sure who they're being measured against. Each week Alabama faces two opponents: one on the field, the other in the sky—the sum talent of all those invincible Bear Bryant squads of the past. The first provides a relative measure of our talents, the latter, an empirical one. By the second standard, the season is already a bust. The loss to La. Tech means we are, in a sense, not in our own league. By the first measure, things aren't nearly so grim. The Tech loss, however embarrassing, was nonconference. Tennessee is our only conference loss, and it only served to put us in the company of the other conference leaders; all have lost one game as well. We are twelfth in the nation. With only three games to go, math intervenes to give us hope where our self-esteem will not. We stand a chance. To get to the conference championship in Atlanta, we just have to beat our opponents, not our ghosts.

On Monday night John Ed and I go together to the weekly meeting of the Tuscaloosa Quarterback Club. John Ed isn't a member, but using the power of his office, he has obtained two invitations on our behalf. Not that he's being altruistic. For a man desperate to unload Alabama-LSU tickets, there is no better place to be than a banquet room full of moneyed Tide fans. John Ed comes prepared. He carries a small stack of tickets bound by a rubber band in his breast pocket, and every few seconds reaches up to feel that they are still there, an anxious gesture that makes him look as though he's having heart trouble.

The meeting is in the banquet room at the Bryant Conference Center, a hotel with an indistinct, Radisson-like interior, but with a feature that makes it the ideal gathering ground for an Alabama booster club: it is adjacent to the Bear Bryant Museum. Meeting so close to this sacred shrine to Bama football gives the members of the Tuscaloosa Quarterback Club an air of entitlement. They are the true keepers of the flame, the gray-bearded orthodoxy. Hardly anyone in the room looks younger than fifty. These are men who knew the Bear personally, and who think that standing up during a game is bad form. These are the old-schoolers.

I sit down next to an elderly man who has retired to Tuscaloosa to be closer to the football. I strain to make small talk, but the man is lost in the contemplation of a corn pone on his bread plate. Who do you like at quarterback, Zow or Watts? I ask. He jerks to life.

"Watts," he says, without hesitating.

"Why?"

He raises his eyebrows. "Why do you think?"

What he means is that Watts is white. As disappointing as it is to hear this, I can hardly be surprised, especially after the incident in Florida at the Alachua campground. It's becoming clear that sports teams are blank screens on which fans project their worldviews—however benevolent or malicious—which means the Alabama of my mind has as little to do with the Alabama of his mind as I do with him. In the uncomfortable silence that follows his remark, I wonder: can enough bad people project enough bad ideas onto your mental screen to blur out your own beliefs and spoil it for you? At what point do you become complicit with bad people just by associating with them? It strikes me as a miniature version of the dilemma citizens face when their governments do terrible things. You can either renounce your citizenship on the spot—pick a new team, as it were—or else you can make as loud and as convincing a case as possible that your government is wrong and hope to persuade others to your side. For better or worse, most people choose the second option. Even during the Vietnam War, when a number of people believed strongly the U.S. was up to some horrific stuff, only a relative handful actually renounced their citizenships and took off for new lands. It's as though once we've joined a group, we're hardwired to stick with it, no matter how flawed the group turns out to be. Maybe that's because leaving something just creates the problem of figuring out where to go next. If I decide I don't like Alabama anymore because some of the fans are louts, am I supposed to start pulling for Auburn? What if their fans are louts? I could spend a lifetime bouncing from team to team, or from country to country, in search of the perfectly compatible group. Most people consider themselves lucky to find even a single person with whom they're compatible for life, and it seems that with groups, the bar is lower. We make allowances. We hang around, and hope our being there brings the averages up. At least with regard to Alabama, there is some reason for optimism. The old guy from Memphis hasn't said he likes Watts "because he's white"; he has said, "Why do you think?" Just enough of a hedge to suggest that he knows there is a chance—at the Tuscaloosa Quarterback Club, perhaps a slim chance—that I might be the sort of Alabama fan who finds such thinking repugnant. Maybe he senses that his worldview is on the wane.

"How about you?" the man says eventually.

"I like Zow."

"Why's that?"

"He's got a better arm."

The man puckers his lips contemplatively, as though I've proposed an entirely novel basis for evaluating a quarterback. He seems at pains to find fault with it, and takes another bite of his corn pone.

"When I say the words 'John Ed' do y'all know what I'm talking about?" The emcee is introducing guests from a raised dais up front. There is a loud groan, and perhaps a quarter of the men in the room say the word *tickets*, not with enthusiasm, but with a kind of world-weary dread. I know instantly they've done business with John Ed.

"Got any?" a man shouts from across the room.

"Yes I do," John Ed says cheerily, patting his breast pocket. He has the eager, slightly devious look of a liquor store owner at an AA meeting.

The evening's speaker is Danny Sheridan, the best-known odds maker in college sports, and the closest thing college football fans have to a Delphic oracle. His forecasts affect much more than simply fans' emotional preparation for the coming Saturday; according to Sheridan, 40 million Americans bet money on college sports. Each week during the college football season, by his estimation, some $5 billion is in play through betting, most of it illegal. Again according to Sheridan, Alabama leads the nation in per capita sports betting, with more bet on college football each week in the Heart of Dixie than in Las Vegas, where betting is legal. I have a hard time understanding why people would bet on their own teams, for the simple reason that betting on your own team puts your heart at odds with your wallet. If I take Alabama over Auburn by six, and we win by one, then Alabama has just beaten Auburn, and I've lost the bet. I can either feel happy while having lost money or feel despondent despite the fact that we've just beaten our fiercest rival by a hair. The first scenario is disturbing, the second simply impossible. Asking the gods to help your team beat both the competition and the spread seems like pushing one's luck.

Interestingly, the topic that gets Sheridan truly excited isn't wagering but Andrew Sorensen, the University of Alabama president. Sheridan denounces him as a "rank amateur." Sorensen's crime? Docking DuBose's salary and taking two years from the coach's contract. Sheridan's argument is that the move undermines confidence in

DuBose, which in the long run will hurt recruiting, which in turn will hurt the team, and ultimately Alabama fans. Sheridan's critique of Sorensen overlooks a small point—that it was DuBose who was sleeping with an athletic department secretary, not Sorensen—but there is a strange consistency to the argument, given Sheridan's job. He is the equivalent of a Wall Street analyst for college sports betting, and like most analysts covering multibillion-dollar industries, he wants less regulation and less oversight. University presidents and provosts with high-minded aspirations for improving graduation rates and disciplining liars only clutter the picture when it comes time to place bets. And anyway, to most gamblers, the fact that a college team is affiliated with a college is an irrelevant detail, like the color of a team's helmets. Thus it is possible for Sheridan to tell the room with a straight face, "Anytime you can name the head of a university before you can name the head coach, you've got a problem at that football program." Far from being offended—this sentiment, if expressed by a school booster, could result in that booster's formal disassociation from his school—the Tuscaloosa Quarterback Club seems titillated; there is applause, and an amen. If polled by secret ballot, probably 90 percent of them would agree with Sheridan's assessment, even if they didn't dare come out and say it themselves. When he finishes, he receives a torrent of applause.

After the meeting John Ed loafs around the hotel lobby, hoping to make a few deals, and I loaf with him. And we loaf. Not only will no one buy tickets from John Ed, they won't even look him in the eye. John Ed rocks back and forth on his heels, anxiously feels his breast pocket for his tickets, and smiles politely at those members he recognizes—but hardly anyone responds. He gets more perturbed with each snub, until finally he says, "Let's go."

"Didn't nobody say no damn thing," he explains to me the in the parking lot, " 'cause, hell, half of 'em have had dealings with me and don't anybody want nobody to know about it." The thinking is that any member in good standing of the Tuscaloosa Quarterback Club should be a paying member of Tide Pride, the booster program, and thus have no need for a scalper's services. John Ed knows exactly who the cheapskates are and that makes him radioactive. They'll buy tickets from him in private, but there is something blasphemous about a high priest of Tide football buying his pieces of the True Cross on the gray market.

John Ed's annoyance doesn't last long. Doing the personal calculus, he seems to conclude that he'd rather have a banquet hall full of customers than of new friends. "I'm pretty much a don't-give-a-rip kind of person," he says, reassuring himself. We climb into his 4Runner; John Ed revs the engine and screeches out of the lot. We're off to Innisfree for a drink.

* * *

Midweek I get an interesting lead. A wealthy Mobile developer flies a jet to Tuscaloosa for every game, I'm told, and there's only one thing he's more obsessed about than Alabama football, and that's getting home to Mobile after the game in less than an hour. Besides being a somewhat bizarre fixation, it's an ambitious one. Mobile is nearly four hours by car from Tuscaloosa. Even with a jet, getting there in an hour is no easy order; on game day it can take that long to get from Bryant-Denny to the Tuscaloosa airport, for all the traffic. So the developer has a strange ritual. With two minutes to go, he and his party leave their seats in the Ivory Club—a tony section for donors adjacent to the President's Box—and walk down the aisles to a portal in the West Stands. When the clock hits 00:00, and not before, they sprint from the stadium to a chauffeured van parked out back. The van ferries them through the still-empty streets of Tuscaloosa to the airport, where the jet awaits with engines running. The plane takes off immediately and, barring bad weather, touches down in Mobile less than forty-five minutes later. The developer is so obsessive about this exercise that he is said to blacklist for perpetuity any guest who slows his exit from the stadium long enough to get the van caught in postgame traffic.

I call the developer, and he invites me to join him in the Ivory Club if I want to watch his escape—on two conditions. The first is that I not use his name—he's Jewish and an active supporter of Israeli causes, and doesn't want attention drawn to himself, he says. The second is that I show up at his box seat before the two-minute mark in the fourth. That's when he begins his exit, he says; he won't wait. I tell him I'll be there if the game isn't too close.

* * *

One of the persistent problems facing students at the University of Alabama is figuring out how to smuggle booze into the stadium on game day. They are frisked at the gate and, once inside, monitored by campus police. Getting busted means being thrown out and possibly suspended—a minor threat when weighed against the punishment of missing the final quarters of a close game. But even so, there is something about the problem of smuggling booze that miraculously imbues the most dim-witted fraternity yahoo with the design genius of a NASA engineer. The most popular solution is to rig booze-filled collapsible plastic bladders beneath the clothes. Local outdoor stores sell them to campers and survivalists—besides being useful on game day, they're apparently handy for the Armageddon. Usually the bladders are placed in the seat of the pants or else around the torso—even beneath the probing fingers of a gate attendant, they feel like genuine sophomore beer bellies. But the safest technique of all is to hide the things inside a date's brassiere, though that poses another risk—getting your date arrested. And yet given the alternative—a football game with no booze—there are plenty in the southeast corner of the end zone who are willing to try. Whiskey is the drink of choice—it mixes well with Coke, if it's mixed at all. Occasionally sorority girls will mix up a batch of drinks for themselves—a mixture of vodka, gin, and pink lemonade called a Pink Panty Pulldown. If you train your binoculars on the student section in the first quarter, you can see them reaching into their necklines for their stash.

The chief nemesis of these students is a tall, clean-cut, and soldierly looking university cop known to everyone on campus and in town simply as Sarge. Typically he can be found during a game on the walkway that bisects the student section behind the end zone, beneath the fraternity seating, a vantage point that gives him a nifty view of much of the game-time mixology going on in Bryant-Denny. His other job is ejecting students who throw their drink cups into the air after touchdowns, a tradition that began a few years back during a big night game and that was banned when a plastic cup full of soda, booze, and ice landed on the head of a dean down below, knocking her out cold. Sarge is an Alabama fan, and would much prefer to watch the game than arrest people, but he does his duty solemnly and politely, and is said to become frustrated and cantankerous only on those occasions when he is compelled to arrest someone during a crucial time in the game.

Beyond football and keeping the peace, Sarge's real passion is a video trivia game at the Houndstooth in which players in bars all around the country compete against each other via satellite. Sarge can be found at the bar on most weeknights with a game console in his hands, staring at the projection TV that broadcasts the questions with the same intimidating look of concentration he wears when scanning the stands for boozers. Sarge recently finished reading the entire works of Shakespeare to boost his score; his goal is to be on *Jeopardy*.

I have a hunch that from his vantage point in the student section, Sarge has a bead on the most ardent student fans. So on Thursday night I stop into the Houndstooth to look for him. He's at the bar, staring trancelike at the projection TV, entering his answers rapid-fire with the click of a thumb. He has the high score against a national pool of dozens. Getting answers from Sarge while he's engaged in a round of trivia is next to impossible, but after a few attempts, I learn that the best way to get a response is to ask a question in trivia game format:

"Sarge—who is the most football-obsessed student in Tuscaloosa?"

"Chpglss."

"What?"

"Chip Glass!"

Ding ding ding!

Chip Glass is happy to hear from me when I say I'm referred by Sarge—"The smartest man I've ever met in my life," he says—and happier still to hear that I want to learn about what he cheerfully calls his "disease." We make a plan to meet at the Houndstooth on Friday evening—I'm to keep an eye out for someone who looks "like Norm from *Cheers*," he tells me, a slight complication given that on most nights at the Houndstooth, half the patrons fit that description. On Friday evening I show up, take a table outside, and begin my vigil. Tuscaloosa is filling up again. RVs choke University Boulevard with diesel exhaust as they roar by on the way to the Law Library lot, and the astringent smell of lighter fluid and charcoal wafts from an RV lot behind the Strip. Students are mothing around the entrances to bars. A limousine pulls up in front of the Houndstooth and disgorges a pack of gold-and-purple-clad LSU fans, who are stumbling and loud, and have the look of a well-fed clown troupe. The LSU fans may not be traveling in their usual numbers, but given that one mad Cajun makes the noise of three Alabama fans, it hardly matters. To my surprise, no one at the Houndstooth seems to mind them, at least not overtly. An 0 and 6 run has gained LSU fans an allotment of charity not usually granted visitors. Or so I think. Glass shows up and shoots the LSU fans a reproachful look.

"I hate these motherfuckers more than Satan," he says before I even have a chance to introduce myself.

Glass is a stocky figure with blue eyes and close-cropped blond hair. He is wearing a red sweatshirt with BAMA on the front in white and looks less like Norm from *Cheers* than a slightly underweight Chris Farley. He seems genuinely flattered to be Sarge's nominee for the most psychotic student fan and takes particular relish in explaining football's power over him. He pukes before games, he says, from nerves. Alabama football frequently drives him to tears. (He bawled in his car for an hour after Alabama went down to La. Tech, overwhelmed with despair; and he bawled after Alabama beat Florida, overwhelmed with joy.) He has lost two jobs because of Alabama football, the first a gig at the local Cracker Barrel—he missed his shift when a game went long—the second at an Applebee's, when he told his boss he was out of town and was subsequently spotted in the stands by a coworker. ("One of the fuckin' employees saw me and fuckin' turned me in," he says.) Glass is both superstitious and boastful of his superstitions for what they say about his dedication to the Tide. He tells me with pride that he has discovered that electrical sockets are bad luck. When he watches games at home, he avoids touching anything that is plugged in. He once busted his lip hugging a fellow fan at an Alabama-Tennessee game that the Tide pulled out in the final moments, and now considers bodily injury a good omen. Glass tells me he frequently has premonitions. "A friend called me before the Tennessee game and said, 'Win or lose?' and I said 'Lose,' " he says, shrugging and shaking his head humbly, as if psychic powers are a burdensome fact of his life. It occurs to me that anyone overhearing will easily conclude that Glass is discussing not football but the reasons for his commitment to Bryce, the local mental hospital.

Glass got his religion the regular way: it was passed down through his family, but his beliefs were refined by time spent in the equivalent of a Crimson Tide madrasa. Glass worked one summer at the Bear Bryant Museum, cataloging videos of the man. Bryant died before Glass was born, so Glass had to rely on that old footage to inform his admiration of the late coach. Glass says he cries whenever he sees Bryant on the JumboTron.

Remarkably, for all his zeal, Glass says he isn't going to the LSU game. A combination of money woes and ghostly inklings are keeping him away, he says; he fears his presence might be bad luck. I don't totally buy it, at least not the part about the inklings. It seems impossible that a fan could like his team so much that he won't watch it. I figure money has more to do with it, and I have an idea. I can buy a pair of tickets from John Ed in the evening—he's desperate to sell anyway—and hand them off to Glass before kickoff, my treat. In return, I could get Glass to agree to let me debrief him immediately afterward about his emotional state. I might learn something. The deal probably crosses some ethical boundaries, like buying a bag of dope for a junkie to see how he behaves when stoned, but I have an ulterior motive: the fan in me can't bear to think of someone like Glass screaming his head off at a television at home on a crucial third-down play when the team—and I—need him in the stands.

Glass is torn. On one hand, it's free tickets; on the other, certain vomiting, possible panic attacks, crying in public, and the potential repercussions of not heeding those inklings. He's mulling it over when the group of LSU fans erupt in naughty snickers, get up together from their table, and scurry out of the bar and into their limousine. Moments later a red-faced college kid in a Bama T-shirt runs out of the Houndstooth.

"Where'd they go?" he shouts.

"They just drove off," I say. "Why?"

"One of 'em just wrote 'Bear Bryant was a queer' on our bathroom wall!"

Glass stands up, teeth clenched, eyes on fire, and looks vainly in the distance. The limo has disappeared into traffic. Glass looks as though he might spontaneously combust, but to my surprise, he exhales, collects himself, and calmly sits down. "Yeah . . . *right*," he says with an uneasy smile. The notion is so preposterous that he isn't going to give it the dignity of a retort. Glass tells me he'll take the tickets.

We make a plan to meet a half hour before kickoff at the large engraved granite wall near the main entrance of the stadium, next to the "B" in "Bryant-Denny."

In the evening I meet John Ed at 4th & 23rd, where, Coors Light in hand, he's on the prowl selling tickets at face value to LSU fans too drunk to know or care that the ticket market is flooded. I can tell from his expression—a blinding permagrin—that he's having success. By the time the LSU fans figure out that they can get into the stadium for twenty bucks less than John Ed has charged them, he'll be in his seat watching warm-ups, wiping the tasty remnants of an Archibald's barbecue sandwich from the corners of his mouth. I'm low on cash, but John Ed agrees to advance me the tickets. "I'll remind you tomorrow, don't worry," I tell him, glancing accusatorily at his Coors Light. The smile disappears from John Ed's face.

"Don't worry," he says gravely. "I'll remember."

* * *

I'm asleep in the Hawg in the Law Library lot the next morning at 7:45 A.M. when my cell phone rings. It's Glass. He wants to know if we're still on. His anxiety over going to the game has been replaced by anxiety that he won't be able to get in. I reassure him and tell him that I'll see him at the "B" in "Bryant," then hang up. I give a few cranks to the plastic stick on the Hawg's metal Venetian blinds, in a vain attempt to shut out the sun. A few minutes later horns playing "Yea Alabama!" break over the early morning quiet of Tuscaloosa, and a few minutes after that there is a knock on my door: Chris, Paula, and Larry with an offering of freshly warmed Tater Tots. I get up and put on the coffee. It's game day.

I spend the rest of the morning wandering from pregame buffet to buffet in the RV lot, and eventually end up at Bobby and Bobbie's, Jerral Johnson's friends. Johnson isn't here—he's off chickening for the weekend. I'm nibbling on potato chips when I strike up a conversation with a willowy-figured man with perfectly combed white hair and a beeper on his belt, like a doctor. He introduces himself as Don Cole, and says he's from outside Nashville, and that he's retired military, from the Air Force. He got into Alabama football while stationed here during the early 1970s, and became a bit obsessed. I gesture toward his beeper and ask him if he's on call for work. Not for work, exactly, Cole says. Eventually, it comes out. Cole is awaiting a heart transplant. His own heart is functioning at around 40 percent, he says, and when his hospital in Nashville harvests a heart that might match, they'll page him. After that, he can expect to go straight into surgery. Cole is wearing the pager now out of habit more than actual need. If he leaves a two-hour radius of the hospital, he says, he's automatically bumped from the list. We're currently about three and a half hours from Nashville, and Cole says he plans to watch the game and to take his time getting back afterward. Not only that, but so far he's made four games this year, and plans to make two or three more, none of which take place within a two-hour radius of his hospital in Tennessee. As Cole speaks, I realize he must be the Heart Guy Skipper spoke of earlier in the season. Startlingly enough, Skipper wasn't pulling my leg after all.

I put the obvious question to Cole. How can he risk missing a lifesaving heart transplant for a football game?

"It's what I always say," he tells me. "If I can't go to Alabama football games, what's the point in living?"

* * *

For the first time in weeks—ominously, since the La. Tech game—I sense an easy confidence in the crowd. I can't possibly list the metrics for gauging such a thing, but you can tell, the way you can tell a friend's mood by a quick look at his face. Zow is still hurt and Alexander is iffy, but even with the freshman Watts starting at quarterback, LSU isn't a credible threat. To go 0 and 6 you have to be both bad and unlucky, a combination that bodes well for Tide fans. And anyway, as any honest fan from either side would tell you, Alabama has LSU's number. In my lifetime, we've never lost in Baton Rouge. The Tigers have picked off a few wins in Birmingham over the years, but not when having seasons like this one. All Alabama has to do is show up, play the team on the field and not get distracted by the one above, in the heavens.

An hour before kickoff, I take off to meet Glass, through the crowd on Bryant Drive, past souvenir stands overflowing with shakers and piles of freshly folded cotton T-shirts. Just across the street from the stadium, there's an old cemetery with graves dating back to the 1800s. In a corner closest to Bryant-Denny, the grave of a departed Alabama fan has been adorned with a red floral "A," which leans to one side on a spindly metal tripod, casting an asymmetrical shadow on the next grave over. In Tuscaloosa on game day, even the dead wear red. Across the street, the ticket sellers have gathered on the concrete apron in front of the stadium. They're waving their extras in the air like folding paper fans. Somewhere, John Ed is gloating: tickets are going for ten bucks.

When I get to the "B" in "Bryant," Glass is nowhere to be seen. But I have company—a bearded creature whose belly hangs over his waistband and whose veiny eyeballs seem to roll backward in his head like bottom-heavy Weeble Wobbles. He too is meeting a friend at the "B" in "Bryant," and until his friend shows up, he says, he's "scopin' 'tang." Sorority Row is just a block away; on any other day, a man like this couldn't get within a mile of the place without getting arrested and sent off to jail as a sex offender. Today he's exchanging smiles and "Roll Tide's!" with a stream of women who look like they're on their way to the Miss Alabama pageant. All in all, it's a startling testament to the aphrodisiac power of college football.

When Glass finally shows up, he's with his wife and wearing a look of icy terror, like a man on the way to the gallows. It's the inklings, he says. For a few moments it seems he might bail, and simply go home to watch the game on TV. And yet: the brassy strains of the Million Dollar Band cascade over the stadium rim; shouts of "Roll Tide!" spew out of the crowd like bottle rockets. A cloud of excitement seems to hover over Bryant-Denny like a head of foam on a freshly poured beer. And then there's weather: clear skies, sixty-five degrees—the first thrilling nip of autumn in the air. This isn't the sort of vibe a fan turns his back on. With a little persuading from me and his wife, Glass takes the tickets. We agree to meet at the Houndstooth afterward for the debriefing, and off he goes, trepidatiously, his wife tugging at his arm.

The student section is already redolent with the aroma of spilled whiskey when I arrive. Sarge is there, staring expressionless at the fraternity section. A student in red face paint and a cape—SuperBama—is sprinting back and forth in front of Sarge, arms extended, howling madly, and Sarge seems not to notice. I sit with the SAEs—the Sigma Alpha Epsilons—who come strolling up the aisles at a leisurely pace with their dates, mostly KDs, bare shouldered, in hip-hugging skirts and teetering on high heels. A pledge has been assigned to hold a poster board bearing a purple dot over his head for the entire first quarter, to help the SAEs locate each other in the crowd. Down below, in the corner, are the GDIs—the "goddamned independents," as those not affiliated with any fraternity or sorority are called. They are distinguished by their red dress—the fraternity kids wear white oxfords and khakis, to a man; the women, pastels and pink and purple floral prints—and by the fact that they are in their seats long before kickoff. Students in the Greek system arrive late from their pregame parties. In the first quarter the student section takes on the feeling of a lunchroom on the first day of school, with women waving at each other and exchanging hugs. The men greet each other with hearty high fives and secret handshakes. From the darting eyes and the furtive whispers, it seems that few people in the fraternity section are dating the person they're most interested in. As mating rituals go, it seems gratuitously chaotic.

Soon, though, all eyes turn to the field. LSU is driving. The chatter dies and gives way to cries for the defense to get in the game. Midway through the first quarter, LSU scores, on a fifteen-yard pass. The transformation in the student section is profound. The social chatter dies away; talking about anything but football now would be a breach of etiquette. Alabama's next drive is a series of inexorable sorties deeper and deeper into LSU territory—a quick out to Milons, a run up the middle by Alexander, a scramble by Watts—until, ten minutes and twenty plays later, Alabama is at LSU's one-yard line on a third down. Watts gives to Alexander and he's flattened. It's fourth down. Alabama comes to the line with the obvious play, Alexander over Samuels on the left side, and there's nothing LSU's defense can do. They're too tired. Alexander blows through for the touchdown. Near the half, Alabama adds a field goal, to lead 10-7. The cocktail party resumes.

In the third quarter, we see the LSU that has gone winless in six tries. Josh Booty, their quarterback, throws two interceptions, and the LSU defense, worn to a nub from that second-quarter drive, can do nothing to slow Alexander and Watts. With a minute to go, Alabama is up 23-7 and DuBose feels confident enough to put Zow in the game. Zow's ankle is covered in so much tape that it doesn't look sprained so much as reattached. But I'm happy to see him and I cheer as loudly as anyone, the image of that codger at the Tuscaloosa Quarterback Club flitting through my mind. Zow takes a snap from the shotgun. It's a screen to the left. An LSU player bats the ball in the air . . . and catches it. Three hundred pounds in gold and blue lope ecstatically down the field, with only the hobbled Zow in chase. *Blam*—Zow is walloped from the side and smeared into the sod. The lineman plods on for an LSU touchdown.

The third quarter ends, and I have to make a decision about meeting that real estate developer with obsessive exiting disorder. Alabama still leads 23-14. I've had my fill of drunk college students (entertaining as they are), so I figure, why not? It will take me half the quarter to get from the student section to the Ivory Club high in the West Stand, so I strike out. I'm on the track at field level when Watts, back in, heaves a wild pass and LSU intercepts. In short order, LSU kicks a field goal. They're within six. Alabama gets the ball back and begins another drive. I take the elevator up to the Ivory Club, a section of armchair seats with glass walls on either side to keep out the rabble, and when I emerge Alabama has moved the ball to the ten-yard line. We can put it away with an easy twenty-seven-yard field goal, with just over two minutes to go. I find the developer and his wife—they're in their sixties, with white hair and matching red jackets, and though gracious, they seem unaware of what's happening around us. They're standing up when Alabama kicks—the ball tumbles right, no good.

"Let's go," he shouts. A row of people stands to let us pass.

The next thing I know, I'm at the end of a line of six people, scraping knees as we shimmy down the aisles of the President's Box, the only way out of the Ivory Club that doesn't take us beneath the stadium and out of view of the game. Alabama leads by six but LSU has the ball. I look up. LSU is at their own forty-five-yard line now, with a minute forty-five to go. We take a right and start down the steps. The crowd groans—flag down; offsides defense. The developer continues down the steps, through the crowd, which is now spilling into the aisles. I look up again. Booty is rolling right. He lofts a pass that seems to hover in the air like a blimp—it's caught. We stop briefly at a portal halfway down the stadium, halted by the presence of an oversized Alabama fan in the aisle who is screaming obscenities at the referee. The developer forges an alternate route, down the aisle parallel to the forty. LSU is now at the Alabama twelve, first down. We continue down the steps. There are twenty-one seconds left. Someone has called time out.

We use the break to scurry to track level, in perfect position to make a run for the van, but in the worst possible position to see what's happening on the field. The helmets of the LSU players obscure my view. If LSU throws they will have two, possibly three tries at the end zone; a score ties, and an extra point wins. The teams jog onto the field. I stand on my tiptoes. It's terrifically loud, that same plaintive caterwauling screech I heard in the final minutes of the Tech game, not a cheer but a desperate cry. I think briefly of Glass—I'm glad he's here, adding some increment of a decibel to noise level; that is, if he's not hunched over puking on his sneakers.

Booty takes the snap and rolls right. A player is open in the end zone, but Booty runs. Yes, he's running for it. Three Alabama defenders stand in front of him, and Booty leaps at the four, so that he's up in the air, twisting, headfirst, like a dolphin. *Wham! Wham!* Again, *WHAM!* He helicopters sideways and drops to the ground—short of the goal. There are ten seconds to go and the clock is moving. LSU is in disarray. I look for the developer. He is sprinting for the van, his commandos in tow. I look back at the field. The referee is waving his arms in the air—*an injury time out??* That would give LSU another play—

"C'MON!" the developer shouts.

Instinctively I follow.

"Hey wait—" I call. *"It's not over!"*

We run through the gate, out of the stadium toward a white van with its doors open. Everyone piles in. The doors shut, and before anyone can even utter goodbye, the van pulls away.

"It's *not over*!!!"

I'm standing outside the stadium, alone. I try to run back in, but a cop turns me away. The only humans in sight are a couple of network PA's smoking cigarettes outside the television production trailer behind the press box. The crowd noise is strange and inconclusive—smatterings of applause more like a tennis match than postgame jubilation. Bits of a pom-pom float down from above. The ramps are still empty. I begin to panic. I've been separated from the herd.

It takes me the better part of half an hour to learn what has happened, and even after being told—by a wiry hyped-up Bama fan with a horseshoe mustache and too much energy to go into much detail—I won't fully understand until I watch the video later on. Booty falls short of the goal line and LSU has no more time outs. The clock winds toward zero; only an official waves his hands in the air to stop the clock—an injury time out. One of the Alabama players who made the play, Marvin Constant, is writhing on the ground, his knee a distended mess. The clock, though, keeps moving, to zero. While the Alabama trainers work on Constant, the referees confer: should they put time on the clock and give LSU another shot at the end zone, or is it over? The fans and players stand there confused, waiting for a ruling, until finally, the refs call the game, a controversial decision, perhaps, but probably a good one. You can't very well give the offense a free shot simply because the defender who made the play exploded his knee in the process. And in fact that is what happened. Marvin Constant will have several surgeries to repair his knee, but they won't take. He will never play football again.

So why go to the trouble of having season tickets, flying in a jet, and the rest of it, if you aren't going to stick around for the end of the game? It makes no sense to me. We had seen the end in technical terms, but we hadn't *felt* it, which to me has always been the point. Maybe I'd been hanging out with the RV-ers too long, but what were quotidian worries like postgame traffic against the ecstasy of a last-second win? In fact, that's the whole point of the RV corps in the first place—to situate yourself close enough to the source of the emotional high of the game so that "real life" can't intervene. The crowd is as much a part of that experience as the score. I have to remind myself that before going to ten games in a row and camping out in stadium parking lots, I wouldn't have thought twice about skedaddling a few minutes early to beat the stadium traffic. I was no less of a fan then, just a fan who thought football was a part of his life, as opposed to his entire life. Now, perspective pleasantly lost, I get a glimpse of how Tony Brandino had the idea to go to five hundred games in a row, and of that feeling Frances described at the Arkansas game, of getting sick at the mere thought of watching a game alone. The more I'm around the game, the more I want to be around it. I'd much rather spend the hour after a Bama game in a folding chair out back of the Hawg than streaking through the skies in a Gulfstream IV. If this constitutes going native, so be it.

I'm quickly reminded that this is not the case for everyone when I go to the Houndstooth to look for Glass. The place is thronged with celebrating fans, but Glass is nowhere to be found. It will take me three days to realize that Glass isn't lost in the crowd, he's avoiding me. I leave several messages for him at home; he doesn't call back. I can only guess that he feels toward me as I feel toward the developer; we've each allowed someone to persuade us into ignoring our hunches and breaking our game-day routines. I should've stayed in my seat in the student section, and Glass should've stayed at home where a man can blow chunks with a modicum of privacy. Going to a game with 83,000 people may be a group experience, but it's one each fan wants to navigate in his own way. Glass and the developer prefer a kind of privacy. They don't depend on a crowd to reinforce it or to make it seem real. The RV-ers represent the other extreme; they feel lost and panicky without their fellow fans. I'd started in the former camp; I'm now in the latter.

This reality is made all the more clear to me on Sunday morning, when I wake up to the sounds of diesels rattling around me. I jump out of my sleeping bag and nervously glance outside my windows, fearing I might be alone. I'm relieved to see RVs on either side of me, blocking out the sun and polluting the air with their thrumming generators. I look at the clock—it's 8:30 A.M.. I put on some coffee and get dressed, and prepare to visit the Bices, still vibrating with the energy of the day before, like a plucked string. Almost simultaneously, the motor homes on either side of me pull away, to reveal that the lot is completely empty, save a single motor home in the back corner with a man on his back underneath. It's broken down. The only thing more depressing than leaving the camaraderie of the lot is watching all your pals leave you behind; you want to pull out early and hit the road before having to confront the emotional and physical desolation of a big tarmac, empty save a few sad piles of garbage. Panicking, I turn off the coffee, toss the metal pot in the sink, and scramble into the driver's seat. The Hawg shudders to life, and creaks and rattles as I pull onto Bryant Drive. I don't know where I'm going exactly, just out of the lot, slightly traumatized, but a little wiser: so *this* is why everyone always leaves so early. I drive to the only place where at this hour on a Sunday morning I think I can locate a concentration of Alabama fans—the Waysider. I'll have a coffee, read the sports pages; maybe even have the pancakes shaped like elephants.

Chapter Thirteen

The Era of Crowds

IN 1895 A FRENCHMAN NAMED GUSTAVE LE BON PUBLISHED one of the first attempts by a modern psychologist to explain the mentality of crowds—*The Crowd: A Study of the Popular Mind.* Le Bon was interested not just in physical crowds—that is, crowds of people actually gathered in the same place—but also in what he called "psychological crowds," groups of people who were in the same frame of mind, regardless of their location. A psychological crowd could be as small as a few people, or in the event of some great national event, millions, so long as they were thinking simultaneously about the same thing. Le Bon theorized that all psychological crowds shared a common characteristic that, with a self-assured flourish, he dubbed the "psychological law of the mental unity of crowds": "Whoever be the individuals that compose a psychological crowd, however like or unlike their mode of life, their occupations, their character, their intelligence," he wrote, "the fact that they have been transformed into a crowd puts them in possession of a sort of collective mind which makes them feel, think, and act in a manner quite different from that in which each individual would feel, think, and act were he in a state of isolation." Such a crowd, he continued, is a "provisional *being* formed of heterogeneous elements, which for a moment are combined, exactly as the cells which constitute a living body form by their reunion a new being, which displays characteristics very different from those possessed by each of the cells singly."

Le Bon was writing during the throes of the industrial revolution, when crowds of workers were mobilizing across Europe and seemed to be gaining momentum against their capitalist bosses. Crowds were ascendant, so much so that Le Bon predicted the coming age would be known as the "ERA OF CROWDS," all caps.

But even Gustave Le Bon would probably be surprised at how accurate his prediction has turned out to be a century later, in the information age. The first ingredient necessary for the formation of a psychological crowd, after all, is information—a crowd needs to know what it's mobilizing for or against, where it's gathering, and to what end. When Le Bon was writing, information was passed by word of mouth and in newspapers. There was a lethargy to the formation of psychological crowds that anyone living in the information age could scarcely imagine. Crowds fizzled because the impetus to form them burned itself out before word could spread to enough people to join up. With telephones, radio, television, and the Internet, that seldom happens now. Technology is fuel on the fire of psychological crowds. If something happens to get excited about, millions of people can readily get excited about it. Free of the old hurdles to their creation, psychological crowds—organized around religion, politics, lifestyles, hobbies, and of course sports—are flourishing. They form in a moment's notice: when Kennedy was shot or the first plane flew into the World Trade Center, vast global psychological crowds instantly convened in front of televisions and on telephones and shared in the surreal emotional trauma of those events in real time. Psychological crowds are no longer even provisional, as Le Bon believed. They're constant. Fans hoping to join the psychological crowd that forms around Alabama football, for example, once had to show up at the stadium to take part. Now—with Finebaum on the radio for four hours every day, with the local news, ESPN *SportsCenter*, and the Classic Sports network playing reruns of old games, with a half-dozen obsessively monitored Internet sites like Tiderinsider.com, Bamamag.com, and BamaOnline.com—the psychological crowd of Alabama fans is *always meeting*. Fans can come and go as they please—or just *never leave*. Indeed for people who are predisposed to join crowds—constant and easy access to the crowd can become a problem. As it did with pornography, auctions, and stock trading, the Internet has made indulging in sports—in psychological crowds of any kind—almost too easy. Sports junkies have the option of becoming like those lab rats who were free to administer themselves doses of cocaine by pressing on bars in their cages; with no external brakes on their pleasure, they hit the bar over and over again until they were comatose. If it feels so good, why stop?

However pervasive crowds are, however predisposed we are to form them, however much they define the age, they tend not to enjoy very good reputations. Historians, psychologists, sociologists, and political scientists who study them tend to view crowds as frightening, depraved, even demonic. The widely held belief is that while individuals can be intelligent, reasoning, and sociable, crowds are dumb, instinctive, and animal-like. Freud disparaged crowds as neurotic on the grounds that, like neurotics, crowds "demand illusions, and in fact can't live without them" and "are guided not by ordinary objective reality but psychological reality." Regretfully, Freud is right at least on the latter point. Try as I might, it's impossible for me to admit that I like Alabama "just because," and not due to an objective reality that establishes Alabama as more worthy of my affection than Tennessee or Auburn. (As I write this, a part of my psyche is battling for control of my fingertips and screaming out *"Oh, yes we are!"*) But why? my rational mind asks. Because we cheat less? (Doubtful.) Because we have better colors? (Absolutely, but if tomorrow we changed to mauve I'd reluctantly go along.) Because we're better than they are? (Some years yes, some years no; the historical tally is still being counted.) Instead I chose Alabama the way a baby bird chooses its mother: it was the first thing I saw. I liked the feeling of belonging to it. The imprinting was complete, and here I am. Maybe Freud wasn't so far off when he wrote that the initial connection of an individual with a group "fits very well with the Oedipus complex."

The general attitude of scholars toward crowds was perhaps most efficiently summed up by a man named George McDougall, author of a 1920 book called *The Group Mind.* Crowds, McDougall wrote, are "excessively emotional, impulsive, violent, fickle, inconsistent, irresolute and extreme in action, displaying only the coarser emotions and the less refined sentiments; extremely suggestible, careless in deliberation, hasty in judgment, incapable of any but the simpler and imperfect forms of reasoning; easily swayed and led, lacking in self-consciousness, devoid of self-respect and of a sense of responsibility." McDougall was just getting warmed up. A crowd's behavior, he coughed, "is like that of an unruly child or an untutored passionate savage in a strange situation, rather than like that of its average member; and in the worst cases it is like a wild beast, rather than like that of human beings."

It's hard to recognize the modern sports crowd in McDougall's description. Crowds have become more mature and self-knowing, thanks in part to the same technology that has been fueling their formation. Video footage of riots and stampedes at European football events has wised up the public about the potentially deadly consequences of a crowd gone wild. No one going to a modern sporting event these days is ignorant or cavalier about what a crowd is capable of. Crowds, as a result, have become self-policing. A group compact, predicated on the understanding of a crowd's power, keeps the peace. When a fight breaks out at an Alabama game, people ease back rather than join in. They wait for the cops to come and boo and hiss at those who would put the peace in jeopardy as they're led down the aisles in handcuffs, no matter what team they pull for.

The compact against violence has a curious effect on the crowd in a stadium: fans feel freer to go nuts over the game itself. They don't need to edit themselves or check their behavior for fear of inciting a riot. You can wear your colors without excessive fear of being stomped. You can go bananas and give yourself over to whatever strange urges emanate from the recesses of the psyche. The bigger a crowd, in fact, the freer we're likely to feel. A large crowd creates an atmosphere of anonymity, which in turn allows people to give themselves to their passions without any social penalty. We can't paint our faces and scream like maniacs at our desks, in the classroom, or at the dinner table with our families, so to be able to do it in public feels . . . well, interesting at first—like making funny faces in a mirror when no one's around—and then . . . positively *titillating.* McDougall thought this liberation from so-called normal behavior was the building block of crowds. It led to a phenomenon he called "intensification." When a man in red face paint and a cape standing next to me screams gibberish and flails his arms, who will notice if I scream at the top of my lungs and beat my chest like an ape? What can I possibly do that will seem inappropriate? The guy next to me sees me screaming like a lunatic and feels free to act a little crazier himself. Perhaps he shakes his head wildly and howls like a wolf. At which point, SuperBama, in his red cape and red face paint, gives in to to the urge to sprint down the aisle with his tongue hanging out and make a sound like an industrial vacuum cleaner. And so on. The effect is the equivalent of an emotional nuclear reaction. It builds exponentially, and races through the crowd generating heat.

A lot has to go right, though, to reach this critical mass. In reality, it happens just once or twice a season. At Florida, it might have happened, but we were the visitors. Being outnumbered ten to one has a way of making you keep your ecstasy in check. The blowouts of Houston and Southern Miss were too gradual, and against LSU and Arkansas, the feeling was more relief than joy. But, at the final home game of the season, against Mississippi State, five minutes into the fourth quarter, I'm finally given the chance to lose myself, to become the untutored passionate savage—the wild beast—McDougall wrote about.

Mississippi State is coached by Jackie Sherrill, a man who made news a couple of years back for taking his team to a bull castration as a motivational exercise. His methods were criticized, but not their effectiveness. What player wouldn't want to perform for a man who felt at ease watching a live animal get its balls lopped off? And in fact, the Bulldogs are 8-0, and lead the division, on the strength of a defense both fast and brutal. The Bulldogs are arrogant in the best ways; they gather on the sideline before kickoff and bounce around in a taunting pack, a performance that inspires a cascade of boos from Alabama fans. It's meant to intimidate, and frankly, it does. Bama players are taught to behave themselves; it's not so hard to imagine them as well-groomed students underneath their uniforms. The hyped-up cavorting of the State players suggests that a peek beneath their face masks might reveal fangs and hairy snouts. I'm jealous.

By the fourth quarter, night has fallen. Moths swirl around the stadium lights like clouds of confetti. The world outside the stadium is black, obscuring everything in the universe but the game. Darkness is the first nudge toward emotional critical mass; our faces carved with shadows like a field full of jack-o'-lanterns, we are even more anonymous than in the daylight, more at liberty to give in to whatever strange impulses pass across our fibrillating frontal lobes. Alabama and Mississippi State have been slugging away at each other for three and a half quarters like well-conditioned heavyweights. The players have gone from fresh to tired to fresh again, the endorphins and adrenaline sluicing through their veins, burning hot and clear, like racing fuel. Alabama leads 13-7, and has a chance to put the game away with a field goal, but the kick soars wide. The Bulldogs get the ball with eleven minutes to go: a touchdown from victory. They begin to drive, to midfield, and now into Alabama territory, jarring the crowd to lucidity. Sensing that our team needs us, we stand and shout. On third down, as the State quarterback approaches the line, there is a sudden roar. It sounds like a massive waterfall, with the steady rumble of stomping feet on the low end and a singeing hiss of clapping hands on the high. My screams fill in the midrange. What am I saying? I have to stop to even notice: *Cmonbamaletsgodefensegobamagobama-godefense.* Gibberish, in other words. And yet, who can tell, or cares? With the sudden spike in noise, the crowd seems to become aware of itself and of its power. It's exhilarating, and the exhilaration inspires us to scream even louder. A moment later, it happens again, as though the crowd is in a shouting match with itself. It's louder still. The decibel level ratchets upward—a graph of it would look like a staircase—McDougall's theory of intensification playing out in real time. Unnerved by the noise, a State lineman hops out of his stance—illegal motion.

Our power is confirmed, and that's all it takes . . . The Bulldogs break the huddle and the roar begins anew, only still louder. Around me, fans are screaming and shaking their heads, mouths open, trying to muscle still more noise from the bottom of their throats, as though trying to shout rocks up a hill. I can feel the rumble through my heels. The State quarterback drops back and jogs right, under pressure. He throws the ball into his receiver's ankles, incomplete. It's our ball. We did it.

A few minutes later, when Zow heaves a ball over the top to a wide-open Shamari Buchanan for a touchdown, the game winner, joy engulfs us like a wave. That chamber of the psyche that houses our ancient tribal instincts is torn open, compelling thousands of strangers to embrace in a frenetic tumble. The glee is pure and uncomplicated, the crystalline contentment of childhood accessed, miraculously, years into adulthood. Besides my team winning, for the first time this season it's possible to feel as though *we* have won—the team, the crowd in Bryant-Denny, the psychological crowd out there connected by fiber optics and radio waves—through a collective effort. Or is this one of those illusions that Freud said a crowd cannot live without—that we actually matter? We've been cheering for ten solid minutes after the game when, at the mouth of the tunnel that leads to the Alabama locker room, there is a commotion. It's the team. They're running back onto the field to cheer . . . *us*. For another ten minutes, the team and the crowd stand applauding each other, the band chugging brassily in the background. It isn't an illusion after all—we *did* do it. DuBose, our charmless resident stooge, improbably, has done it too. How this happened is a mystery beyond all reckoning, but it's one we're content not to get hung up on. We're a single game away from playing for the conference championship. Auburn is next.

After the game, I head back to the Law Library lot to connect with the Bices. They're not at their RV, so I wander around a bit, dodging golf carts as they whiz silently by, and peeking around corners into various parties to see if I can spot them. Eventually, I find them near the entrance to the lot, not at an RV but a pickup truck. A local Tide fan has set up speakers and a couple of CD players, and is playing DJ to anyone who bothers to come along. There are about fifteen takers, strangers mostly it seems, torquing and twirling with each other on the grass, beneath an old oak tree. Chris and Paula are in the middle—Chris is getting down with his big plastic go-cup, and Paula is dancing with her lucky red Alabama shaker. A stranger hands me an unopened beer can, which I crack into delightedly. I take a sip—it's deliciously frigid—and wander into the pack and start dancing. When he sees me, Chris makes a funky face and offers a hand for a high five. Paula twirls past, smiling a smile as bright as a stadium light bulb.

I've spent a month in Tuscaloosa. When I arrived, I didn't especially want to be here; now, I don't especially want to leave. Besides the city's subtle beauty—the slowly oozing Black Warrior and its morning blanket of mist, the clatter and moans of old freight trains, the crimson flora of game day—the real allure of Tuscaloosa is its simplicity. Life here is built around the proposition of winning or losing, which, boiled down, is the basic proposition of life. Out there beyond McFarland Boulevard, in the "real world," the game is a lot tougher. When you walk into a cocktail party or your office, it's often hard to distinguish friend from foe. The person who's nicest to you at work might be scheming for your job. A close friend may secretly have designs on your mate. But when you drive down Bryant Drive during football season, it's all so clear: red RV—friend; blue RV—foe. Is it any wonder that people can't get enough of it?

On my last day in town I decide to stop by the Bear Bryant Museum. It's as much a shrine as a museum, after all, and it seems only right that I end my visit to Tuscaloosa by spending some contemplative time among the holy relics there, to see what secrets they might give up. The curator, a thirty-seven-year-old Bama grad named Taylor Watson, agrees to show me around, but only if I'll meet him for lunch first at a soul food restaurant called KSV—short for Katrina, Sabrina, Veronica, the names of the three owners—in the black section of Tuscaloosa, near downtown. "It's gonna be high in fat," Watson says on the phone, not as a warning but as an enticement.

We are the only white patrons in KSV, which is delicious, if a bit risky to the heart; even the veggie plate—black-eyed peas, collard greens, corn, sweet potatoes, and corn bread—is butter drenched, leaden, and despite it all, irresistible. Watson's job, he says, is to catalog the Bryant Museum's sprawling collection—ten thousand photographs, twelve thousand cans of 16 mm game film, tapes of the play-by-play of every Alabama game since 1949, a menagerie of trophies, and an amalgam of between five and six thousand Alabama football "artifacts," among them strange offerings from fans, like a life-sized mannequin of former head coach Gene Stallings with a small, angel-winged Bear Bryant doll on its shoulders. "We get a lot of folk art," Watson says. "Some of it's pretty weird."

Watson played only a few downs of football in his life—when he was seven he took a hit rounding the corner in Little League practice, told his dad that it hurt, and quit the team and football for good. After that, he was content to be a fan, and like a lot of young men growing up in Alabama during the seventies, he fell under the spell of Bear Bryant, and under the coach's lofty prescription that in life as in football you should strive to be both sportsmanlike and a "winner." The highest calling of all was to show "class," a word that when thundered forth by the Bear took on a kind of holy aura. Class was the code of the gentleman warrior, and that was the Bear's ethic. As a kid, I fell under the same spell, but nearly twenty years after Bryant's death, I can remember feeling awe toward the man, but I can't remember the man himself. The particulars of his gait, his expressions, his stentorian cadence have drifted over my memory's horizon. Watson can't forget. Bear Bryant walks through his every day. He has old audiotapes of the Bear at pep rallies, talking not in that nearly inaudible grumble of his later years that could rattle the nails out of floorboards, but stridently, clearly. And he has tapes of nearly every episode of *The Bear Bryant Show*, the Sunday morning ritual my father took me to on my birthday. It was where Bear celebrated the tough hits—*"Bingo!"*—and took the blame for the failures. ("I call all the bad plays.") Watson offers to cue up a few old videotapes for me to refresh my memory. We finish lunch and head across town to the museum. There are some listening booths in back.

For the next two hours I sit at a cubicle with headphones on, just me and the Bear—the ghostly soundtrack of my youth sputtering between my ears like a spark between poles. Watson has pulled Bryant's appearance on *The Dick Cavett Show* in 1981, just before he broke Stagg's record for wins, and then *The Bear Bryant Show* from the day after number 315 against Auburn in 1981. Watson gives that tape an enthusiastic shake. "He's in rare form," he says. The Bear is rosy cheeked and beaming. To his surprise, the producers play a series of congratulatory messages from Bob Hope, and then the governor. Presidents Reagan and Carter had called him in the locker room afterward. In the Cavett tape he's slow and grumbling, like a freight train pulling out of the yard, but a year later, after the big win and all the attention, he's positively chipper, a 33 running at 45. Even in his latter years, it's possible to glimpse his secret power—the dry wit and charisma that caused people to remember verbatim their every encounter with him. When reporters probed his coaching secrets, he had a stock response: "I don't know, and if I did I wouldn't tell you." It was both humble and reticent, just oblique enough to perpetuate the mystery of his being, the mystery carried in those craggy, squinting eyes that hid in the shadows of the brim of his lordly houndstooth fedora. Before the Cotton Bowl in 1980, a reporter asked Bryant if there was anyone he feared, and Bryant had answered grimly: Grafton Hocutt. The reporter nodded knowingly, and when the interview was over, got on the phone to New York to put his researchers on the trail of Grafton Hocutt, whoever he was. Sometime later the word came down: Grafton Hocutt was a Tuscaloosa undertaker.

In a *Sports Illustrated* profile published the week before Bryant broke Stagg's record against Auburn, two years before Bryant died, Frank Deford wrote, "So when the Bear goes, it will not just be that one more link to the past will be broken, that a little more of that curious Southern combination of eternal knighthood and childhood will fade. It will be harder for football ever to mean so much again in Alabama. Not even winning will be the same." Football means as much there now, but Deford was right—it's different, contemporary, real, no longer mythic, which is probably a healthy thing. But for a couple of hours on a weekday afternoon, care of some old videos and an indulgent museum curator, I'm able to link once again to the past . . . the vision of eternal knighthood and childhood comes fleetingly back into focus.

Before pulling out for Auburn I drive the Hawg to John Ed's office. The Downtown Gallery next door is crowded—the team's good fortune has prompted a late-in-the-season buying spree; Sherrill Barnes is having the best week of her best year yet. Things are going very well for John Ed too. He's long on Auburn tickets, and they're selling for between \$200 and \$300 apiece. Not only that—John Ed has at least one deal in the works that promises to net a huge gain. A woman has called in desperation because her husband, a local lumber salesman, has promised his boss and two clients that he has box tickets to the game. The man has no such tickets; his boss has just found out and his job is now on the line. As a backup, his wife has located four tickets in a row on the forty-yard line—for \$450 apiece. She's hoping—praying—that John Ed can find tickets in a sky box.

"This is a case of someone's alligator mouth overloading his hummingbird asshole," John Ed tells me. "This could lead to some serious money and some serious *somethin'* down the road. I mean, she's *desperate.* Money will be *no object.*" A desperate wife with her desperate husband's credit card and no spending limit: John Ed's vision of heaven.

A while later a Jaguar whips into a parking space out front and out pops a beamy character with slicked back hair, deep-pleated black trousers, and tasseled loafers that ride low on the forefoot—a get-up that clashes with Tuscaloosa as strikingly as would an Auburn track suit. John Ed says it's a local doctor here to pick up his tickets. The man blows into the room as though he were about to announce an emergency. Then, panting, he undoes his belt buckle and lets his trousers fall to the floor.

"I'm dropping my pants, John Ed," the man says, "Go ahead and fuck me."

Alas, there are few options to those in Tuscaloosa who would protest the cost of scalped—brokered—tickets. This is what it has come to, and it's not pretty.

John Ed smiles, not the smile of someone going along with

someone else's joke, but the smile of someone laughing silently at his own joke.

Four hundred dollars, he tells the man, and deals two tickets on the desk.

The doctor grimaces. "It's a pleasure doing business with you," he says, handing over the money, his cheeks flush. Then, weakly: "Can I zip up my pants now?"

Chapter Fourteen

Chief Got Wet!

RIDING IN THE HAWG DOWN THE NARROW ALABAMA TWO-lanes toward Auburn feels less like driving than hurtling in a bobsled down a chute; I don't steer the thing so much as point it and hope for the best. At stop signs in little towns like Centreville and Lawley I get a brief chance to take stock of my surroundings. Central Alabama is beautiful and green, the hills straight and steep like roller-coasters. Judging from the rifles and shotguns mounted in the rear windows of nearly every pickup I see, however, it seems like a rotten place to grow up a varmint.

After three hours on the road, I arrive in Auburn. The red brick clock tower on Samford Hall at the center of campus is bathed in late-afternoon sun, which casts a crosshatch of shadows beneath the building's white eaves and recesses so that it looks ancient and austere, like a building in Red Square. The stadium lights are on, projecting an eerie column of blue light into the sky over town. The fraternity porches are full, and the sidewalks on College Street are bustling with students. The air smells faintly of cut hay and manure, aromas that go some way toward telling the story of the Alabama-Auburn rivalry.

Auburn is a land grant university—a cow college—created under an 1862 law that set aside money from government land sales to finance schools that taught "agricultural and mechanical arts." Alabama, with its antebellum aesthetic, is a society school, or so the thinking goes. The stereotype holds that kids go to Alabama to learn how to cocktail and schmooze before moving on to law school or to take over their father's insurance business, while kids go to Auburn to learn about things like erosion control and worming cattle. Up close, the stereotypes don't hold—Auburn has plenty of bright kids from Atlanta and Jackson and Birmingham who've come to study engineering or architecture, and Alabama has plenty of students who've grown up on farms. But in the context of the football rivalry between the schools, the stereotypes are everything. Competition, after all, stokes the human urge to find and exaggerate differences, even if those differences are more imagined than real. Both sides play along. Alabama fans—even those sons and daughters of farmers—sing "Old MacDonald Had a Farm" during the Auburn alma mater, refer to Auburn fans as "barners," show up at the big game with signs that read CULTURE VS. AGRICULTURE, and make redneck jokes at the expense of the Auburn crowd. Auburn fans embrace the stereotype in their own way, by assuming the mantle of the perpetual underdogs, have-nots at war with the haves to upset a system of privilege and favoritism that has neglected them. If the Alabama psyche is hung up on an antebellum fiction, the Auburn psyche is hung up on a postbellum reality. Auburn fans have all the bottled-up resentments and inferiority complexes of a defeated people. In other words, Auburn's relationship with Alabama is like the state of Alabama's relationship to the rest of the country.

The average Auburn fan's conviction that he is downtrodden and neglected has led to the one actual difference between the fan bases of the two teams: Auburn's fans are much rowdier. Once you've been dismissed as a lowlife and a redneck, there's a certain defiant pleasure in acting like one. To put on airs of gentility and to prattle on about "class" and sportsmanship would be to validate the Alabama fans' worldview. So instead, Auburn fans embrace their lot. They act crazy. They misbehave. They're hostile toward outsiders. This last detail is of particular relevance to the Alabama RV-ers setting up camp in Auburn; we are those outsiders.

The Bama RVs are in a field near the school's cattle barn, and I edge the Hawg along the wet, sucking mud of the rutted dirt road that leads down a slope onto a carpet of damp grass. The lot is bordered on two sides by busy campus roads and, on the back, by a darkened forest. I park in the back corner, near the woods and far enough from the roads that I feel I'm safe from any projectiles—beer cans, eggs—that might fly from passing cars. I lurch the Hawg onto its fluorescent red plastic levelers, turn off the engine, and a languorous quiet takes over. I'm among friends, it turns out. The RV closest to me belongs to the man I parked next to at Oxford weeks before, the one who ran off vandals by waving his pistol. It's a measure of how my attitude has changed that at Ole Miss I felt alarmed to learn my neighbor was packing heat, and now I feel reassured. Skipper is nearby too, but Donnie and the rest of his gang are nowhere to be seen. They hate Auburn so much, Skipper tells me, that they won't set foot here. So they stayed home? I ask. Hell, no, Skipper says. They're spending the weekend at a campground in Clanton, ninety miles away. They're going to watch the game there on satellite TV. For hardcore RV-ing fans, the cognitive dissonance of their predicament must have been excruciating. As Auburn haters, they won't come here, but as Alabama RV-ers, they can't possibly stay home. So they've compromised—unwilling to go to the game but reluctant to miss it, they've decided to simply go near it.

A childhood friend named Chandler Busby lives in Auburn, so I call him up to suss out the local mood. He went to school here and stuck around to become the local bagel magnate. Chandler suggests a drink at the Mellow Mushroom, a pizza and beer joint, so I'm off. I haven't seen him in years, but besides the fact that he has blond hair and is almost pathologically cheerful, the one other detail I remember about Chandler from childhood is that he pulls for Auburn. Growing up in Alabama, team allegiance is a signature trait.

The clientele of the Mellow Mushroom is a clan of contentedly belligerent college kids in low-hugging blue jeans, flannel shirts, muddy L.L.Bean duck boots, and bent-brimmed baseball caps pulled low over the eyes. Conversation is limited almost to a single affirming word: *solid.*

"How's it goin', bro?" Chandler asks a friend.

"Solid."

"Solid," Chandler responds.

Over a beer, I ask Chandler if he suspects there will be any violence over the weekend. Only if two unlikely things occur, he tells me: first, if Alabama wins, and second, if Alabama fans then try to roll Toomer's Corner. Toomer's Corner is a tree-lined intersection on the main drag in Auburn in front of the old Toomer's Drug Store, and when Auburn wins, tradition holds that students turn out in a horde and drape the arbors there with toilet paper. Auburn fans view the rolling of Toomer's Corner as a private ritual, Chandler says, and as he's sure Auburn will beat Bama—Alabama has yet to win at Auburn in its five tries there since the game was moved from its neutral site in Birmingham—he doesn't expect much of a problem. If Alabama wins, they go to the SEC championship game in Atlanta, and there's no way Auburn's going to allow that to happen. But if some accident of the cosmos occurs and Bama pulls it out, he says, a mob of students and probably even the local cops will surround Toomer's Corner to protect it from Alabama fans with any funny ideas. There've been rumors, he says.

History backs up Chandler's prediction. Years before, when a mob of Auburn football fans gathered near Toomer's Corner, the local fire department chief ordered firehoses turned on the crowd to disperse it. Some college students managed to wrestle a hose from the firemen and turned it on the chief, who was knocked down and washed down the street by the force of the water, as the crowd chanted, "Chief got wet! Chief got wet!"

Indeed, trouble seems to loom. When I get back to the Bama RVs, one of my neighbors proudly opens a compartment beneath his RV to reveal several dozen rolls of toilet paper, which he bought in bulk at

Wal-Mart—something like the Lifetime Supply Pack. A bid in the conference championship is at stake, and he expects a victory. When it comes, he has a plan.

"We gonna roll Toomer's Cohnah," he tells me confidently. "Word's been sent 'round on the Innernet."

Later in the evening, I'm in the Hawg in the back corner of the field near the cattle barn, when I hear a flurry of voices. A group of Alabama fans, weary of the barrage of taunts from passing Auburn students, has decided to take over the intersection at the opposite corner of the lot. Taking the intersection means, more or less, standing in it and dodging oncoming traffic. Perhaps fifteen Alabama fans do this. For a few minutes they are jubilant—dancing about with their pom-poms as though they've taken Iwo Jima—then quickly, they are bored, and worse, out of beer. They migrate back into the field. Quickly the horns and taunts resume.

Just after 11:00 P.M., there's a knock at the door: it's Chris Bice, just arrived from Greenville, along with Jimmy, the sleepy-eyed, perpetually sunburned Bama fan who nearly punched my lights out after the La. Tech game. Jimmy is all too happy to see me now; he can't remember my name so he just calls me "Noooooo York City"—repeatedly. They want to know why I've parked so far from the action. Jimmy and the Bices have set up camp in the corner of the field right next to the intersection. Those horns and taunts are for them. Chris says he's saved a spot for me.

Maybe the weekend will pass more smoothly if you're out of throwing range, I tell them.

"We're all set up and we're not gonna move," Chris says defiantly. Besides, he says, getting yelled at and having eggs thrown at you is "part of the fun of being at an away game." There is an implicit challenge in the remark, which is utterly effective. I don't want to seem like I'm not game. I'm here to be in the middle of it all, I remind myself, and what damage could anyone really do to the Hawg, which looks so thoroughly vandalized already? A few minutes later, I'm bouncing over the ruts and dirt clods and weaving through the maze of RVs with

Jimmy and Chris as my ground crew. The commotion causes people to get up from their folding chairs and to peek from beneath the curtains inside their RVs. I'm now the neighborhood nuisance. Pulling the Hawg perpendicular to both the Bices' and Jimmy's motor homes, I form a kind of RV fort, which also has the effect of making us a large, easy target for the local egg hurlers. Several times in the night, I wake to the tympanic *thwump* of an egg crashing against aluminum siding, and to screams from passing cars—interestingly, half of them delivered in the night-piercing cackle of female voices. When it comes to shouting obscenities at perfect strangers, Auburn is an equal-opportunity town.

The next morning we wake to survey the damage—or rather, the fun of being at an away game. Mostly it's innocuous—a henhouse full of broken eggs, crusty splotches of dried yolk on the sides of nearly all the RVs within throwing distance of the road. Miraculously, the Hawg is egg-free, no doubt because the Auburn students had calculated that to egg the Hawg would be to waste an egg. Some chairs have been stolen, along with a cooler of beer left outside overnight under an awning, which reflects better on the thieves than on the victim of the theft; no one else in the lot was stupid enough to leave their beer outside overnight. The victim of this crime decides to bear witness: he posts a sign on the side of his RV that reads AUBS STOLE MY BEER. One of the RVs down the line has been graffitied with blue spray paint. If the blue scribbles spell anything, no one can decipher it.

More distressing is that some students climbed on top of an RV and torched two Alabama flags, which were made of a synthetic material that dripped into a molten puddle onto the motor home's roof. The prank could've led to something serious—it wouldn't take much to turn one of these mostly plastic motor homes into a large can of Sterno—so a congress is called in the middle of the field to discuss our options. Skipper says he's ready to head to the Clanton campground, in part because he is fed up with Auburn and in part because he's afraid he'll get in a fight and get arrested. A man in a red jumpsuit makes the entirely reasonable suggestion that we simply not raise flags over our RVs, as a safety precaution, and is immediately denounced for "caving in." We agree that we should call the police and agitate for protection. A woman calls the Auburn police department from her cell phone. The officer at the other end of the line is unsympathetic. Specifically, he tells her that we wouldn't be vandalized if we had just stayed home.

If there was any doubt that this is more than just a football game—that it is anything, in fact, less than a battle between the forces of righteousness and evil, that officer has set the record straight. We've come for a football game; we're now at war. For the next three days, relations between the Alabama corps and our Auburn hosts devolve further. I make a list of incidents:

- An RV down the row is attacked by Auburn students with paint guns.
- An Alabama fan in the lot says "Roll Tide!" to a passing pedestrian. The pedestrian responds, "Fuck You." The Alabama fan then deploys a six-inch deer knife and threatens "to gut you like the pig motherfucker you are."
- At 2:00 A.M. on Thursday night, a half-dozen Bama fans and I climb in the back of a pickup truck owned by Paula Bice's cousin, then drive through the Auburn RV lot blowing the horn and shouting obscenities. Auburn fans respond with obscenities and several partially filled cans of beer. The mission is deemed a success.
- We hear there's a party at Benji's Place, a bar at the local Quality Inn. We show up—it's an Auburn party. Upon seeing a clutch of Alabama fans, a blond woman in her twenties grabs one of her breasts, points it at us, squeezes it, and sneers, "Fuck y'all." My first assault by lactation. A drunken member of our party later tries to get the woman's phone number.

Through it all, what strikes me is how comfortable people seem in this state of conflict. Far from being distressed by it, the fans seem reassured. Having enemies—especially formidable ones—gives life structure, a way for people to orient themselves. Ironically, nothing creates friendships like having enemies. The woman who called the police department, for example, and the man with the deer knife—

they're now my bosom buddies, if only for the curious reason that someone out there wants to throw eggs at us and steal our beer—no small threat, to be sure, but still one incongruous with the depth of our connection. It's not that I expect everyone in orange and blue to be hostile, only that because there's no reliable way to differentiate the friendly Auburn fans from the ones who might heave an egg my way or try to lactate on me, I assume they're all dangerous; I latch on to my kind. Maybe this is how racism begins—with just a twinge of fear of the Other that snowballs into an ideology. In strict terms, I'm actually predisposed to like Auburn fans. Politically, I sympathize with the underdog. I admire the school's founding ethic—that hard work and the land are things of real value—especially when compared with Alabama's Old South fetish, which borders on creepy. But these are rational considerations, quickly overridden the second a threat is registered.

* * *

Like the sight of the Bices departing for the Vanderbilt game early in the season, the vision of Auburn, Alabama, through the mist on Saturday morning gives the lie to the idea that sports fans are passive types who prefer watching to doing. In three days, the fans have built a city, and not a simulacrum of a third-world city of cardboard and canvas like Woodstock, but a functioning modern metropolis, with plumbing, electricity, space-age materials, and a first-world telecommunications system of cell phones, walkie-talkies, satellite dishes, wireless Internet hookups. Most impressive of all are the grills—not dainty backyard jobs of pressed sheet metal, but spectacularly masculine contraptions of welded iron, with tires, tow bars, and chimneys like industrial smokestacks. Over there toward the woods, a haughty, bearded Alabama fan is toiling over a slaughterhouse's worth of ribs on a home-crafted pit the size of a pickup truck. Across the street, an Auburn fan is cooking butts on a grill made of two oil barrels cut in half lengthwise and welded together. As far as the eye can see, grills spew little tornadoes of smoke skyward, calling to mind the oil well fires of Kuwait. Up the hill, some Auburn fans have constructed a stage and a wooden dance floor, beneath an orchard of hanging electric lanterns. A national park's worth of picnic tables perforates the landscape. Then there are the plastic living rooms, golf carts and Harleys, and three folding chairs for every backside. Even John Ed is impressed. He pulls up in his red 4Runner and surveys the scene.

"Son, I've been to the Sugar Bowl, the Super Bowl, two World Series, and a goat fuckin'," he declares, with his hands on his hips. "And I ain't never seen anything like this."

I take a walk around the lot at lunchtime and pass by Skipper's RV, which is parked toward the back of the lot. Skipper is outside watching a game on television, uncharacteristically alone, since the rest of his crew has parked an hour outside of town. To my surprise, he waves me over, and to my further surprise, he offers me a barbecue sandwich. He seems keen to chat with someone about the game. Whether because he's alone or because he's seen me at eleven games now—including this one, which even his hardcore buddies have flaked out on—Skipper's attitude toward me is markedly different. Don't get me wrong—he's hardly lovey-dovey, and he still disagrees with nearly everything I have to say about the game—but he seems to view me with something less than utter contempt, perhaps in recognition of my fortitude, and for that, I can't suppress a tiny blip of pride.

My seat for the game is high in the corner of the stadium where Alabama fans have been exiled. I'm surrounded by familiar faces. As cohorts hearty enough to drive to the swampy reaches of Gainesville and the red clay plains of innermost Alabama, we share the esprit de corps of warriors. We are outnumbered, surrounded, and given that there are just a handful of two-lane roads out of Auburn, more or less trapped—all of which heightens the sense of danger and the illusion that we are as much a part of the game as the players. We trade high fives and comradely nods, and an uneasy energy percolates through the ranks: in three hours we'll either be at Toomer's Corner on a toilet paper binge, or getting howled at, egged, and spray-painted—possibly torched—by throngs of jubilant drunks. The emotional slingshot is drawn back, and we'll either be launched into the stratosphere, or the band will break.

Alabama manages a field goal early, but already there's a disturbing sign. Zow's passes are going wildly high again, over the heads of his leaping receivers. As the first quarter winds down, we get a gift when Tommy Tuberville, the Auburn coach, calls a fake punt in his own territory. The kicker's pass is off target, in the receiver's ankles, and four plays later, the Tide adds another field goal to go up 6-0.

In the second quarter, things begin to go badly. Auburn drives, first by sending their speeding truck of a fullback up the middle, then by throwing long downfield. They're at our eleven when Ben Leard, the Auburn quarterback, runs to his right, drawing the attention of the blitzing Alabama defenders, then throws left, to an open receiver for a touchdown. The stadium shakes to life beneath a canopy of blue and orange pom-poms. There are over ten thousand Alabama fans, but given the horseshoe of blue that faces us, it's possible to feel very alone.

Alabama gives the ball back, and again Auburn drives—alternating runs with quick passes to nimble receivers. From the fifteen, Leard throws a short pass to an underneath receiver, who shoots past a frozen Alabama defender for another score. Auburn leads 14-6.

I need a dose of optimism so at the half I seek out the closest thing Alabama has to offer in relentless cheerfulness to the Sri Chinmoy: Chris Bice. The Bices are down low, near the thorned hedge that separates the crowd from the field, and they're crammed uncomfortably against two yelping Auburn supporters, who are cavorting to the band. I scoot down the aisle, and the three of us stand jammed together in a space reserved for two.

"What is *that*?" Chris shouts over the din.

Oh yeah—I've got a red and white Alabama shaker in my hand, my first in nineteen years, since Alabama's 7-0 loss to Notre Dame in Birmingham, when it was proven beyond a doubt that shakers for me are bad luck. I'd told Chris and Paula about the shaker curse on our first weekend together, when we compared superstitions, and Chris remembers. He gives me a condemning look, then glances toward the scoreboard: it's my fault. My explanation—that I thought maybe this particular superstition had expired—falls flat, and causes even me to cringe. The Alabama-Auburn game isn't the time to test the will of the gods. I'd always thought of superstitions as all-or-nothing propositions—they either worked or they didn't. In Chris's view, superstitions are cumulative; there's a kind of cosmic superstition ledger—if I use a shaker, some Auburn fan has to lapse as well, to cancel me out—and the most pious side wins. It's like an election: it's easy to think your vote doesn't count, until a close race. Chris yanks the shaker from my hand and flings it in the puddle of Coca-Cola and bourbon at our feet, like a preacher casting away demons.

Miraculously enough, in the third quarter, the karmic pendulum slowly begins to swing our way. Auburn drives deep into Alabama territory, but misses a field goal. When we get the ball back, Watts comes in at quarterback to replace Zow and leads us on a seventy-five-yard drive to the Auburn six. On four consecutives tries, we're stopped, and the ball goes back to Auburn. But on the next play, Leard drops back into the end zone and is sacked for a safety. In short order, we've gone from the possibility of being down by two scores to being down by exactly one; it's 14-8 Auburn. The Tigers kick off after the safety, and we start at midfield, Alexander running fifteen yards, then fourteen and two more. On a fourth down and three yards to go, Jordan-Hare Stadium begins to shake with such violence that it seems it might fall instantly into a heap of girders. There's a shared premonitory feeling that this is it: if Auburn can't stop Alabama now, they never will. The thing is getting away from them, and all the noise and tumult of the moment is an expression of their desperation. Alabama breaks the huddle, and Watts sprints off to the right; Milons, our rabbit-quick flanker, steps into the quarterback position, grabs the snap from the air, and streaks into the left side of the line, popping out some seven yards downfield. It's a first down. A play later, Alexander gets the ball and ghosts through the Auburn defense for a touchdown. With just under twelve minutes to go, Alabama leads, 15-14.

Auburn's next series is a disastrous string of penalties and blown plays, and in no time, Alabama has the ball again, at midfield, and with Alexander resting on the sideline, we take it right at the wearying

Auburn defense, with a series of fullback draws up the middle. With the Tiger line softened, Alexander is sent back in. He takes the ball on a sweep to the left and he's in: 22-14 Bama.

Auburn fights back for a field goal, but their defense has no energy left to fight with, and with just over a minute left, Alexander gets the handoff again, this time to the right, and high-steps into the end zone. It's Alexander's third touchdown of the night, on an incredible 182 yards of rushing. Alabama has won 28-17.

The slingshot is released. For half an hour, we sing, hug, high-five, do the Rammer Jammer cheer, snip off pieces of the thorny hedge as souvenirs. The moment the celebration begins to tire, the team comes out to thank the fans, and it begins anew. A throbbing chant of S-E-C! S-E-C! gives way to another, one that seems to have begun faintly in the madness down low behind the end zone, and now takes us over: Too-mer's! Too-mer's! Too-mer's! Soon we're tumbling and bouncing down the ramps like spilled marbles, down onto the wet shining asphalt and toward town. Rolls of toilet paper miraculously appear from beneath coats, out of purses and knapsacks. But emerging from behind the campus buildings, we run headlong into a intimidating sight: half the town of Auburn has turned out to guard Toomer's Corner.

The crowd, perhaps a thousand or two—it's hard to tell who's there to be at Toomer's Corner, and who's simply passing by—has formed a large circle. The half near Toomer's Corner consists of a pack of angry young men prowling beneath the arbors, like caged cats. The other half of the circle: the Alabama crowd, drunk with glee and carrying armfuls of toilet paper. Jostling through the hot bodies, I stumble over, of all things, a man in a wheelchair. He's wearing an Alabama cap; a woman in an Alabama sweatshirt, and with a tall black hairdo like a shrub, is pushing him through the mob. There's a commotion, then a shriek. I turn in time to see a college-age kid in blue jeans and a baseball cap dart into the pack; he has ripped the man's watch from his wrist. I can't decide which seems more craven, stealing a watch off a man in a wheelchair, or pushing your wheelchair-bound husband into a drunken mob.

Something is holding the two sides of the circle apart from each other, and it's not until I've made my way to the seam between them that I see what it is: a lone cop. He's standing at the center, wild-eyed, knees bent, and hands out, like someone playing defense in basketball. When one side of the circle surges forward, the cop pushes it back, then retreats to his spot in the middle, and back into guard position. The crowd heaves forward, and I feel a heavy weight against my back. I'm jammed between an AP photographer who has been alerted to the possibility of a riot, and an Auburn student whose breath is a sirocco of barley spirits.

"It's gonna clash here in a sec," he tells me excitedly.

A roll of toilet paper streaks overhead, tailing through the air like a comet. The Alabama crowd is just out of range of the trees, but a scrap of paper breaks off in flight and floats down over a branch. Cheers from the Alabama side.

"That shit's in our tree, man!" an Auburn student shouts. Inspired, one of his comrades shoots up the tree like a monkey, then leans out on the branch and collects the paper. Cheers from the Auburn side. A man to my left is carrying a garbage bag over his shoulder, like Santa Claus: it's full of toilet paper. He reaches in, grabs a roll and a crowd clears to give him room for a long throw.

"Don't do it," someone shouts from the Auburn crowd. "Y'all won. Now go on home."

He does it anyway. More cheers.

"It's gonna clash, it's gonna clash," the Auburn student repeats.

As absurd as this exercise is—and it is profoundly absurd, except for the possibility that a massive brawl could occur at any moment—it is undertaken with the utmost seriousness. Sherman never met such stone-faced and determined resistance. The strange, dour exercise continues for fifteen minutes, the cop holding the circle back from itself like a spoke, until an Auburn student jumps up on a brick stanchion with a plastic Alabama shaker in one hand and a cigarette lighter in the other. The crowd begins to chant, "Burn it! Burn it!" and so the student dutifully flicks the lighter and the shaker begins to ignite. At this moment the lone cop attacks him, yanking him down from the stanchion and heaving him facedown into the wet sod—

"He did a Rodney King on his ass!" the drunk kid shouts in my ear.

As a crowd control move, the takedown is profoundly effective. The violence of the maneuver is enough to deter anyone else from inciting a riot. Moments later the reinforcements arrive, batons at the ready, and the crowd quickly begins to back up, and then to disperse. No toilet paper hangs in the trees. Auburn fans may have lost the game but they've successfully defended their campus from a tidal wave of t.p.

I make my way back past the stadium, through the game-day detritus—old shakers clumped together like mops, game programs soaked wet and splayed on the asphalt like banana peels, and thousands of discarded cups, as at the finish line of a marathon. The town is flooded with traffic, which hardly moves. From the road that passes the cattle barn, I see the tops of the Alabama RVs, peaking up from the bog like the backs of hippos in a pond. A drunk Bama fan is standing at the intersection nearest the lot, propositioning any woman who happens to stop there with her window down. The line is always the same: "You so purdy, I'd go to bed with you even though you' an Auburn fan." The testosterone high of the win deflects the sting of a thousand rejections.

The air smells of cigarettes and wet charcoal. The lot is quiet—not empty, but oddly calm, in an exhausted, postcoital repose. It's all I can do to drag my weary body into the Hawg, and to stretch out on the rust-colored, faux-crushed-velvet cushions inside. Even the cheerleader in my brain is spent, passed out prone across my frontal lobes. The little gold dots on the roof paneling swirl together in a blur.

In this deeply pleasing moment of tranquillity, my thoughts turn to Mike DuBose. My instinct from the beginning of the season was to feel embarrassed by him. He spoke poorly and had a dufusy quality that repelled on its face, the more so because a coach represents the fans the way a president represents a country. I felt his social handicaps reflected on me. Instead of overturning the unflattering stereotype of an Alabamian, he confirmed it. The affair with the secretary repelled further, not because I'm a moralist, but because it was craven and untidy and threw the football season into chaos. As the coach, though, DuBose was like an unpleasant relative; there was no brushing him off or denying our connection, which put me in a strange position emotionally. My discomfort at having DuBose as my representative began to put me at odds with my love of my team, so that after the Tech game, like many Alabama fans, I was ready to make a bargain: I'd happily endure the upheaval and resulting losses that would come with firing a coach midseason simply to get rid of him. Then, shockingly, DuBose won in the Swamp. He beat LSU and Mississippi State, and now he has led Alabama to its first win ever at Auburn. There's a sense with DuBose that it could all go wrong at any moment, but those wins show conclusively that, like many fans and certainly Paul Finebaum, I underestimated him. I never thought he had the mental equipment to come back this way. I still can't square the Tech loss with the wins at Florida and Auburn, but more remarkable than the dissonance of those outcomes is the idea that DuBose could get knocked down so hard and still get up to fight again, so that he's now taking his team to the conference championship for a rematch against Florida. It seems like a miracle. As miraculous: I like him again. Or at least I think I like him; I like him for now. Winning changes everything.

It's a given that winning feels better than losing, but lying on the towel-thin rear cushions of the Hawg, the only sound now an occasional "Roll Tide!" sung out to the clouds like a coyote's call, it's easier than ever to get in touch with ancient origins of that basic emotional fact of life, and perhaps, even something like an explanation for all this, an answer. In the eons between our ectomorphic beginnings and the now of plastic laminates, cell phones, and televised football, there was only one real problem that mattered to our forebears, and that was the problem of survival, which played out in an endless regimen of battles, tiny and huge. There's one grub left, or one banana, or one rib, and two hungry creatures want it. The winner eats, the loser goes hungry. The winners survive to breed, the losers die off. In this state of affairs it makes sense that the desire to win would be selected for, since the will to win—the awareness that winning is important—is a powerful step toward actually winning. What better insurance could there be against losing than a feeling of intense pleasure at winning? And so it is that the rib, with its savory allotment of calories, produces pleasure when it's eaten; but *getting* the rib also produces pleasure, in the form of a surge of hormones—testosterone, endorphins, dopamine, and adrenaline, that little waterfall of natural chemicals that sets the frontal lobes alight and the cheerleader in the brain to dancing. (Before evolving, she was probably a perky, decently attractive cavewoman.)

At some point along the way from ectoplasms to our present state, we developed into social creatures that divided labor and assigned the big and burly with the task of fighting on our behalf. Since our fate was tied to theirs, we began to feel their winning as our own. When they failed, we failed as well. In the present, there's less need to fight over ribs; we pick them up at the supermarket and grill them on the Weber, or else at the drive-through window (where they're called McRibs). Our socializing instinct has taken over. It ensures that the poor and the weak are tended to, that those around us have access to the basic staples of survival. Wars are no longer won on strictly physical terms, but on intellectual power, and the power that money brings. As revolutionary as this reality is from our primal beginnings, it's wildly new, at least compared against the millennia of our development. But our animal beginnings lurk just behind that civilized scrim, and no circumstance quite awakens them like being placed face to face with a rival in a zero-sum game. Two groups wanted the same thing tonight, but only one could have it. Our civilized selves understood it was all play—that's probably why there was no riot at Toomer's Corner—but our animal selves reacted as they always have. The desire to win took over, and we experienced the contest the ancient way: testosterone levels plummeted with a loss and soared with a win; the dopamine flowed in a torrent or it went dry; winning feels ecstatically good, and losing empty beyond imagining—same as it ever was.

"Y'all havin' fun?" the cop asks from inside his cruiser. It's Sunday morning, and as the Alabama RVs pull out around us, a small group has rounded up several rolls of the toilet paper that went unused last night and gathered around a rather pathetic-looking twig of tree near the intersection at the front corner of the lot. It now stands more or less encased in toilet paper, which, heavy with the morning mist, congeals over the branches like papier-mâché. The cop has pulled up just as Chris Bice is heaving our last roll over a high branch.

"Time for you all to move on," the cop says, more lazily than sternly.

And so we do. I give Chris a final high five and Paula a hug. We'll see each other next in Atlanta, for a rematch with the Florida Gators for the conference championship. The Hawg cranks easily. I pull out of the lot, bouncing through the ruts and onto the main road. The glee of last night moderates into a glassy serenity, as smooth and rolling as the ribbon of highway ahead of me.

I can already feel myself wanting more.

Chapter Fifteen

Muckety-Mucks, Out of Control

WHEN THE SUN RISES ON THE HAWG ON MONDAY MORNING in Birmingham, I notice something odd: those brand new front tires I bought just a month ago are completely bald, all the way down to the steel belting. So I drive the contraption down to Saab Tire and Automotive and drop it off for the guys there to have a look. We're all on a first-name basis by now, and they greet me like old friends. A few hours later I get a call from Jack; it's not good news. The front axle is bent in such a way as to point the front tires outward. My RV is duckfooted, and those tires haven't been rolling along the asphalt of various southern highways so much as scraping against it. Jack tells me they have a machine that can bend the axle straight. I'll need a new set of front tires. The whole thing will cost another $500 and will take a couple of weeks.

In actuality, it's all right. The SEC championship game is played in Atlanta at the Georgia Dome; there's no RV parking there. And anyway the SEC championship game is the sort of highfalutin event that might inspire even a dedicated RV-er to spring for a hotel room. Not the Bices, though. They plan to drive the Hurricane from South Carolina and to park at an RV campground just outside of Atlanta across the interstate from Six Flags. I book a room at the Omni, across the street from the stadium. I'll have company, a clerk at the hotel confirms; several hundred other Alabama fans are staying there as well.

The University of Alabama has an allotment of around thirteen thousand tickets, perhaps a fifth of the total sought by Alabama fans. Atlanta is just over three hours from Tuscaloosa, though, truth be told, if the game were being played in Alaska, demand for tickets would not have suffered much. Alabama fans are feeling optimistic, and there's still something to prove. The win in the Swamp was spun as a fluke by many sportswriters, who still portrayed Florida's coach, Steve Spurrier, as a kind of demigod of the gridiron. Finebaum, in a column earlier this season, raised the possibility that Spurrier was as great a coach as Bear Bryant, a remark that prompted more hate mail and more calls for his firing. As for this time, Finebaum has been telling anyone who will listen that the idea of DuBose beating Spurrier twice in one year is "beyond comprehension." On his radio show, Finebaum has picked the Gators to win by ten.

In Tuscaloosa, students begin camping out for tickets on Sunday night, though they aren't scheduled to go on sale until Tuesday. The fraternity brothers make the best of the situation by dragging sofas and lounge chairs, and eventually even TVs and Sony PlayStations, to the waiting area in front of the Coleman Coliseum ticket office. Others bring tents, sleeping bags, and of course coolers. Since many students have classes and exams on Monday, a couple of enterprising young student government types propose a system: everyone signs a list, saving their place in line during the day. Roll is taken three times, at midnight, 2:00 A.M., and 5:00 A.M., and anyone missing a roll call loses his spot. Eventually, about a thousand students join the party.

The party though comes to an abrupt and unpleasant end on Monday evening at 6:30 P.M., when two university administrators show up accompanied by school police. Students unwilling or unable to join the line have been calling the administration to complain that they shouldn't be penalized for going to class and going to bed in their dorm rooms at reasonable times, and their argument sways the administrators, who are eager to promote such responsible behavior. Speaking to the mob through a bullhorn, an administrator named Sybil Todd announces that the student-run list will not be honored by the school. "You may be angry and you may fuss," she says in language suggesting she has misjudged both the rage and the maturity level of the mob in front of her, "but you must have civility between students."

"I bet you have a ticket, don't you?" an angry voice shouts, to cheers.

Immediately, civility disintegrates. The mob crushes its own against a row of police barricades and begins chanting an old football cheer—H-O-L-D, Hold that line!—as Todd looks on in dismay.

"This is a riot in the making," a business school student named Joey Parker says, surveying the mayhem. There are scuffles, some beer bottles fly, and one of them lands on a young woman's head, opening a bloody gash. As the administrators confer, some students make signs—WE WERE HERE SUNDAY: WHERE WERE YOU? one of them reads, in hasty red lettering on orange posterboard—and jab them in the air, so that for a little while the scene takes on the look of a political rally. Ms. Todd returns to say she's standing firm, to more boos. Eventually the mayhem quiets and the crowd begins to disperse angrily, with a promise from the administrators that the school will announce a new ticket-buying policy in the coming days.

There's one person for whom news of a ticket riot is music to the ears, and that's John Ed Belvin. Tickets to the SEC championship have been sold out since the beginning of the summer, in no small part thanks to ticket speculators like John Ed. If Alabama had not made the championship game, he'd simply have unloaded his allotment to dealers in the towns of the schools that had. They all know each other, and like traders on Wall Street, the best among them know that a rival today can be a customer tomorrow, so they maintain a friendly rapport.

As it stands, John Ed is in the catbird seat. His early-season gamble on conference championship tickets is paying off in a big way. When I stop by Need One Ticket, John Ed has the oversized tickets spread neatly on his desk like a man playing solitaire; he's looking at the seating chart and trying to decide which of his favored customers will get the best seats—at $300 a pop—and which will be relegated to the upper deck and the end zones. The phone is ringing incessantly with callers looking now not just for tickets but for hotel rooms, transportation, catering advice, and any inside skinny they can glean from John Ed about the Tide's chances. He's now less a ticket broker than a full-fledged travel-agent-cum-psychic. All the phone calls, though, are getting on John Ed's nerves; every time the phone rings he forgets how he's allotting his supply of tickets, and he has to start over again.

Sherrill Barnes, his next-door neighbor at the memorabilia shop, stops in for a moment. She's on the way to the courthouse for an interview with a district attorney who has enlisted her help in tracking down four stolen Daniel Moore prints. With Alabama in the conference championship, sales are booming, and she doesn't want to lose any more business than she must. John Ed and I tell her that if anyone stops by the shop, we'll encourage them to come back later in the day. She's off with a cheerful little wave and a "Roll Tide!"

John Ed lets me in on a secret. He's working a deal, he says, to get a $5,000 skybox—the entire thing—at the Georgia Dome for the game. He says he'll have to sell several of the places in the box to local muckety-mucks to finance the deal, but he has a plan for getting me in. He's also worked a trade with the Bices—I'd introduced them—taking their tickets to sell now against a promise for slots in the box at the game. They'll be in on the plan, too, he says. It all sounds a bit complicated and cryptic, and when John Ed sees a look of doubt beginning to creep across my face, he quickly holds up both hands like a traffic cop ordering a vehicle to halt.

"Like Coach Bryant said, son," he tells me, "you gotta believe in me."

So on Thursday I check into the Omni Hotel in Atlanta, upstairs from the CNN Center. At lunchtime, I wander to the mall and food court downstairs to find it teeming with Alabama and Florida supporters in full fan regalia. They're watching the live taping of the CNN town hall show *Talk Back Live*, but against the presence of all the other fans, world events can't compete for their interest. Anyone distractible enough to find himself engaged by the show is quickly distracted back to the action in the food court, where wave after wave of peacocking fans wend their way through the fast-food lines for their afternoon supply of fries and bucket-sized soft drinks. It's hard to draw conclusions from a single food court, but it seems Alabama fans outnumber Florida fans by a good two to one. Perhaps the Gator faithful are simply healthier.

A few blocks away in a place called the World Congress Center there's a family-oriented event going on called the SEC FanFare. It's put on by the conference office to provide something to do for those fans who'd rather not spend the afternoon before the game drinking and shouting at each other in the local sports bars. Predictably, it's poorly attended. A few dozen families stroll listlessly in a cavernous room better suited for a boat show than an intimate afternoon out with the kids. Over there is a moonwalk; there's a kicking game where kids and some childlike adults have the opportunity to make field goal attempts. I walk past a line at the funnel cake stand and, to my surprise, stumble upon Paul Finebaum. He's broadcasting his show live from the FanFare, sitting rather miserably with his headphones on as Alabama fans walk by glowering at him. A father stands with his son about fifteen feet away from Finebaum's table, pointing at him as one would at a threatening beast at the zoo. That, the father says to his horrified child, is the man who compared Steve Spurrier to Bear Bryant.

Finebaum seems relieved to see a friendly face, and he invites me to have a seat at his table and to don a pair of headphones so I can hear the abuse being piped in via satellite hookup from callers in Birmingham. The first caller I hear is "Tim, on a car phone."

"When exactly did you lose your credibility, Paul?" Tim asks bitterly.

"Who ever said I had any?" Finebaum answers.

Next is Shane, a regular caller and a die-hard Bama fan. Shane quickly lays into Finebaum for his prediction on the game, and goes on to accuse him of being on the take from wealthy Auburn boosters. Then I see something I haven't seen before: Finebaum loses his cool on the air. He angrily calls Shane an idiot, then, when Shane objects, he replies, "I shouldn't have called you an idiot. I meant to call you an imbecile." As Shane shrieks in response—specifically, he calls Finebaum a "mush-brain"—a flustered Finebaum turns to his producer and slides his finger across his throat—he's done with Shane. At the commercial break, Finebaum takes his headphones and sighs a world-weary sigh. "Wow" is all he can say.

Later, over a bite to eat at a nearby restaurant, Finebaum tells me he's stressed out. There's a lot of tension in the air, he says, and he fears it could get "out of control." The day before, his last in Birmingham before coming to Atlanta, he'd replayed a days-old interview with the Auburn coach, Tommy Tuberville, in which Tuberville answered questions about the loss to Alabama. Listeners were most likely too caught up in the Schadenfreude of hearing Tuberville stumble through an explanation of why he called a pass play on first down deep in his own territory—the play when Alabama sacked Leard for a safety, turning the momentum of the game—to realize that Finebaum's purpose in playing the interview was to free himself from taking live calls from Alabama fans who wanted to remind him of the last time he picked Florida to win. Finebaum tells me he replayed the interview "to cool it down." I take leave of Finebaum, and wish him luck, telling him perhaps I'll try his cell phone after the game. I don't say anything, but I too am worried about his safety.

I've offered my room as a meeting point for the Bices and John Ed before the game on Saturday because I'm the closest to the stadium, and have told them to invite their friends. So on Saturday afternoon, I have only myself to blame when a dozen hardened Bama fans show up at my door, each carrying a twelve-pack, except for Chris and Paula, who come armed with a Tupperware container of Bama Bombs and a pair of walkie-talkies. The walkie-talkies, I'm told, aren't for fun. We all have tickets into the Georgia Dome, but we're short on the pricey passes required to get into the skyboxes. The plan is that we enter the stadium together; once everyone is in the skybox, Chris will assess the situation, gather skybox-level ticket stubs from those already inside, and bring them down to those of us with lower-level tickets, so that we can then enter the premier level. The walkie-talkies are to help us locate each other once we're inside the stadium. Again I have my doubts, but John Ed gives me the look that causes me to remember Bear's mandate: I gotta believe.

The scene outside the hotel door is even more unruly than the one in my room. The Omni has interior balconies that look down onto a central interior courtyard, and it's there that a mob of giddy fans has gathered to shout and holler. We head downstairs to join them, and out we go into a crowd of thousands that encroaches on the Georgia Dome with the inexorability of a glacier. We split up, the skybox crowd to the left, the rest of us to the right. I turn on my walkie-talkie and try to raise Chris. After a few tries a voice comes blathering through the machine; it's Chris, repeating a single phrase: "I can't hear shit." Eventually Chris finds a pocket of quiet that allows us to coordinate the handoff of the skybox stubs. He directs me to the ramp just behind where I'm standing, and says he'll meet me at the gate there in ten minutes. The handoff goes off without a hitch and a few minutes later we're in the box: Chris and Paula, John Ed and his business partner Tony, the muckety-mucks, and assorted familiar faces. There's also a bottle of tequila, the bucket of Bama Bombs, and several cases of Coors Light.

The first Alabama game I attended, consciously anyway, was against SMU in Birmingham, September 18, 1976. I was six, and I remember the day well, thanks perhaps to the pictures my father took that day with his old Yashica 35mm; they're somewhat faded prints, with round corners and a matte finish. He let me take a few; they're all of the players, tiny red specks on the green background of the field. They were the fascination to me then; the spectacle in the stands around me hardly registered against the glow of the team's aura. I knew who Bear Bryant was; I remember my father pointing to him on the sidelines and remember that I could never quite make him out, though I said I did. We won that game 56-3. A little over two years later, we won the National Championship on a fourth-down stop of Penn State in the Sugar Bowl. I watched that one in the living room with the neighborhood kids and a babysitter; I remember my parents had gone to watch the game with friends. A year later, there was another National Championship, this one against Arkansas, again in the Sugar Bowl. By the time I met Bryant in 1982, I'd watched or listened on the radio to dozens of games, and acted them out—especially the running back over-the-top dives—in my bedroom, with pillows serving as the defense.

I went to Bryant's funeral in January 1983, insisting that my mother take me out of school. After that, there was the last-second loss to Penn State there, on a bad call in which the ref ruled Preston Gothard out of bounds in the back of the end zone. There was the Kick—Van Tiffin's fifty-two-yard last-second field goal to beat Auburn, and the Sack, Cornelius Bennett's stuffing of Notre Dame quarterback Steve Beuerlein, in Alabama's first win over Notre Dame. The first of those I watched on television, and stuck my hands through a ceiling fan when I leapt into the air in celebration; the latter I watched in person, the first game I drove to myself. When I didn't come home immediately afterward, my parents called the police fearing I was lost; I was simply out at my first genuine postgame celebration. There was the blocked field goal attempt at Penn State on the last play of the game that preserved a lead; that one I watched in person. And in 1992, that magical year, there was the interception for a touchdown against the Gators in the SEC championship in Birmingham, then the rout of Miami in the Sugar Bowl, which I watched in a crowded New York apartment with friends who'd joined more to watch me act like a fool than to watch the game.

Since then, there was less to celebrate, thanks in part to sanctions for recruiting violations. We'd had losing seasons—which to me felt as abnormal and jarring as natural disasters—but I hung on. I'd been spoiled for my youth and adolescence, those truly formative years when the seasonal rhythms take hold and form expectations, or worse, a sense of entitlement. The nineties were the karmic payback time. I'd like to say I have enough control of my emotions that I'm able to resist the sentimental and fundamentally nostalgic position that a conference championship would amount to some sort of restoration of order, but I can't. I see the Tide run onto the field, and that red and white line of players is the same line that runs backward through my life, a strand on which hang the beads of experience.

So imagine the bolt of misery that shoots through me just one minute thirty-seven seconds into the game when the Gators score their first touchdown. They've started by heaving the ball downfield as we feared—going right after our weakness, our defensive backs—and before the bite of those grain alcohol–soaked Bama Bombs has subsided from my sinuses, we're trailing. The muckety-mucks in the box include a couple of Tuscaloosa lawyers and their very attractive, prim dates, who shift awkwardly at the torrent of profanity that pours from our mouths at the score. But for the rest of the quarter, we hold the Gators, even as they hold us. The season-long quarterback controversy between the white Tyler Watts and the black Andrew Zow resolves neatly, though; the two rotate, switching out on each change of possession. In the second quarter we manage a field goal, then another, to trail 7-6, and just before the half, Zow drops back from the twenty-seven and guns a ball at a tumbling Jason McAddley, who makes the catch for a touchdown. Now the lawyers and their dates squirm at the torrent of profanity shouted in glee. We lead 12-7.

At the half, we're indulging ourselves in pizza and beer and Bama Bombs and tequila when at the door of the box, a surprise visitor appears: it's Andrew Sorensen, the president of the University of Alabama. Sorensen has a reputation as a schmoozer, and figuring that only powerful and wealthy supporters of the school could find their way into the $5,000 skyboxes of the Georgia Dome, he's making the rounds. Sorensen takes two steps inside the box and quickly realizes he's not in a box of wealthy, powerful university boosters but of hardscrabble scammers who happen to have a friend in the ticket business. Before anyone can so much as say hello, he's gone.

In the third quarter Alabama adds another field goal, but more important, the Florida offense can't get anything started. The quarterback's throws are off; Alabama is stopping the run cold and blitzing to bring pressure on the already flustered QB. We have the ball on our twenty-three-yard line three minutes into the fourth quarter, when Milons, normally a flanker, lines up at quarterback and takes a snap, as he had on the crucial fourth down against Auburn. Milons takes off down the line to his left and runs headlong into a pack of Florida defenders; suddenly he stops, pivots, and darts back the way he came, down the line toward his right. The Florida defense, weary now and slow, gives chase, but they've committed themselves, and Milons turns the corner. The fuse hits the fuel and he's off, whizzing and skittering down the sideline with no one in front of him and no one on the field nearly fast enough to catch him. Before I see him score, I'm lost in a tangle of arms.

A play later, Florida's quarterback drops back and, under pressure, throws a pass squarely into the raised forearms of our lineman Reggie Grimes, who miraculously grabs on to the ball, and prevents it from hitting the turf. Then, like that, he's lumbering right toward our skybox at the back of the end zone, an improbable, wonderful sight. It takes him forever, it seems, to run the thirty-eight yards for the score, but when he finally makes it, even the muckety-mucks and their dates join in the heap of embraces. The band blasts our song. The cork is unstoppered and for long minutes we are suspended in a clean effervescing flow, little bubbles tumbling through the air within an exhilarating rush of a tincture of perfect joy.

In the end, it's the most unusual type of win there is, and maybe the best. With eleven minutes to go, Alabama leads 28-7. The Florida offense is hopelessly inept. It's apparent to everyone in the arena that the game is over. The Florida fans are dashing for the exits across the way, tiny rivulets of orange flowing upward toward the gates—and yet there is so much time left to savor winning. Some victories like this get boring, the joy fading in proportion to the inevitability of the outcome. But against an opponent you feared would win, every moment of the winning feels fresh, so that for the twenty minutes it takes for the clock to finally wind down, we're suspended in a state of hilarity. There's even another score, which strikes us—Chris, Paula, John Ed, and myself—as even more hilarious. We can't stop laughing, long, childlike peals of laughter. When the display of wonderment that is the fourth quarter finally ends, we've won 34-7. The conference championship is ours.

The party continues in the stadium for half an hour, as the band plays and the players run around the stands to give thanks to the fans, and it continues outside, moving into the bars and hotel lobbies and any other place humans can gather without being told to move along by the police. Half an hour outside of Atlanta, at a McDonald's at the Douglassville exit, a crowd of Alabama fans attacks a WIAT news van on the assumption that Finebaum is inside. He's not, though; he left Atlanta toward the end of the third quarter, fearing the Alabama crowd in the Georgia Dome might turn on him.

Outside the stadium, I'm swept into a crowd of revelers, and we sing our way to a bar called Jocks & Jills; the name, like every thing we encounter, is also hilarious, but so is that stop sign, so is that drunk person, so is that nondescript office building over there. There's nothing that's not utterly wickedly wackily funny. A hip-hop mix throbs. The patio is now a dance floor. And we dance—hundreds of us, all with beer bottles in our hands, swaying and commingling like the tentacles of anemone in a brisk current. The air is cool and clean, a beautiful late-autumn night in the South so perfect as to seem custom ordered from heaven. The women, all their pretty Southern pretense having left them sometime in the middle of the third quarter, twirl and shout. Wild tangles of hair brush unexpectedly against my face. Chris comes over and I try to speak, but I'm too hoarse. So I close my eyes and dance; I can see it in my mind as though it's happening now: Milons around the corner, the fuse hits the fuel. He's gone.

Epilogue

I ALWAYS FEEL A MIXTURE OF MISERY AND RELIEF AT THE end of football season. Like a boozer thrown in the tank for a forced dry-out, I miss the elixir even as I know that it does me good to go without. There is, after all, the not insignificant matter of having a life, of earning enough money to buy food and shelter, of doing all the things necessary, in other words, to keep myself alive until next season. Pro teams continue to play for a few weeks after the college season ends, which helps ease the craving; but to mix addiction metaphors, the NFL for me serves as a kind of methadone; it's football even though I don't exactly care who wins—the drug without the high.

For the RV scene, the end of the season is unnervingly abrupt. The morning-after routine is the same—everyone wakes early and blows out of the lot, fearful of being the last out—only there is no next week, just next season, nine months of waiting. The RV-ers disperse, driving back home to South Carolina, New Mexico, Tennessee, and every county in Alabama, and, it turns out, few of them keep in touch. With football season dormant, so are the relationships that revolve around it. The psychological crowd breaks up.

Just outside Atlanta on their way home from the Florida game, the Bices experience another kind of break up: their RV comes apart. Chris is at the wheel when he hears a terrible grinding sound and then a crash; the driveshaft of the Hurricane has broken loose and is pogo-ing down the interstate behind them, bashing into oncoming cars, threatening to impale their drivers. Amazingly no one is injured, but five cars are damaged and the Hurricane knocked out of commission indefinitely. The Bices hire a lawyer and threaten to sue.

Perhaps no one is as affected by the end of the football season as profoundly as Paul Finebaum. Without football to generate controversies and scandals, he has to improvise—sometimes desperately—to keep listeners tuning in for four hours a day. Not long after the season ends, I stop by the studios to see the desperation firsthand. Finebaum is holding a trial of sorts for Phyllis from Mulga, one of his most frequent callers, for saying the word *balls* on the air and in the words of his mock indictment, for being "over-emotional and overly sentimental, indeed downright sappy, about Coach Gene Stallings." It's a kangaroo court of course, and Phyllis, despite a passionate defense of herself, is found guilty and banned from the show for life. But Finebaum, it turns out, is even more desperate than that; a few weeks later, he issues a pardon.

For John Ed, too, the end of football season is especially difficult. Tuscaloosa in the winter months grows eerily, depressively quiet. The ticket business grinds to a halt; those few tickets John Ed does sell—to concerts in Birmingham, for example—don't bring any special social cachet in Tuscaloosa, and so give him little pleasure. I meet John Ed on a cool winter night at Innisfree, and the place, usually throbbing during football season, is nearly empty. The Alabama-LSU game from the year before is on the tube, and we grab a couple of Coors Lights and take a seat near the window.

"For a week after football season, I get depressed," he tells me.

"For three months my life is *Bam Bam Bam*, and then all of a sudden it's nothing. I see it coming every year and still I can't do a damn thing about it."

There is one mitigating factor to John Ed's blues: the fact that he made an absolute killing selling tickets this year. He won't tell how much, but it's certainly enough to live on comfortably until next season. He's got a beach condo in Florida where he plans to spend time, and every year in the summer he takes a trip to a ranch out west.

"I plan to head out to Wyoming and tell the world kiss my ass," he says.

Despite his best efforts to remain single, Tuscaloosa's oldest teenager, as he likes to call himself, accidentally falls in love not long after the season ends. His girlfriend, a spunky legal secretary named Brenda, is a Tuscaloosa native and, of course, a hardened Alabama fan. They get married at a small country church outside of Lawley, where John Ed was born. Wedding invitations come in the form of tickets: Admit One to the Nuptials of John Ed and Brenda.

Alabama finishes the season ranked eighth in the AP poll. Mike DuBose, who was perhaps one play from losing his job during the Arkansas game, is named Southeastern Conference Coach of the Year for his championship performance. Would that that were the end of the story. In the next season, the wheels come off his Crimson Tide. Alabama goes into its first game, an away match against UCLA, ranked number two in some polls—some thirty thousand Tide fans and one hundred RVs make the cross-country trip to California for the game. I meet up with the Bices beforehand—with the Hurricane out of commission, they've flown—and we are giddy with expectation. On the first punt return early in the game, Milons does an amazing reenactment of his touchdown run against Florida, and Alabama goes up by a touchdown, confirming all our optimism. It turns out, though, it's the season's lone moment of glory. Alabama loses that game 35-24 and, two weeks later, is stunned 21-0 in Birmingham by Southern Miss. All the off-the-field turmoil caused by DuBose's fling with the secretary comes due: the team is undisciplined and out of shape; assistant coaches assail DuBose to the media in off-the-record conversations. After losing homecoming to Central Florida 40-38, DuBose is told he will be fired at the end of the season. He goes on to lose in Baton Rouge to LSU—breaking a winning streak there that extended to before I was born. After losing by ten points to Tennessee, DuBose tells the media that for a few days afterward, he blamed the loss on God—a comment that still sends shivers through even the most devoutly religious Tide fans. The dreadful finale to our dreadful undoing comes on a dark, sleet-filled Saturday in Tuscaloosa when Auburn shuts us out 9-0. I'm there to see it in all its brutality. Alabama's record for the season is an astonishing 3-8.

It gets worse. Under the DuBose regime, a rogue Alabama football booster allegedly paid a high school coach in Memphis to steer a star recruit Alabama's way. DuBose himself was never implicated, but the school is penalized with a two-year bowl ban and the loss of a substantial number of scholarships, which affect the talent Alabama is able to attract for the next several years. DuBose eventually takes a job coaching football at Northview High School in Dothan, Alabama, and goes a full year there without a win. Today his time at Alabama is associated with the awful unraveling, more than with his championship season. The Lord giveth and the Lord taketh away.

There is a bright spot though in the midst of that miserable season: I save my first life. I stop by the Bices' RV before a game in Tuscaloosa, to have a beer and to catch up. I see an older man at the RV next door—his name, I learn shortly, is the Dean—bent over at the waist, rubbing his throat and belching repeatedly.

"What's with him?" I ask Chris.

"Says he's got real bad heartburn," Chris says.

A few minutes later, the man is still retching when he turns toward me and I get a good look at his face, which is the color of putty.

"He needs to go to the hospital," I tell Chris.

"His son's been telling him that all day, but he won't listen to him," Chris says. "Maybe you could try."

When I tell the Dean he needs to go to the hospital, he quickly gives in; he'd been holding out, apparently, for fear of missing the next day's game, but the pain has grown too intense. We shuffle the Dean into his son's pickup truck, and then drive him to Druid City Hospital—all of three minutes away. Perhaps he feared the place because it was where Bear Bryant died. At any rate, the next morning I wake up to find I've got a message from Chris on my cell phone.

"Hey man—good call on the Dean," he says chirpily on the recording. "He was havin' a heart attack. They did angioplasty this morning. Said he's gonna be all right."

The Dean missed the game, but his boots still walk.

Don Cole, the Heart Guy, isn't so lucky. Cole finally got a new heart in the spring, but he suffers complications, and catches pneumonia. He remains in the hospital for the summer, and into the next football season. He tries to watch Alabama games from his hospital bed, but his son Jeff tells me it's not the same. "It was like he didn't care that much anymore," Jeff says. "Mainly I guess because he wasn't there." Don Cole, who'd told me that life without Alabama football wasn't worth living, never gets out of the hospital; he dies in late December. "That's how he looked at it," Jeff says. "Football was the main thing he lived for."

Jerral Johnson, Show Chicken Man, visited Don several times during his convalescence. He has a lot of free time these days; after setting his sights on winning Exhibitor of the Year, Jerral won going away. When he won the next year, he said, it started to get boring. "I accomplished what I set out to accomplish," he tells me matter-of-factly when I catch up with him in the lot before a big Alabama game against Oklahoma in Tuscaloosa. "Sold all my chickens," he adds. "Bought some goats."

At the end of the season, I decide to divest myself of the Hawg. I check in with Jack at Saab Tire; he'd been so impressed with the Hawg that he'd asked for first dibs. But in the meantime—perhaps because he's seen what a regular customer I've become—he's changed his mind. So I put an ad in the *Birmingham News* classifieds asking $5,000, and a few weeks later, I've got a taker—though for $4,000. But for $1,500, plus an additional $1,500 or so in repairs and upkeep, I've made it through a season—perhaps not quite as cheap as staying in hotels every night, but certainly more fun.

Not long after I arrived in Tuscaloosa, I stopped by the Northport townhouse of a retired Episcopal minister named Ray Pradat. He was locally legendary for delaying the start of autumn weddings until halftime or a lull in the action, even as the congregation fidgeted in the pews. For big games, Pradat set up a television just off the sanctuary so he could watch the action from the altar. He followed Alabama basketball, softball, and gymnastics as well, and confessed to me an obsession with "anything where you keep score."

That phrase still echoes in my head. Humans seem almost instinctively fascinated with keeping score, in the arenas of society, economics, and of course, sports. We compulsively want to know where we stand. I'd set out to try to understand this phenomenon, with the hope perhaps of becoming something like an enlightened fan, all the while aware that that term would strike many—myself included—as an oxymoron. Being a fan, some would argue, is about embracing one's unenlightened self, giving in to the instinctive compulsion to keep score and, of course preferably, to win. Well that's certainly true *in the moment*, but the fact is, fans spend 99.98 percent of their time *not* in the moment—simply going about their business, at work, home, at the wheel of their RVs—and maybe in these times it's possible to achieve some clarity about being a fan and, perhaps, some perspective.

In the end, I didn't come up with anything so pat as to amount to advice about how to be an enlightened fan, but I've certainly come to understand better how the bargain works, and what I'm willing to put down to have access to it. I don't imagine, for instance, that I will forgo a much needed heart transplant just to go to a football game (though I might consider postponing surgery until, say, Sunday, with the hope that I might be recovered enough to watch a game on television the following Saturday). One simple truth I've come upon is that the more you immerse yourself and identify with the team, the higher the payoff of a win, and the greater the cost of a loss. Getting an RV and going to every game, to put it mildly, amounts to upping the ante. I was an obsessed Alabama fan to begin with, but I became even more obsessed when I joined the RV scene. The La. Tech loss early in the season was as dismal a loss as I'd experienced since childhood, and the wins against Auburn and Florida supremely gleeful. The next season—particularly that first game against UCLA—brings home the ugly reality, not just of the team, but of the emotional calculus of being a fan. Going 3-8 immediately after winning the SEC championship is a neatly constructed lesson in the downside of immersion. I'm not part of the RV scene, but I still know all the players' names and numbers, their speeds in the forty-yard dash, their heights and weights, and I know the names of every position coach on the team. I'm in deep. And anyway, one needn't go to every game in a motor home to qualify as a hardcore fan; sports sites on the Internet offer ample opportunity for immersion from one's desk. However a fan has come to immersion, whether online or in a parking lot, the equation for the emotional consequences of winning and losing is remarkably perilous.

Between the cold (if clever) opportunism of Finebaum and the perhaps self-negating devotion of the Heart Guy, Don Cole, I figure I've outlined the extremes of attitudes present in sports fans. I also figure that, of all the fans I met, the Bices have it about right. They leave the door open for the unmuddled glee of winning, and manage to limit the downside of losing, so that while they never seem particularly happy about a loss, neither do they seem paralytically distraught. I imagine that on some level, this might be a quirk of biology—perhaps they both have the happy gene—but absent the happy gene, I've come up with a few strategies to help manage my obsession—to be cheerier—which is in itself a strategy for perpetuating it. I only root for one team in one sport these days, for example. I've given up entirely on the Knicks; I watch the Yankees with practiced detachment (though in a bit of relapse, I paid $600 for a pair of World Series tickets to—who else?—John Ed). I've given up entirely on the Cowboys, the only pro team I ever pulled for. So all told, I'm in the emotional balance a mere twelve Saturdays a year, a manageable number. I make a point not to follow recruiting very closely; I figure I'm stuck with rooting for Alabama no matter who the players are. I've grudgingly forced myself to admit that there are *nnnnnnn . . o. . . . e.m.ppppppp.i.r.i.c.a.l. . . . rrrrrrrrr.e.a.s.o.n.s*—the words take considerable effort just to type—that Alabama is better than everyone else, not our stadium, not our cheerleaders, not our uniforms (well, maybe our uniforms)—but I've made my peace with the idea that for three hours on twelve Saturdays a year, I can expect my id to disagree passionately with this premise. And I've also made my peace with the notion that when it comes to sports, empiricism is overrated.

Despite these adjustments, I rarely miss an Alabama game. If I'm stuck in New York, I always watch on TV, and with as many fellow Bama fans as possible. I was on assignment in New Zealand recently and had to listen to the Alabama-Auburn game over the Internet, pretty much as I'd done in college fifteen years before, when I listened to the game over a telephone. A sign of progress: listening to an Alabama game online from New Zealand these days is easier than listening by telephone from New York fifteen years ago—there are no long-distance charges. And whenever I can—usually two or three times a year, I fly home for games; a few weeks before I write these words, for example, I was out on the town in Tuscaloosa with John Ed on a Friday night, and I crashed in the Bices' RV, with Larry at my side. The Bices settled with their RV builder, by the way, and bought an even bigger model, a thirty-seven-foot Coachmen Cross Country, so even accommodations have improved.

We've had a rough few seasons since DuBose left, and whenever I feel a bit down after a loss, I turn to the Bices for a little optimism and a reminder that, as Paula said, it's only a ball game. (I need reminding more often than I'd like to admit.) As a source for a brighter point of view, the Bices never fail me. We are in Miami, for example, for the last game of the season, the Orange Bowl against Michigan. The game goes into overtime, and just like that first game against Florida, comes down to a final kick. The Alabama kicker makes contact and the ball arcs left just outside the uprights; Michigan wins. Before I can even drop my head in my hands in despair, Chris puts his arm around me and jerks me upright.

"Thing is," he says, "we were four and seven two years ago, seven and four last year, and ten and three this year. That's three better each season. You know what that means, don't you?"

I nod. "Next season, we'll be undefeated," I say, grimacing through the pain.

"That's right," Chris says. "And I can't *wait* until next year."

Inspired by Chris's cheeriness, I stave off the encroaching depression, at least temporarily, and say the only words I know that can give me comfort.

"Roll Tide," I tell him.

"Roll Tide!"

ACKNOWLEDGMENTS

This book could not have been possible without the insightful research of a number of scholars who've studied and written about fans and their behavior. I'm especially indebted to Daniel L. Wann, Merrill J. Melnick, Gordon W. Russell, and Dale G. Paese for their original work and for their comprehensive review of the research on fans in *Sport Fans: The Psychology and Social Impact of Spectators* (Routledge, 2001). I'm also deeply indebted to professor Allen Guttmann of Amherst College for his excellent and concise book *Sports Spectators* (Columbia University Press, 1986), which I relied on heavily for historical material. Thanks also to Richard Smith at the University of Kentucky for the insights on Schadenfreude and fans; to Kathryn S. Oths, a professor of anthropology at the University of Alabama, for leading me to "Meanings and Interpretations of Paul 'Bear' Bryant," an intriguing bit of research on the particular psychology of Alabama fans by her students Vanessa L. Fuller, Pat McElroy, and L. Nyman; and to Christian M. End at the University of Miami for sharing with me his research on reflected glory.

In the course of my reporting I was the beneficiary of an incredible amount of unprovoked kindness. I'm especially thankful to Chris and Paula Bice, for inviting me into their lives (and their RV) and for their genuine curiosity and enthusiasm for this book. I'm also grateful to Jerral Johnson, Skipper, Donnie, Robbie, Larry, Jimmy, Frances, Bobby and Bobbie, Freeman and Betty Reese, Bill and Louise Reid, the late Don Cole, and others in the RV lot who tolerated me, and who made sure I never went hungry; to John Ed Belvin, for his hospitality, sense of humor, zest for life, and not least of all, that Auburn ticket; and to Paul Finebaum, for the leads and laughs, both of which he provided in abundance.

Many in Tuscaloosa provided me invaluable help in finding my way around both town and the history of Alabama football. I'm thankful to Sherrill and John Barnes, and to Sue Barnes for showing me around town, taking me to the Indian Hills Country Club and showing me the very bar stool where the Bear enjoyed his cocktails. Taylor Watson and Ken Gaddy at the Paul W. "Bear" Bryant Museum offered research help and access to tapes of *The Bear Bryant Show*. The staff of the *Crimson White* opened the paper's archives to me; Trip at Innisfree and Sarge gave me the lowdown on life in Tuscaloosa; the ever-vocal members of Tider Insider provided the up-to-the-minute skinny and a reliable source of entertainment; the members of the Hollyhand Sewing Circle offered company and lore by the platterful; and the staff of the Waysider regularly served the baddest breakfast, as John Ed might say, in four counties.

I'm also grateful for the hospitality extended to me by the Fightin' Gator Touchdown Club in Gainesville, the Monday Morning Quarterback Club in Birmingham, and the Tuscaloosa Quarterback Club; to Chandler Busby, my solid guide through the wilds of Auburn; and also for the help extended to me by those at the sports information offices at the University of Alabama, the University of Florida, and the University of Mississippi. The people at Saab Tire and Automotive in Birmingham deserve special credit for helping to keep the Hawg on the road—against all odds.

A number of friends gave moral support, camaraderie, and editorial advice, among them William Hinds, Rob Fox, David Fox, Vincent Muehter, Brian O'Keefe, Chris Knutsen, David Bennahum, Mark Harris, Gabrey Means, Max Calne, Alex Kuczynski, Jim Rutenberg, Ward Hendon, Mary Claire St. John–Butler, Edward Butler, and Scott and Susanna Davis. Gates Hinds provided all of the above, as well as a futon and working shower on those many nights when the Hawg was up on jacks. I'm grateful to Katrina Heron, Howell Raines, Trip Gabriel, Barbara Graustark, and Bill Keller for indulging me in this extracurricular activity, and to Sarah Wyatt, my crack researcher and fact-checker, for helping me get away with it.

I've also been blessed with the incredible fortune of having the wise, supportive, and relentlessly energetic Elyse Cheney as my agent, and having publishing's equivalent of a Bear Bryant National Championship team in Crown Publishing. A Bama Bomb's worth of thanks are due to Steve Ross, perhaps the only publisher in the history of the industry to catch a 5 A.M. flight on New Year's Day in order to accompany one of his writers to a college football game—Hall of Fame stuff—to Doug Pepper, who never let his preference for hockey over college football dim his wit or his zeal for getting it right; to Christopher Jackson for the wise and calming counsel; to the relentless Brian Belfiglio; to Web wizard Alex Lencicki; and to Cathy Calvert, Tina Constable, Jill Flaxman, Doug Jones, Kristen Kiser, Genoveva Llosa, and Philip Patrick.

And to Nicole Maurer, whose total indifference to football never once impeded her support for me or this book, thanks for everything. I'll make a Bama fan of you yet.

ABOUT THE AUTHOR

Born in Birmingham, Alabama, Warren St. John is currently a reporter for the *New York Times*. He has also written extensively for *The New Yorker*, the *New York Observer*, and *Wired*. He went to Columbia University and lives in New York.

PRAISE FOR

RAMMER JAMMER YELLOW HAMMER

"Part amateur anthropology, part new journalism. . . . [*Rammer Jammer Yellow Hammer*] is thoroughly fun to read. These fans are nuts and St. John vividly, but without condescension, presents them in the full frenzy of their nuthood."

—Maureen Corrigan, NPR's *Fresh Air*

"Warren St. John barrels headlong and shrieking into the mind of fandom and the heart of Southern football mania."

—*Vanity Fair*

"Unique and hilarious . . . Despite St. John's often wicked humor, his book is a serious search for a more balanced life. You couldn't ask for better company in a stadium parking lot."

—*Sports Illustrated*

"A great sports book, thanks to [St. John's] feel for the Deep South milieu and his superb way with words. . . . Like a Southern version of Nick Hornby's soccer memoir, *Fever Pitch*."

—*The Onion*

"A very funny and engaging book. You don't need to be an enthusiast of college football to enjoy this book. . . . Whether you're from the North, uninformed, or otherwise oblivious—*Rammer Jammer* is a great place to jump in."

—*Atlanta Journal-Constitution*

"If you've ever done an end zone dance around your own sofa, this book is about you too."

—*Maxim*

"Strangely riveting . . . By the end of the book, the insanity makes just a little bit of sense."

—*Men's Health*

"A marvelous journey into the soul of sports in America. Warren St. John captures our passion with hilarity, absurdity, and poignancy. He just gets our religion. A great ride in the tradition of Hunter Thompson and an even better read."

—H. G. "Buzz" Bissinger, author of *Friday Night Lights*

"Sports fandom is a phenomenon that has so far baffled the field of psychology. The professionals haven't a clue. They should read this book. Warren St. John takes us to where the rubber meets the road."

—Tom Wolfe